Elizabeth Horodowich is an associate professor of history at New Mexico State University. She earned her BA from Oberlin College in Ohio in 1992 and her Ph.D in European history from the University of Michigan in 2000. She has published articles in journals such as *Past and Present*, *Renaissance Studies*, and *The Sixteenth Century Journal*. Her first book, *Language and Statecraft in Early Modern Venice* (Cambridge, 2008) considers speech acts and foul language in sixteenth-century Venice. She has received scholarly grants and fellowships from numerous organizations, including the National Endowment for the Humanities and Harvard University's *Villa I Tatti*. Professor Horodowich lived in Venice for six years and always looks forward to returning to the watery city.

Titles available in the Brief History series

A BRIEF HISTORY OF

VENICE

A New History of the City and Its People

ELIZABETH HORODOWICH

ROBINSON

RUNNING PRESS
PHILADELPHIA · LONDON

Constable & Robinson Ltd
3 The Lanchesters
162 Fulham Palace Road
London W6 9ER
www.constablerobinson.com

First published in the UK by Robinson,
an imprint of Constable & Robinson, 2009

A copy of the British Library Cataloguing in Publication
Data is available from the British Library

UK ISBN 978–1–84529–611–7

1 3 5 7 9 10 8 6 4 2

First published in the United States in 2009
by Running Press Book Publishers

US Library of Congress Control Number: 2009920962
US ISBN 978–0–7624–3690–3

Running Press Book Publishers
2300 Chestnut Street
Philadelphia, PA 19103–4371

Visit us on the web!

www.runningpress.com

Printed and bound in the EU

To Steve and Louis,
and all my friends in Venice with whom I have shared the city.

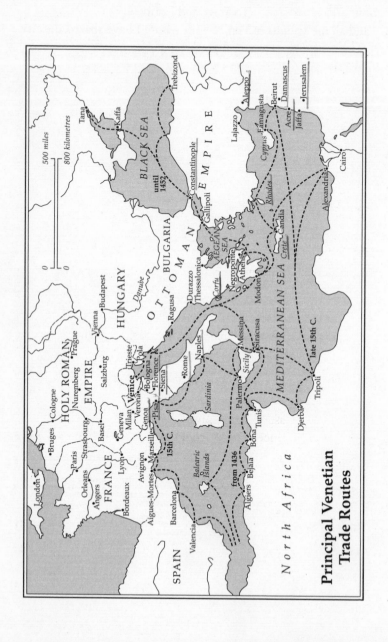

Principal Venetian Trade Routes

CONTENTS

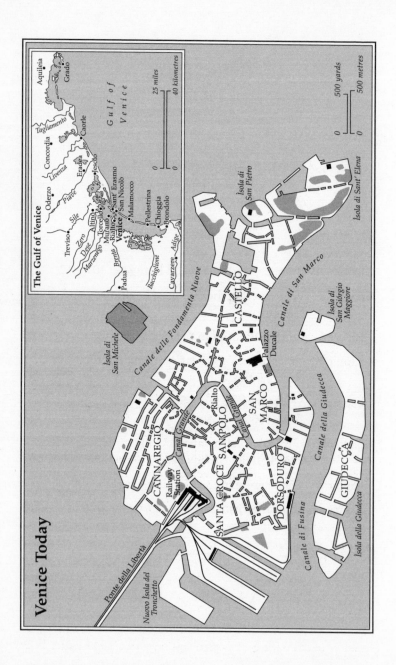

Venice Today

The Gulf of Venice

Aquileia
Grado
Tagliamento
Concordia
Caorle
Oderzo
Eraclea
Jesolo
Piave
Sile
Altino
Torcello
Sant' Erasmo
San Nicolò
Treviso
Murano
Rialto
Venice
Pellestrina
Zero
Dese
Marzenego
Chioggia
Brondolo
Brenta
Padua
Bacchiglione
Cavarzere
Adige

Gulf of Venice

0   25 miles
0   40 kilometres

Nuovo Isola del Tronchetto
Ponte della Libertà
Railway Station
CANNAREGIO
Isola di San Michele
Canale delle Fondamenta Nuove
Isola di San Pietro
CASTELLO
Isola di Sant' Elena
SANTA CROCE
SAN POLO
Canal Grande
Rialto
SAN MARCO
Palazzo Ducale
Canale di San Marco
Isola di San Giorgio Maggiore
DORSODURO
Canale di Fusina
GIUDECCA
Canale della Giudecca
Isola della Giudecca

0   500 yards
0   500 metres

INTRODUCTION

The first time I went to Venice was in the autumn of 1991 as an American exchange student from Oberlin College in Ohio. Like other college students, I had studied Venice and its art and architecture, and had read about its gondolas, canals, pigeons and museums. I had seen many images of the city – of the alleys and public squares, the 'Bridge of Sighs' and the Ducal Palace – and had come prepared (or so I thought) to see it for myself.

I arrived in the city by train: an approach that does not afford the grand spectacle offered to visitors who arrive by boat, as most have done throughout the history of the city, but an approach that is perhaps even more perplexing. Leaving the station, despite my preparation and book knowledge of the city's topography, I nevertheless instinctively expected to smell exhaust and hear the buzz of traffic as in every other major Italian city. I wearily shook off the lull of the train and prepared to steel myself against the clamour and confusion of urban life outside the station. Instead, I stepped out into a quiet world. Not that it was silent, but something seemed amiss. When things came into focus, I noticed that between me and a row of buildings, where a street should have been, there glittered instead a wide green canal lapping at its banks and a boat or two streaming along it in either direction. The impression of the scene was powerful. Despite the fact that I had seen similar images in slides and textbooks and in my mind's eye hundreds of times, somehow nothing could have prepared me for the first impact it made in real time. As I stared, I began to understand more profoundly than before that things here were not put together in any normal way. Though perhaps not as dramatic as a panorama from a mountaintop or a sweeping vista down a wide and bustling urban avenue, the effect of this landscape was entirely disconcerting, no matter how many times I had seen it reproduced before. I put down my bag for a moment, blinking into the dazzling glare of light, stone and water, and taking in the seemingly incomprehensible. This could not be – a city of water and boats instead of streets and cars – and yet, it was.

My experience was, of course, hardly exceptional. Writers and historians through the ages have commented on the breathtaking nature of their arrival in the city of Venice, whether by boat, train, bus or plane, and on the sense of wonder and confusion generated by this city perched on water. It is not just the shifting light and colour of the sea that startles; Venetian architects and builders have seemingly defied the properties of stone so that the city's palaces and churches, its squares and towers, appear to float rather than sit on the surface.

Introducing a history of Venice with such a description is not meant to romanticize it. Like many other cities, Venice is both wonderful and difficult, delightful and frustrating, accessible and outrageously expensive. The Venetians are both friendly and (as we shall see, perhaps justifiably) rude. I describe my sense of confusion associated with my first moments in Venice because I believe it neatly reflects the sense of bewilderment that many scholars have experienced in approaching the city's history. Almost everyone who has poured over its records and read its texts has come up with more questions, paradoxes, myths and mysteries than concrete conclusions or exacting, stable narratives. Jacob Burckhardt, the nineteenth-century Swiss art historian and one of the first modern scholars of Italian culture, famously stated that while Florence was 'the city of incessant movement, which has left us a record of the thoughts and aspirations of each and all,' Venice, in contrast, was 'the city of apparent stagnation and of political secrecy [that] recognized itself from the first as a strange and mysterious creation.' Not unlike the dazed tourist who looks upon the incomprehensible, Burckhardt remained bewildered by what he perceived as the ever-shifting and impenetrable nature of the Venetian world. Rather than try to unwrap its mysteries, he focused the bulk of his scholastic energy on Florence and the Italian courtly cities and left Venice largely untouched.

The sense of bewilderment associated with this floating city has proved so powerful and pervasive that it has earned itself a title, the 'Myth of Venice': the term modern scholars have used to refer to Venice's seemingly unique historical capacity for peace, piety and republicanism. In brief, Venetians and their rulers appeared to demonstrate a remarkable degree of political unity and civic stability. To this day people wonder, why? Some of the questions and paradoxes include, how did Venice survive as a republican state for nearly a millennium when its neighbours did not? Why, for this same thousand years, was it never conquered by an outside power, despite the fact that the city had no walls, battlements or ramparts? How was it possible that among its population, 90 per cent of whom were workers and labourers, there wasn't a single, significant popular revolt? How did its female population, with no formal political role, also contribute to its civic stability? How could this city have been both so pious – as the historian Edward Muir observed there is 'a virgin on every street corner' – while appearing so clearly stamped with the mark of the Muslim Orient? And was Venetian peace due to Venetian piety, to a sense of political and social justice that was equally imparted to all, or was it the result of a system of ruthless policing that forced its residents into trembling submission? Entire libraries have tried to answer these questions, and the results are still debated. Mythically, if not mystically, Venice's historical appearance of serenity, independence and freedom, as well as its beauty, religiosity and long-standing republican nature have caused generations of historians, like the tourist staring for the first time at the Grand Canal, to wonder, how could this be?

This book by no means aims to answer fully these questions. Thousands and thousands of pages written by professional historians have already been dedicated to that task, which naturally begs the question, why another book on Venice? How can we possibly propose yet another volume on a city that has already been overly studied and excessively scrutinized? The answer to this question is twofold.

First, despite the thousands of volumes on Venice, ranging from the highly focused and specialized historical monograph to the slim guidebook, there is still no complete history of Venice from the city's foundation to the present day in a single volume. Yes, there are many masterful histories of the city in the English language, but none is aimed at the general reader. Those interested in studying the history of republican Venice in great depth should read Frederic C. Lane's *Venice: A Maritime Republic* or John Julius Norwich's *A History of Venice*. But both are demanding in their attention to detail and focus on political, economic and maritime history. Indeed, most general histories of Venice tend to be political histories with an occasional nod at art, leaving much to be said about social and cultural history that this volume, in contrast, considers more at length.

Elisabeth Crouzet-Pavan's *Venice Triumphant: The Horizons of a Myth* organizes the history of Venice thematically and culturally, but extends her story only through the sixteenth century. Indeed, many general histories conclude their narratives with Napoleon's arrival in the lagoon in 1797, such as Peter Lauritzen's *Venice: A Thousand Years of Culture and Civilization* or Alvise Zorzi's *Venice 697–1797: A City, A Republic, An Empire*. Other excellent surveys such as Margaret

Plant's *Venice, Fragile City: 1797–1997* cover instead the modern segment of the city's past. Peter Mentzel's *A Traveller's History of Venice* offers an excellent general synopsis of the arc of Venetian history, but again is primarily a political history written by a historian of the Ottoman world with a perspective that does not tend to reflect the pressing questions that have driven more recent generations of Venetian historians. The best general and brief histories of the city to date are in Italian by Gherardo Ortalli and Giovanni Scarabello (now in English translation, though not readily available) and in French by Christian Bec.

My aim has been to provide a general history of Venice from the city's foundation to the present day and tackle the questions that have puzzled scholars for decades. While some historians and writers have deliberately broken with traditional narrative histories and taken a thematic approach – as in Jan Morris's grand essay, *Venice*, or Garry Wills's *Venice: Lion City* – I have stuck to a traditional, chronological format. And though I occasionally consider art and architecture, the history of Venetian art is simply too vast and complex to do justice to it here. My tale is primarily historical. I've therefore struck a balance between breadth and depth, between the grand battles and everyday life. Most importantly, I've tried to make complex historical questions and the latest research accessible to the non-specialist, partly by using narrative explanation rather than academic notes. But how can I claim to do so much in one concise volume, to break new ground where thousands have gone before? Only by recognizing that you can't have one, singular, exhaustive, complete or completely objective history of Venice.

So many stories, tales and anecdotes in Venetian history make it more than apparent that it is often impossible to establish 'the truth'. So much of Venice's history is shrouded in dubious accounts with a variety of stories explaining Venetian landmarks and traditions. For example, is the body of St Mark still preserved under the high altar in the basilica of the church that bears his name, or was his body destroyed in a fire in 976? Is the *Campo dei Mori* – 'the square of the Moors' in a neigh-bourhood on the north side of the city – so-named because there was a Moorish warehouse nearby, because of the Moorish statues placed here in the walls or because a prominent family that once lived here came from Greece, then called Morea? Was Marco Polo's famous account entitled *Il Milione* to describe the 'millions' of riches he brought back from the Orient, or for the wearisome 'millions' of lies and exaggerations it contained? And what is the origin and meaning of the *ferro*, the eerily shaped six-pronged prow of the gondola? Is it descended from Roman galleys, an emblem of the decisive axe of Venetian justice, representative of the Grand Canal, or of the six *sestieri* or neighbourhoods of the city? Any two gondoliers or guide-books will offer two different answers to these questions, and there are hundreds of other, similar questions. In many instances nobody really knows the answers.

As in many other cities, it is often difficult to appreciate the density of the past in the physical remains of the city since on any given plot of ground, buildings have been built, razed, rebuilt, embellished, their decorations chiselled out and sold, and then restored or re-created and pasted back in. The city's art and architectural fragments, in many cases, have been taken from Venice to Paris, Vienna, or Brussels and brought back again, or have been replaced by replicas or acceptable substitu-tions. The function of any given building that we see standing now could easily have changed many times, from a church to a hospital, factory, mill, stable, movie theatre, mask shop, or bar today. Because of these complexities and the essential impossi-bility of finding 'the truth' in the past, good historians always recognize that their craft entails constructing history, as if with clay, rather then trying to reflect history to modern readers as if with a mirror.

The second reason for another book on Venice is that there still exists the need for a comprehensive history of Venice with more tourists – for better or worse – visiting than ever before.

On 1 October 2006 the *New York Times* reported that from 15–18 million tourists had visited Venice that year, and the numbers keep on rising. During Carnival week there can be as many as 150,000 visitors a day. Venice has been used to tourism since the Middle Ages because it was the great take-off point for pilgrims and crusaders travelling to the eastern Mediterranean, but such numbers overwhelm today's population of about 60,000. In their book *Venice, The Tourist Maze: A Cultural Critique of the World's Most Touristed City*, Robert C. Davis and Garry R. Marvin understand the benefits that Venetians glean from such tourism while lamenting the physical and cultural problems. Tourists, they claim, 'are consuming not so much Venetian culture, but rather the images of that culture, and consuming them, for the most part, as quickly as possible.' Statistics show that most visitors come to Venice for just a day trip. To help the tourist who wishes to stay longer know more about the history of Venice, the final section of each of the following chapters describes the locations around the city and the lagoon where the history in that chapter is made visible. This allows visitors 'to read' the city's stones in person: stones and monuments that recount and relay the city's past more directly and often more poignantly than any written text.

Before delving into the riches of Venice's past, a brief word about the location and topography of the city. While this isn't a guidebook, establishing a basic understanding of the city's layout will make it easier to understand events as they unfold. And of course that layout is bizarrely based on water. The modern city exists on a series of interconnected islands in a lagoon in the northern Adriatic. This lagoon is an unusual and unique natural environment where brackish water is created by the mixing of fresh water from nearby rivers with the waters of the Adriatic that enter the lagoon through three principal channels. The islands that form Venice are protected from the sea by a series of barrier islands that separate the lagoon from the Adriatic and act as a breakwater. To the north and south of the centre of Venice the lagoon is peppered with islands, rocks, mudflats and uninhabited shoals of waving reeds and grasses. Though the lagoon is vast, much of its waters are shallow and can only be navigated by shallow craft and by those who know its sandbars and channels.

✗ Venice may look like one geographic whole – especially from the air – but the central city is actually composed of about 120 islands, spanned and connected by more than 430 bridges that cross 170 canals (called *rii*, or *rio* in the singular). In terms of its overall shape, as the Venetian writer Tiziano Scarpa has pointed out, '*Venezia è un pesce*' ('Venice is a fish'), which it really does resemble from above. Its backbone is the Grand Canal, which weaves through the city and divides it into two. To date, in 2009, four bridges cross this canal.

Unlike other Italian cities, Venice does not call public squares and streets *piazze* and *strade*. Instead, Venice's open spaces are called *campi*, and its narrow and often winding streets are *calli*. A small alley is a *ramo*, and a street that used to be a canal but has since been filled in is a *rio terrà*. In Venice the only *piazza* is that of San Marco, the city's ceremonial and civic centre. The names of Venetian streets, spaces and canals – that often refer to the craft, profession or activity that happened there – are frequently in Venetian dialect. And the final point to note is that in the twelfth century Venice was divided geographically into six municipal zones called *sestieri*: San Marco, Castello, Dorsoduro, San Polo, Santa Croce and Cannaregio. In each of these districts, houses are numbered consecutively.

Chapter One considers who the first Venetians were, where they came from and how they formed an unusually independent political state by the middle of the ninth century. Chapter Two traces how this city of humble fishermen and salt traders came to control the economy of the Mediterranean through conquest and commerce, beginning with the theft of the body of St Mark in 828 through the thirteenth century. Chapter Three tackles the same time period, but considers political and social developments in the city. Chapter Four investigates the spectacular events of the fourteenth century that made Venice the polity it remained to the end of the republic. Chapter Five examines Venice during the early modern period, otherwise known as the Renaissance. In particular, it will question how and why Venice became a mainland empire and look at the city's complex and productive relationship with the eastern Mediterranean in terms of political and cultural diplomacy. Chapter Six looks at the history of Venice in the seventeenth and eighteenth centuries, and explains how Venetian culture and politics changed as the city's economic status began to decline. Chapter Seven covers the nineteenth and twentieth centuries when Venice was violently thrust into the modern world with the arrival of Napoleon, followed by the end of the Venetian republic, the onset of Austrian rule, the unfolding of the *Risorgimento* (the founding of the Italian state) and the wars of the twentieth century.

Underlying all these topics is one persistent question: is Venice fundamentally similar to or different from other cities? Should it seek to emulate them and their paths towards modernization, or should it focus primarily on protecting and shoring up its past? Such questions date far back into the Middle Ages when Venetians first considered whether to build a mainland empire. Most medieval cities had a *contado* or surrounding territory that buffered them against foreign powers. Venetian politicians debated whether they too should conquer a territorial empire, or continue to focus their resources and capital on the sea, the traditional source of their wealth, defence and success? Later, in the wake of the Enlightenment, Venetians in the eighteenth and nineteenth centuries often wondered if they should emulate the liberal political ideas emanating from Paris or stick with their age-old aristocratic rule. Daniele Manin, the city's revolutionary leader in 1848, even suggested selling off some of the city's paintings and other works of art to finance the new, modern, political configuration of a democratic regime. However, the art historian John Ruskin, one of the city's most influential

visitors and writers on Venice, famously scorned modernization in Venice, from gas pipes being laid over bridges to
arriving in the city by train. For him, it was more crucial to
preserve the city's unique past than to bring it up to speed with
other cities in the modern age.

Following his ideas, it is interesting to note that the three
biggest and potentially most significant modern architectural
projects proposed for the city in the twentieth century (a
centre for students on the Grand Canal by Frank Lloyd Wright
in 1953, a new hospital by Le Corbusier in 1964 and a new
conference centre by Louis Kahn in 1969) were all ultimately
rejected by the city's politicians and urban planners. Change
and modernization in many ways always ran counter to the
survival of the city; indeed, today we are grateful that the
Venetians did not opt to install a subway (or underground) a
project that was discussed at length in the later twentieth
century. Change, however, has been necessary to the city's
survival. Debates about change and modernization in Venice
are ubiquitous in discussions about art and architecture
(conservation or restoration?) and in arguments about how
best to protect the lagoon from flooding (leave it alone or opt
for the MOSE project, a series of flood gates?).

It has always been hard for Venice to find its way between
the old and the new, or between the lagoon and the rest of the
world. Is the city a museum or a modern city? As one writer
put it, does it survive or does it live? These questions and
conflicts are embodied in the symbol of the Lion of St Mark
that, in Vittore Carpaccio's painted rendition, has two paws on
land and two on the water. Venice is like other cities, but at the
same time, it is not, because of its curious history and singular
position on water. These tensions characterize all of Venetian
history, from its foundation to the present.

An understanding of the history of Venice has much to offer
the modern reader. If one believes that the past offers insights
into the present, the lessons of Venetian history teach us about
cosmopolitan life and multicultural interaction. Historically,

many Venetians lived abroad and large communities of foreigners lived in Venice. In this way, Venetian history has much to tell about cultural exchange, immigration, and the politics involved in sharing a dense, limited, urban space – topics that constantly confront the contemporary world. Furthermore, we shall see that the Christian state of Venice managed to maintain a tense but productive and pragmatic relationship with the Muslim East, perhaps offering insights into similar relationships in the modern world. Venetian history also serves to inform us about the relationship between republics and despotisms, and potentially, how republican politics survive in an otherwise dictatorial world.

For those who think that we rarely learn from the past, the history of Venice – like all good history – offers a Copernican understanding of time and the world. Just as Copernicus suggested that the earth was not at the centre of the universe, so history destabilizes our sense of ourselves as unique or important. Where else has a population lived so differently, travelling by boat not by land, living from the sea instead of farming? Where else has people's work interacted with water in such a peculiar way?

And perhaps most pressingly, the recent history of Venice has much to tell us about the relationship between politics and the natural environment. Like New York, Calcutta and other coastal cities, Venice is at the forefront of concerns about climate change. Is it sinking, is the water of the lagoon rising, and what efforts are being undertaken to understand and cope with such phenomena? While this is an enormous topic, Chapter Eight includes discussions about Venetian efforts to cope with a variety of environmental, political and economic crises that have challenged the city in recent decades. In this way, we shall see that for all its uniqueness, modernization has impacted on Venice, as it has on much of the rest of the world. Venetian creativity and ingenuity in confronting these challenges will ultimately demonstrate the degree to which Venice is as unique and mythical as it has always claimed to be.

I would like to thank several colleagues and friends for reading portions of this manuscript: Linda Carroll, Bill Eamon, Frederick Ilchman, Ken Hammond, Margaret Malamud, Dwight Pitcaithley and Marsha Weisiger.

I

ROMANS, BARBARIANS AND
REFUGEES: 400–812

Walking the streets of Venice today, it is difficult to imagine what the landscape must have looked like several thousand years ago, or to envision the slow, painstaking process behind the city's construction and development. Perhaps the one visible clue giving us an indication of the challenges involved in building this city is the maintenance that is always being carried out. We constantly see workers dredging canals to clear away the build-up of mud and silt. Buildings often have to be restored to repair the leaning and crumbling produced by shifting foundations and dank air. In fact it is almost impossible to look around any *campo* or down any street in Venice without seeing scaffolding covering the façade of a building, or a canal being dammed to hold back the water, so that silt and debris can be cleared away and the foundations repaired. No piece of the city can be allowed to sit for too long before nature begins to eat away at the built environment. All this work offers a small window on to how hard it must have been to come and live on these marshy islands in the first place. Why did people leave the comforts of the Roman world – its roads, aqueducts, theatres and baths – to undertake a much more laborious existence on the barren mudflats of the Venetian lagoon? As the beloved Venetian poet Diego Valeri put it, when 'our saintly forefathers [came here] more than a thousand years ago, they must have had both an enormous supply of stubborn will, as well as a generous grain of insanity.'

Venice was not founded like other European cities where people came together at the intersections of trade and commerce, or gathered around ancient holy sites as they re-made them into Christian ones. It did not grow outward from a market or forum, did not grow inward from defensive walls and, though Venice eventually emerged as one of the greatest European commercial capitals, it did not spring up at any Roman crossroads; it was instead deliberately founded as far away from them as possible. Its islands possessed no hallowed ground, and the city's inhabitants would have to invent, and steal, their political and spiritual legitimacy. Understanding how the first Venetians came to inhabit the islands of the lagoon, their relationships with Rome and Byzantium and their relationship to their physical and natural environment are crucial to grasping the history of the city.

Venice, as we shall see, first formed as a city of immigrants with ties to both Rome in the West and Constantinople in the East: ties that influenced the foundation myths of the city and the way that Venetians saw themselves. However, as these settlers built up their confidence and wealth by repelling outside invaders and harnessing the lagoon's resources, the city slowly emerged as a powerful, independent state in the northern Mediterranean. In turn, Venetians developed a narrative about their inborn sense of freedom and independence, a narrative that more than any of their cultural ties to Rome or Byzantium defined their identity and their understanding of themselves. The events surrounding the first large-scale migrations to the lagoon, as well as the way that subsequent generations of

Venetians interpreted the foundation of their city, are defining moments in early Venetian history.

Tracing the origins of Venice's first inhabitants requires delving into a murky past where myth and history overlap, and it is often impossible to separate one from the other, not least because there is little documentary evidence from the Venetian lagoon in late antiquity and the early Middle Ages. Very little was written down about Venice during the Roman Empire, and the Roman and Greek historians who did write about the lagoon, such as Livy and Strabo, only discussed it in passing. While archaeological studies have added greatly to our understanding of how populations grew on the lagoon's islands, there are still many questions about the first residents of these islands whose answers remain unclear. Who were the first inhabitants of the Venetian lagoon, where did they come from and why did they leave the mainland in the first place?

The First Venetians

The name of the city, Venezia, derives from the name given to this Roman region in the northern Adriatic: *Venetia*. *Venetia* was the *Decima Regio*, or the tenth of eleven regions (not a province, which was a territory outside Italy that was governed by Rome) established by the Roman Emperor Augustus. *Venetia* represented essentially all of north-eastern Italy, roughly from the Alps to the Po River and from the Adige River to the Adriatic Sea. According to one sixteenth–century writer, Francesco Sansovino, Venetia was derived from the Latin phrase *veni etiam* meaning 'come back again', or 'return to see this beautiful place'.

Some Venetian historians and chroniclers in the Middle Ages claimed that the first Venetians came from Gaul, emphasizing ties between Venice and France. Others argued they came from Troy, suggesting either that the Trojans found refuge in Venice following the sack of their city by the Greeks, or that the descendants of the Trojan leader Antenor founded the city of Padua on the mainland and then later came to the lagoon. It is also said that Antenor founded the mainland town of Aquileia, in the same way that Aeneas founded Rome in the wake of the Trojan War. Yet another story claimed that Antenor found protection in the lagoon and built a castle on one of the islands, now in the Venetian neighbourhood known as Castello. Possible Trojan origins were a big plus since they suggested that Venetians, like Trojans, were subject to no one and would rather flee their homes than be ruled by outsiders. A different myth, focusing on Rome rather than Troy, claimed that a group of three consuls from the Roman city of Padua founded Venice on 25 March 421, the same date that marks the beginning of the first month of the Roman year and also the feast of the Annunciation to the Virgin.

While these foundation myths proved crucial to the way all future Venetians imagined and described themselves, we need to look for the origins of Venice much closer to home, in the lagoon. In all likelihood, the earliest inhabitants of Venice were not Roman consuls or Trojan refugees but humble, local fishermen and hunters arriving from nearby Roman towns on the mainland. While some archaeological evidence suggests that people have inhabited the islands of the lagoon since Neolithic times, radio-carbon dating has shown that the islands of San Francesco del Deserto in the northern lagoon and the area around the *Piazza San Marco*, for instance, were first inhabited in the fifth century and sixth century AD, respectively. On the island of San Francesco, archaeologists have discovered evidence of a port where Romans received goods from traders in the Adriatic and then ferried them to mainland towns a few miles to the west. Some studies have also suggested that there was a fixed Roman colony on the island of Torcello (also in the northern lagoon) in the pre-Christian era. These island populations were by no means large, and it is unlikely that people initially inhabited the islands regularly or year-round since few people wanted to live far from the benefits and comforts of Roman civilization.

In the early Roman Empire the islands of the lagoon were thinly populated by boatmen. They crossed the waters in shallow craft and returned with their catch to the bustling cities of Aquileia, Altino and Oderzo on the Roman mainland. While some recent archaeological theories have argued that this entire region was not lagoon but farmland irrigated by a network of canals, and that the lagoon formed as a result of a natural catastrophe at some point in the early Middle Ages, this seems unlikely. Most historians and archaeologists tend to agree that the lagoon and its islands existed during the Roman Empire and that they were sparsely populated by fishermen, duck hunters and the occasional party of picnickers and weekend revellers. The mythical idea that the first Venetians moved to an uninhabited place is surely false, though popular since it affirmed Venetian ideas about their independence and denied any pretence of rule by foreigners or outsiders. For many centuries, people came and went among the mudflats and reeds and the obscure, anonymous islands of the Venetian lagoon quietly remained outside of history.

All this changed, however, with the arrival of the barbarian tribes. The period of the barbarian migrations in Europe lasted from approximately the fourth to the seventh centuries when a series of Eastern, Germanic and Central Asian tribes – including the Huns, the Visigoths and the Ostrogoths – moved into the territory of the Roman Empire. The barbarians are best known for supposedly having contributed to, or even caused, the fall of the Roman Empire, but here they had another important effect. Imperial authority was decadent and incapable of defending its subjects in north-eastern Italy against these invaders. Fleeing the violence and destruction of these tribes as they moved down into the Italian peninsula, the populations of Roman cities in the northern Adriatic took refuge on the islands of the lagoon and became the first Venetians.

No one knows which barbarian groups caused the greatest waves of immigration or when settlement in the lagoon became permanent. Some have argued that people first fled to the Venetian islands in large numbers when the Visigoths, under Alaric, arrived in the area in the early fifth century. On their way to attack Rome in 410, the Visigoths first sacked the wealthy Roman city of Aquileia in the northern Adriatic in 402. One of the major trading posts between Rome and the East, Aquileia was the Roman administrative capital of this region and one of the largest and richest centres of the Roman Empire, with a population as high as 100,000 at its peak in the second century AD. Its wealth attracted barbarian tribes seeking profit and plunder, forcing Aquileians to leave for the safety of the nearby lagoon, about 6 miles (10 km) away. These barbarian invaders were excellent horsemen but were completely unfamiliar with seamanship, leaving them unable and unwilling to attack at sea. When the danger passed, Aquileians returned to the mainland and resumed their usual way of life.

Alternatively, some believe that the first major migrations occurred during the Italian campaigns of Attila the Hun who swept into Italy in 452 and sacked the town of Aquileia on the way. It is said that Attila was so terrifying that he did not speak but barked like a dog and, wherever he passed, 'the grasses no longer grew'. After Attila passed through north-eastern Italy, Aquileia never regained its former status as a Roman imperial city but presumably most locals did return to live there. Interestingly, one of the remotest islands in the northern lagoon, the small and mysterious Monte dell'Oro, or 'mountain of gold', is the site of a legend about Attila. According to tradition the King of the Huns buried his immense riches on the island and had them guarded by a demon. Even today, local lore claims that fisherman continue to fear this island because, at night, you can still see the souls of the Huns guarding their treasure.

It's very likely that the Venetian lagoon was first colonized with a series of improvisory and gradual movements back and forth between the mainland and these nearby islands, when people seeking refuge from invaders tried living in the less exposed Adriatic. The Visigoths and Huns were clearly part responsible, but most scholars now think that the first major migrations to the lagoon happened not in the fifth century but in the sixth and seventh centuries, as a result of the Lombard invasions. The Lombards (sometimes called Longobards, meaning 'Longbeards') were a Germanic tribe from Northern Europe that some historians believe had agreed to offer their military services to the Byzantine Empire in the territory of Pannonia (now Hungary) in exchange for land in Italy. In 568 the Lombards moved south across the Alps to claim this territory in the valley of the Po River, marking one of the last major movements in the period of the barbarian migrations. Unlike the Visigoths or the Huns, the Lombards founded a permanent kingdom in Italy that lasted until Charlemagne conquered it in 774. The Lombards gave their name to the modern region of Lombardy in north-western Italy after they eventually conquered Milan and made Pavia their capital.

A consensus now suggests that when the mainland residents along the coast of the northern Adriatic realized that these barbarian invaders intended to stay, they established the first permanent communities in the lagoon. The locals saw their world die around them as the barbarian scavengers of the Roman Empire swooped in and conquered their homes. With the arrival of the Lombards, the inhabitants of many mainland towns along the northern Adriatic coast moved to a series of islands in the nearby lagoon in large numbers, bringing as many of their belongings as they could, including the tools of their trade and their civil and religious institutions. They carried their relics, sculptures, vestments, chalices and even funerary inscriptions to the islands, saving them from otherwise certain destruction. They were no longer temporary guests but immigrants intending to stay.

Archaeologists have been able to determine with a fair amount of certainty the exact routes and migration patterns that these refugees took. On any map of the area at this time, moving from north to south, you can see how the peoples of Friuli and Aquileia moved to the town of Grado at the extreme end of the port of Aquileia. Aquileians, with the residents of Concordia, then moved to Caorle. As the Lombards threatened Oderzo, further south, its inhabitants moved to Eraclea and this population expanded outward to the island of Jesolo. Moving closer to what is today the city of Venice, the inhabitants of Altino (just north of Venice's modern Marco Polo airport) fled to the island of Torcello just a few miles to the east. Altino, like Aquileia, had existed at the intersection of several major Roman roads. When its residents moved to the lagoon, Torcello became the largest commercial centre of the early island communities: a source of supplies for Byzantium as well as an outlet for Byzantine goods in the lagoon. The inhabitants of Treviso and Padua moved to Malamocco and Chioggia, and the populations of the towns of Este and Monselice, even further to the south of Padua, fled there as well.

Although we have no contemporary testimony that describes this exodus, we can imagine people from the entire arc of this shoreline, from Grado in the north to Cavarzere and Chioggia in the south, fleeing to the lagoon after the arrival of the Lombards. The founders of the islands of Venice were immigrants and refugees, and while they did not travel as far from home as many refugees do today (on a clear day, you can see Altino on the mainland from the island of Torcello), they nevertheless left their native towns under duress, seeking safety and protection in the coastal marshes. Whereas most people once wanted to live close to the routes along which Roman trade and culture spread, it became suddenly necessary to move as far away from these routes as possible since it was precisely these paths on which the invading barbarians travelled. As the Lombards completed their conquest of the Adriatic mainland, these settlements in the lagoon became the last remnants of the Roman Empire in North Italy. Under King Alboin, the Lombards conquered Friuli and much of north-eastern Italy including Aquileia, and King Rotari completed the conquest of the region by eventually taking the cities of Oderzo and Altino on the mainland near the lagoon by 639.

Amidst the conflicting evidence surrounding the earliest inhabitants of the lagoon – who these people were, and when and why they left the mainland – we can draw some conclusions about the symbolic meaning of these accounts for Venetians in later generations. Many of the city's foundation myths sought to link Venice's origins directly to Rome to demonstrate that Venice had mythically inherited the greatness of that ancient civilization. Roman origins gave Venice a powerful civic pedigree. The story of later migrations to the lagoon further emphasized the 'Romanness' of Venice since such narratives claimed that Venice was born in opposition to the violence of the barbarian tribes that came to destroy the last vestiges of Roman civilization. Viewed in this way, the first inhabitants of the lagoon – the first Venetians – were the noble preservers and transmitters of Roman culture, transporting the physical scraps of their lives to a barren new world. This description suggests that in the twilight of the Roman Empire, Venetians represented some of Rome's last surviving descendants. A thousand years later, historians living at the height of Venetian cultural and economic supremacy would argue that the virtuousness of Venetian citizens stemmed in part from the noble Roman families who immigrated to the lagoon during the period of the barbarian migrations.

But what was life like on these islands during the period of the first major settlements? While there are very few records from before the year 1000 there is one famous letter that offers a glimpse of the experiences of the first Venetians. The Roman official Cassiodorus – a minister to the barbarian King Theodoric in Ravenna – wrote a letter 'to the tribunes of the maritime population' of the lagoon (i.e., the local military men who governed the region) around the year 537–8. The letter ordered Venetians to help transport supplies of wine and oil from Istria to the Byzantine capital at Ravenna, and gives a striking account of life in the lagoon. Cassiodorus described the landscape of the marshes – the reeds, brackish waters, aquatic birds, currents, flooding, tides and silt – as well as the fragile houses of these first inhabitants that, he said, were 'like [those of] aquatic birds, now on sea, now on land'. He explained how these people made their living through hunting, fishing and making salt. Compared to the hustle and bustle of Roman cities, the lagoon was nearly deserted and the inhabitants lived in 'permanent, tranquil security' largely because they were free of the Roman Empire and the Roman Church. Though the lagoon's inhabitants were for the most part poor, according to Cassiodorus, 'rich and poor live together in equality. The same food and similar houses are shared by all; wherefore they cannot envy each other's hearths, and so they are free from the vices that rule the world.' Freedom, nobility but noble simplicity, according to Cassiodorus, were the political and social characteristics that defined life in the early lagoon.

As the historian Frederic Lane has noted, Cassiodorus' letter reads like the daydreams of a harried bureaucrat staring out his window during an especially busy day at the office. Surely life among the earliest inhabitants of the lagoon was neither easy nor peaceful. Even if there once was some type of primitive egalitarianism among these island dwellers, this soon came to a close after the Lombard invasions when various local noble families established themselves in the lagoon and determined to control the best fishing holes and salt beds. It was not long before rich local landlords established dependent tenancies. Whatever the case, Cassiodorus does at least give some idea of how the first Venetians lived and what their environment looked like. And he helped fuel the myth that the first inhabitants' virtuosity was steeped in their state of independence and some form of democracy.

Political Life Between Byzantines and Franks
What type of political structures defined life in the early lagoon? From its inception Venice was governed by the political powers in Byzantium, the Eastern Roman Empire. At the beginning of the fourth century, the Roman Emperor Constantine founded a

separate Roman capital in Constantinople (now Istanbul). When the Western Roman Empire collapsed at the end of the fifth century, this eastern half of the empire survived. While the roots of Byzantine civilization were clearly Roman, the Byzantine world and especially its church (which became the Eastern Orthodox church) grew to become quite separate and distinct from Rome in the West, both politically and culturally, especially after the fall of Rome. The territory of the Venetian lagoon fell under the jurisdiction of Byzantine rulers. Since Constantinople is a long way from Venice, the city was governed by a local administrative functionary of the Eastern Roman Empire called the Exarch of Ravenna (a type of civil and religious Byzantine governor who oversaw the empire's lands in Italy). When the western Roman Empire disintegrated at the end of the fifth century, Ravenna remained an outpost of Byzantium or the eastern Roman Empire in Italy. By answering to the Exarch of Ravenna, Venetians were political dependents of the Byzantine Empire and as such, Venice maintained economic and cultural ties with Constantinople from early on in its history. Venice was also controlled in the fifth century by local governors called maritime tribunes – the same officials to whom Cassiodorus wrote – who were subject to the Byzantine emperor.

The establishment of the first doges or dukes in the lagoon reinforced Venice's subordinate political relationship to Byzantium. Not surprisingly there are competing theories about who was the first doge since records are fragmentary and confusing. According to one legend, Venetian dignitaries convened in Eraclea in 697, called by the Patriarch of Grado to discuss the persistent threat of the Lombards. This assembly decided to replace the existing system of military tribunes with a single leader or duke called a *dux* (in Latin) or *doge* (in Venetian). Legend claims that the first doge, Paoluccio Anafesto – the Exarch of Ravenna – was elected in 697 during this assembly, and he was given the title of doge when Byzantine authorities decided to make the entire Venetian lagoon subordinate to one military ruler, though he continued

receiving orders from the emperor's local representative in
Ravenna. For this reason, the first doge was merely a representative of Byzantium, making the first 'genuine' Venetian doge
Orso Ipato. During the iconoclasm controversy of the early
Middle Ages, the Eastern Emperor Leo III the Isaurian
(717–41) prohibited the use and cult of sacred images and
ordered their destruction. Rome did not agree, and the
Venetians sided with the West. Again according to lore, the
protesting Venetians then armed, revolted and nominated their
own duke or doge – Orso – in 726, making him the first (or
according to the Anafesto tradition, the third) doge who was
elected without Byzantine authority and without outside
intervention. The election of Orso signified the first big step
Venetians took away from the Byzantine sphere of influence.

It was not until the eighth century that Constantinople first
accepted a locally elected doge, and even eighth-century dukes
continued to maintain some political allegiance to the Exarch
of Ravenna, much as before. It is true that the highest
Byzantine officials given the task of governing Venice were
distant – they were either in Ravenna or Pola (now Pula, across
the Adriatic in modern Croatia) – but the lagoon was overseen
by a series of military officials who represented the Byzantine
Empire in the lagoon during the period of late antiquity. The
first Venetians might have come from the nearby Roman
mainland, but politically Venice was Byzantine. Until Venice
achieved a greater degree of political independence in the ninth
century, many Venetian administrators were Byzantine
appointments that were subject to the approval of Eastern
exarchs, military leaders or emperors. In addition, the earliest
doges were more likely mid-ranking military generals and
mercenaries in the Byzantine chain of command than princes
or dukes.

These early political ties to Byzantium had a profound
cultural impact on the rest of Venetian history. Venice's
cultural roots were Byzantine more than Roman. Its streets
and urban organization would never reflect Roman planning

so that there never existed in Rome a Roman city layout with a grid like Ostia's, urban quarters as in Florence, amphitheatres like those of Verona and Arezzo or baths and aqueducts like those in Rome. Venetians never fully adopted Roman law, they were often at odds with the Roman papacy and they were slow to take up the revival of Roman classicism that interested so much of the rest of Italy during the Renaissance. While some accounts of Venice's foundation emphasize its Roman roots and while Venetians at times wanted to emphasize their Roman pedigree, they also found themselves to be very different from Rome and often sought to emphasize this difference. This paradox – of wanting to be Roman while wanting to be distant from Rome – represented one of the great tensions defining Venetian history throughout the Middle Ages and the Early Modern period.

This strong connection to Byzantium meant that Venetians would form lasting and complex cultural ties with the Eastern Mediterranean. Venetian architecture, for instance, was first modelled on Eastern rather than Roman designs. One of the city's most representative buildings, the church of *San Marco*, with its brick and rubble walls, low-domed roof and small windows, is in stark contrast to luminous Western cathedrals that reach for the sky. Like much Venetian architecture, *San Marco*'s design is unmistakably derived from eastern models. Venetian trade was also primarily with the East, Venetian ambassadors spent much of their careers in Constantinople and Venetian artists were heavily influenced by the Byzantine tradition of mosaic production while artisans in the East learnt how to blow glass from their Venetian counterparts.

Following their initial subordination to Byzantine politics, however, Venetians slowly began to assert their political independence as Byzantine authority in Italy began to decline after the middle of the eighth century. The Lombards captured the Byzantine capital of Ravenna and the exarchate – the lynchpin of Byzantine control in Italy – collapsed in 751, effectively terminating any Byzantine presence in Italy. Without a mainland base, the Eastern Roman emperor's control over Venice became remote and with the fall of Ravenna locally elected doges in the lagoon began to exercise real political power.

The most decisive event solidifying Venetian political independence however was the Venetian defeat of the Franks in the early ninth century. The Franks, the ascendant barbarian group in Europe by the eighth century, succeeded the Lombards in Italy after 750. Towards the end of the eighth century, Charlemagne, the King of the Franks, entered the Italian peninsula with the aim of conquering all the Lombard territories and incorporating them into his kingdom that was by then well established in Gaul. Charlemagne is perhaps best known for the way in which he fashioned himself as a new, Western Roman emperor and forged the largest territorial empire in the West since the fall of Rome in 476. Based on its established eastern–political orientation however, Venice resisted Roman rule under the Emperor Charlemagne and remained loyal to its established ties to Constantinople.

Twice in the first decade after he was crowned emperor in Rome in 800, Charlemagne's armies tried to conquer Venice, and his attacks on the Lido settlements – the outermost islands separating the lagoon from the sea – almost succeeded. After defeating the local Lombards, Charlemagne decided to make himself lord of the lagoon primarily because it was the last corner of Byzantine territory not yet subject to the Franks. He proclaimed his son Pepin the King of Italy, and Pepin tried to conquer Venice in 810. Pepin destroyed Jesolo, Eraclea and Grado and then prepared a fleet in Ravenna to attack the Lido town of Malamocco. The battle raged for over six months, and the Frankish fleet eventually entered the lagoon, but the Venetians thwarted Pepin's attack in part by removing the shallow water markers along various channels in the marshes, thereby grounding the Franks' boats and preventing them from penetrating the lagoon's centre. With their flat-bottomed boats, the Venetians could practically fly around the Franks and were able to attack with much greater agility and speed, fighting off the invaders with arrows, rocks and boiling pitch. The Venetians decimated the Frankish fleet and, as the story goes, the waters turned red from the slaughter and, the canal that crossed this part of the lagoon, was named the 'Canal of Orphans' since the battle left so many Frankish children fatherless. The Franks eventually agreed to stop the siege of the city when the Venetians offered Pepin an annual tribute in exchange for their permanent withdrawal. The Venetians had narrowly escaped being subjected to a feudal power. Its lands would not be split up into baronial estates, the inhabitants were not made into serfs and farmers, and the city continued to rely on the sea for its existence. Through a series of treaties signed between 812 and 840, both Constantinople in the East and the Franks in the West slowly recognized greater degrees of Venetian political independence and the Venetians became conscious of the nascent power of their state.

The Venetian defeat of the Franks was significant not only because it earned the Venetians their freedom, but also because it was precisely in this period that the population of the lagoon moved to the islands that today comprise the city of Venice. In 742 Venetians had transferred their political centre from Eraclea (where the first doge was perhaps elected) in the northern lagoon to Malamocco on the outer islands of the Lido. Political crises within Byzantium had forced the transfer of the doge's seat, Malamocco being a good choice because it was even further away from the mainland and therefore safer from foreign conquest and invasion by land. However, with the naval threat of Pepin and the Franks, the principal families of the lagoon were forced to move again, this time to protect themselves from threats by sea. Once again fearing for their lives, these families turned inward from Malamocco to inhabit the muddy, flood-prone islands in the centre of the lagoon that had not previously been major areas of settlement. These islands formed the archipelago of the Rialto, the 'rivo alto' or high bank. They were the vestigial bed or sedimentary banks of the Brenta River that lay a few miles to the west and offered the

most elevated land in the area that was best suited to habi-
tation. It is these islands that form the dense urban centre of
Venice today.

With this second migration to the islands in the centre of the
lagoon Venetian history truly began, as these refugees in the
eighth and ninth centuries laid the first foundations of the city
that exists today. In addition, this movement from various
lagoon communities to the islands of the Rialto encouraged the
growth of a common civic identity. Before the settlement of the
Rialto, the inhabitants of the lagoon maintained a variety of
family and kinship allegiances rooted in the mainland cities
from which they came. When they inhabited the Rialto islands,
however, those from Eraclea, Torcello, Jesolo and Malamocco
left the more peripheral islands in the lagoon, including their
animals and fields, and merged their families with their historic
adversaries to try and forge a single civic entity on what was
then a deserted mudflat. While it would take many years for
Venetians to develop a real shared sense of identity and for
Venice to spring to life, once they moved to the Rialto together
these people became perhaps for the first time Venetians with a
distinct sense of shared purpose.

While Venice clearly had both Roman and Byzantine roots,
the events leading to a new degree of Venetian political independence by the ninth century would also contribute greatly
to the myth of Venice and suggestions that it was free and independent. Commentators like Cassiodorus believed that Venice
had a 'natural' tendency towards political independence. They
argued that the first Venetians prized their freedom so much
that to preserve it they fled their mainland homes for the
islands of the lagoon. This, however is clearly wrong. The first
Venetians did not found a city based solely on the noble virtue
of independence. They fled the mainland in desperation and
misfortune as terrified refugees running from the destruction
and chaos resulting from the arrival of various barbarian tribes
and the disintegration of the Western Roman Empire. They
were by no means free but were politically subject to the

Byzantine Empire for several centuries following the first mass migrations to the lagoon. However, in a rather singular fashion, Venetians defended themselves against the encroaching Franks about the same time that they managed to wrest their freedom away from the Byzantine Empire.

Nestled between Byzantium in the East, which maintained its political sovereignty over the Adriatic and its coast, and the incontestable dominion of the Franks on the Italian mainland, Venetians found themselves strategically located on a string of marshy islands on the margins of both empires. Their watery location on the borders of these worlds allowed them slowly to chip away at, and extract their freedom, from both sets of over-lords and eventually collaborate with the Muslim Orient. Venice would become a great cultural mediator between the worlds of Christianity and Islam. By the middle of the ninth century, Venetians had managed to carve out an embryonic but stable form of political autonomy. Such independence was unique in a world where few lived outside the dominion of the larger kingdoms and empires that dominated the Western and Mediterranean worlds. Venice's peculiar geographic location, as well as the fact that it became a tiny, independent republic amidst otherwise sprawling empires, were powerful factors influencing the way in which Venetians understood themselves as political actors throughout their history. This permitted the developing city to possess a type of political power and imagi-nation very different from its mainland counterparts.

Primitive Life
Most histories of Venice skip rather quickly from the migra-tions to the lagoon and the events leading up to Venetian political independence directly to the high Middle Ages and the explosion of Venetian commercial success in the Medi-terranean. In doing so, these histories confirm that mythical Venice was born seemingly perfect and fully formed. As the historian Ennio Concina put it, Venice appeared to emerge as if it were an 'independent shard of history'. It is important to

emphasize, however, the great degree of struggle that these early Venetians undertook not only to establish their political independence but also to simply survive in the hostile environment of the lagoon. This is, in essence, the same struggle that Venetians are engaged in today as they try to maintain and protect their palaces and canals against shifting ground and rising tides. The lagoon did offer its refugees peace, safety and protection from a variety of invaders, but it was also an extremely challenging if not repellent environment in which to try to build and preserve a community. It was desolate and barren: a vast, swampy, brackish marsh of mud, silt and sand bars inhabited almost exclusively by birds and mosquitoes.

Venetians laboured painstakingly for centuries to stabilize and conquer the lagoon's inhospitable bogs and mudflats. They did not reap the benefits of traditional Roman planning or engineering, or of being able to build on a pre-existing site. What little land existed above water was tenuous and fragile. It needed to be drained, filled with mud, raised and enclosed with dykes, its banks and shorelines built up, in order to construct stable shelters and buildings that would last. Mud had to be dredged from channels in order to make them navigable. Wells had to be built to collect drinkable rainwater. Perhaps the most pressing problem was that little would initially grow on these islands (contradicting the theory that this area was irrigated farmland). Though much of the produce at the Rialto market today comes from the islands of the lagoon (artichokes and lettuces, for instance, are often labelled as 'St Erasmo'), these islands originally had no viable farmland to fill to feed their inhabitants let alone to provide agricultural goods for export or profit. Early local farming primarily involved simple gardens and small vineyards, making Venetians almost entirely dependent on long-distance trade for food supplies. As one Italian proverb put it, however, the Venetians were a strange people because 'they never planted or harvested, but always had their silos full'.

Determined settlers, they slowly learned how to carve out a place for themselves in the economy of the Mediterranean through hunting, fishing and, in particular, trading in salt. As Cassiodorus' letter explains, the first Venetians did not farm; 'instead of ploughs and scythes they used rollers to pack the base of salt pans'. The earliest fishermen quickly realized that the waters of the lagoon produced a valuable resource in salt, thanks to the high salinity of the lagoon's shallow waters. Venetians built dikes to enclose areas of the lagoon, and the dikes contained locks and moveable doors to allow salt water to enter special bays where it began to evaporate and transform into a dense, salty liquid. This liquid passed into other smaller bays where the last of the water was left to evaporate and the salt concentrated into crystals. These crystals were collected and deposited on nearby docks or quays to be broken up with mallets and sent to warehouses to be stored and sold. As the islands of the lagoon slowly became peopled in the seventh and eighth centuries, island dwellers increased their salt production since then, as now, salt was indispensable for flavouring and preserving meat and fish. For the earliest Venetians, salt provided a formidable natural resource with which to trade for other goods, including grain, oil and wine, that they could not supply for themselves. While Venice would eventually become one of the greatest maritime empires as a result of its trade in luxury goods, such as silks and exotic spices, it is somewhat ironic that the humble resource of salt provided Venetians with their first substantial commodity for exchange. Salt represented the coin of the first Venetians and the original source of their wealth.

Venetians traded their salt along the rivers of Northern Italy. After they sacked the nearby rival city of Comacchio on the Adriatic coast, just south of Chioggia in 886 and again in 932, they obtained access to the mouth of the Po River and control over the mouths of all the major rivers leading into the Adriatic from Northern Italy. They began transporting large amounts of salt up these rivers into the mainland interior in exchange, at first, for agricultural goods, especially grain. They also soon discovered that clay from the more solid islands of the lagoon could be fired into good bricks, and began navigating their rafts upriver to trade with them as far away as Pavia near Milan. By the ninth century they were also transporting large quantities of timber, largely from the oak, ash and beech groves on the plains near Venice, but also larch, pine and fir from the foothills of the Alps. After mastering this river trade, ensuring their food supply, and slowly but surely reclaiming the habitable land on the islands around the Rialto, Venice stood poised to make a grand entrance into the greater economies of Europe and the Mediterranean.

Exploring Venice today, how can we get a sense of the raw, stark world of the first inhabitants of the lagoon and their origins? The mainland towns around the arc of the northern Adriatic – and the civic museums of Altino, Oderzo and Aquileia in particular – exhibit the humble but stirring remains of the Romans who lived in this area before migrating to the lagoon. In addition, the patriarchal basilica of Aquileia boasts the largest paleo-Christian mosaic floor in all of Europe: a breathtaking reminder of the Roman world from which the first Venetians came from. Other remains include archaeological fragments and extant patches of Roman roads, such as the via Annia and the via Claudia, the formidable highways that once linked these towns in the Veneto to the larger Roman world. Patches of these once great arteries are now almost invisible and lie quietly among the overgrown weeds around these mainland towns.

In the lagoon itself, virtually no architecture from the period of the earliest inhabitants of Venice survives, largely because the Venetians' first houses were most likely wooden huts built on stilts to protect them from the tides and flooding, to wait out a storm, and to temporarily store supplies. There remains little or no trace of these structures since, elementary and spontaneous as they were, shifting marshland reclaimed these first buildings ages ago. The first fishermen to inhabit the lagoon probably built these shelters as described by Cassiodorus, using larchwood poles that were sharpened and then forced into the mud to form walls with a roof of reeds or straw. Fishermen in the lagoon still build similar structures on piles called *cavane* to shelter their boats and nets, and you can occasionally see these huts around the minor islands of the lagoon. Amidst the buzzing speedboats of weekend visitors, looming ferries transporting tourists and commuters back and forth among the islands, and the airplanes that come and go in the background, these huts offer a quiet reminder of the fragile world of the first Venetians.

The place that today offers the best image of archaic Venetian life is the island of Torcello in the northern part of the lagoon. Archaeologists think that the lagoon basin was colonized to some degree long before the arrival of refugees fleeing the barbarians. Many Roman objects have been found on the islands in the northern lagoon, especially on Torcello, suggesting that there may have been a Roman colony here emanating from nearby Altino. Torcello preserves a sense of the primitive world of the early settlers from long ago.

The cathedral of Torcello is one of the oldest surviving buildings in the lagoon, founded around 638–9 when the Bishop of Altino transferred his seat here and various families from the mainland followed. In front of the cathedral today are the remains of the original seventh-century round baptistery, where the refugee catechumens (those studying to become Christian) would have been made Christians – perhaps by candlelight, as was the practice in Ravenna – in this stark world far removed from civilization. Set into the left-hand wall inside the church is a stone tablet recording the dedications and consecration of the church in 639. This inscription, which includes the names of the bishop and the exarch, is perhaps the oldest authentic document of Venetian history (though some say this inscription does not refer to this cathedral but to another church in the mainland town of Cittanova). According to legend a monumental stone on the island not far from the cathedral was actually once the throne of Attila the Hun, though it was more likely the seat of one of the local governors or tribunes. Though fewer than 100 people permanently live here today (by some accounts, not even 30), at its height in the twelfth century the island was home to 20,000–30,000 people (a plaque on the main quay of the island says 50,000). Torcello was abandoned in the later Middle Ages when silt built up from nearby rivers and created marshlands that bred mosquitoes and malaria.

According to legend, as the Lombards approached, the residents of Altino did not know which saint to call on to ward off this impending danger and, desperately, they decided to hold a public prayer in the town's central square. Suddenly they saw a flock of birds taking off nearby carrying in their beaks their newborn chicks. This extraordinary event was interpreted as a portent and everyone unanimously decided to follow them. Preceeded by two tribunes, Ario and Aratore, and members of the clergy, the Altinese followed the birds to Torcello where upon their arrival, the lord spoke to them from a cloud and told them to erect a church on that spot. According to one theory the island of Torcello was named after one of the gates to the city of Altino, *Turicellum*.

Today Torcello helps us envisage the flight of those first exiled from the mainland to the lagoon. The immigrants from Altino brought on their backs the relics of their local saint, St Eliodoro. Near the main altar of the cathedral of Torcello you can look down through a grate in the floor and see a sarcophagus decorated with pagan images containing the body of this saint, brought here in haste and under duress to protect this island. His image is also found among the apostles in the apse mosaics. The church is studded with Roman columns and Corinthian capitals, stone most likely salvaged from the mainland during the Lombard invasions.

Links to Altino and the Roman mainland are visible in numerous classical inscriptions, especially the Roman funerary monuments in the Torcello museum, again taken primarily from the area around Altino. While they could not bring everything, the immigrants dismantled as much of Altino as they could, stone by stone, including the paving stones from

the Roman roads that ran through the town, moving them to
Torcello to recreate their city in the early seventh century.
Looking at all these remains, we can imagine these immigrants
from the mainland looking around their homes and communities to decide which of their belongings they could manage to
pack up and bring to the lagoon as the Lombards approached.
The great nineteenth-century art historian John Ruskin aptly
described the cathedral of Torcello as being like a ship: a
Noah's arc that saved people from an otherwise certain
destruction. More than in the richness of the Venetian arsenal
or the pomp of its palaces, he argued, merely ascending the
crude steps that encircle the altar of Torcello allows us to experience the original heart of Venice.

Beyond the cathedral and the archaeological remains associated with it, the surrounding landscape of the island also
gives us a sense of the world inhabited by the first Venetians: an
experience that is no longer possible in the architectural
density of today's Venice. Here you can see the desolate terrain
that once confronted these first refugees. Looking around,
there is almost nothing in sight but sea and sky, especially from
the top of the church's bell tower. You can hear little besides
the rustling reeds, lapping waves and the occasional bark of a
seagull. Though this may be picturesque if not blissful to the
modern tourist, this landscape represented the bleak and
remote world (compared to the pleasures and comforts of the
Roman Empire) to which the first Venetians came to remake
their lives.

A variety of other small details around the other islands of
the lagoon, and in the city centre, show us the remnants of
early lagoon life. The baptismal font of the church of *Santi
Maria e Donato* on Murano, for instance, came from the
Acilio family in Altino, according to its Latin inscription.
Similarly, settlers transported a series of octagonal Roman
pilasters, originally made in the second century BC, to Murano
from the mainland and applied them to the outside of the
church. Various Roman bricks or artefacts, sometimes called

altinelle because they originated in Altino, can be found randomly around the city: An antique Latin inscription with several Corinthian columns inserted into the façade of a building near the *Ponte del Paradiso* at *Santa Maria Formosa*, a Roman tablet from the mainland placed in the base of the campanile of the church of *San Vidal*, a set of blind arches with a tooth-patterned border and a series of winged animals located along the *Riva del Carbon* near the Rialto. In addition, the Venice Archaeological Museum houses a handful of Roman statuettes, each no more than 30 cm (12 inches) tall, from both the Veneto and the lagoon: a bronze Achilles made near Oderzo in the first century BC, a Poseidon from the second century BC discovered near the Lido town of *San Pietro in Volta* and a Hercules from the third century BC unearthed near Malamocco. These scraps and fragments might be small and humble, but remain potent vestiges and reminders of the Romans who first came to Venice.

2

VENICE IN THE MIDDLE AGES: LEGITIMACY AND EXPANSION

At the magnificent height of the Roman Empire, the city of Venice was nothing but a group of barren, grassy islands uninhabited except by fishermen and hunters. Even at the start of the ninth century, Venice still only contained groups of families huddled together on a series of muddy tidal flats: families who prayed for survival against the elements and for their attackers to pack up and go. By the thirteenth century, however, Venice had become a world power: the centre of the Mediterranean economy and the envy of all Europeans who both admired and jealously eyed the city's wealth and opulence.

Over the course of the Middle Ages, Venetians organized their system of government from one based on clan loyalties that was subservient to the Byzantine Empire to a republican state that employed elaborate government mechanisms to manage its inhabitants and its resources. How did these remarkable transformations happen? How did Venetians evolve from a humble community of salt traders and fishermen into a city of world-class merchants, bankers and statesmen? And how did this happen when Venice, unlike most other Italian states in the Middle Ages, did not even have a king or an emperor to make it an equal player on the field of European politics?

Venice and the Mediterranean in the Early Middle Ages
Venice had already achieved a new degree of political independence by the early ninth century. Byzantine power in Italy had declined and the Franks had been defeated. After routing Pepin in the lagoon in 810, a series of treaties between the Franks and the Byzantines in 814 – the *Pax Nicephori* (named after the Byzantine Emperor Nicephorus) and the Treaties of Ratisbon and Aquisgrana – stated that the Byzantines would recognize the Franks as the rulers of the West, but that the Franks in turn had to renounce their claims over Venice and recognize that it was subject to Byzantium. These agreements stipulated that Venice was required to pay a tribute to the Franks in exchange for its independence from Western rule. For the first time, in the wake of these treaties, Venetians began to govern themselves like an independent state. As an island world in the space between two great empires, Venice had quietly begun to carve out its unique political niche, independent from both. However, becoming independent was not enough to make these islands a European power; they needed something to validate their political importance, and the crucial event that first gave Venetians a European presence was their theft of the body of St Mark.

At the start of the ninth century Venice was still technically a Byzantine territory and subject to the patriarchal jurisdiction of Aquileia and Grado, other Byzantine outposts in the area. While it is impossible to argue that there was a conscious Venetian desire to assert its power over these and other cities, some Venetians surely had a sense that they would need symbols and relics of greater significance than these towns possessed in order to surpass them in political and religious importance. In 828, as reported by Venetian chronicles, two men managed to sneak the relics of St Mark the Evangelist (and the writer of the Gospel of Mark of the New Testament) out of the eponymous Coptic church in Alexandria and transport them to Venice. Mark had founded this church in Alexandria and was martyred in the city in 62/3 AD, and that's where his remains had lain ever since.

While accounts of this story vary, it seems that two merchants, Bono from Malamocco and Rustico from Torcello (sometimes called Tribunus and Rusticus), were either swept into Alexandria by a storm or deliberately entered despite a ban on trade with the city at the time. Local caliphs had been destroying Christian churches around Egypt to use their materials to build a palace in Alexandria, so these Venetian merchants were in a hurry to seize the relics before they were lost or destroyed forever. After days of negotiations when the merchants tried to convince the church's clergymen to hand over the body – both for its protection and in exchange for potentially great rewards from the doge – the merchants were permitted to remove the body from its sarcophagus, most likely replacing it with the body of another saint that was handily nearby. While they may have obtained tentative permission from the overseers of the church, they nevertheless had to sneak the body out from under the eyes of the civic guardians of the city and those who oversaw trade. Legend claims that they conveyed it safely out of the city by hiding it under slabs of pork, offensive to both Muslims and Jews, and sneaking it safely on to a ship. The only problem was a storm on the return journey near the Calabrian town of Cropani, on the shore of the instep of the 'boot' of Italy. Apparently the merchants promised to leave Mark's kneecap in the village in exchange for safe passage from their city and, as a result Cropani's traders were uniquely exempt from Venetian taxes during the Middle Ages.

The choice of St Mark was important. According to legend he had once preached on the shores of the lagoon, when Christ told him in a vision that he would one day find his final resting place there. Another legend claims that after ordaining the first patriarch in the town of Aquileia, a storm forced Mark to take cover in the canals among the islands of Venice. He got out to pray, perhaps in the exact spot where the Ducal Palace would eventually exist. An angel appeared to Mark in that moment and said *'Pax tibi Marce evangelista meus'*, meaning 'be at rest here' that could be interpreted to mean both 'do not be afraid of the storm' and 'this will be your final resting place'. Venetians, naturally, heard the second interpretation and to this day the motto is visible everywhere in the city, under the paw of the heraldic winged lion, the symbol of the evangelist that became the symbol of the city of Venice. The arrival of the relics of St Mark had the crucial effect of allowing Venice to usurp the political authority of its nearby rivals, Aquileia and Grado. With St Mark's body in its princely palace, Venice was now more powerful than its neighbours.

The merchants delivered St Mark's body to the doge Giustiniano Partecipazio (r. 827–9), who then lived in the recently erected Ducal Palace. As scores of historians have pointed out, it is significant that the merchants gave the body to the doge and not the local patriarch. In most early medieval cities before the development of stable governing institutions, the bishop was the centre of most local governments. Venice, however, as a part of its Byzantine heritage, had an early history of subordinating the clergy to secular rulers, a trend that would become very important in its later history. In addition, the patriarch of the area was resident in Grado at the other end of the lagoon and was technically not the Bishop of Venice. The local bishop in the lagoon somewhat oddly resided on the island of Olivolo in the district of Castello, far removed from the Ducal Palace, all of which meant that Venetians, by the ninth century, turned to the doge and not an ecclesiastical authority as the leader of their community. The doge immediately decreed that a church worthy of the relics should be built. Four years later, Mark's body found a home in the completed private chapel of the doge that was then named *San Marco*.

This church was built to honour the arrival of these relics and, as the doge's chapel, it represented a powerful symbol of the marginalization of other spiritual authorities in the lagoon.

The theft of St Mark's body also represented a symbolic preview of Venice's future. As we shall see, Venetians earned much of their wealth but they also stole quite a bit of it. Mark's body was perhaps the first great instance of what would become a long tradition of Venetian theft.

With the arrival of St Mark, Venetians switched their allegiance from their first patron saint, the Greek St Theodore. Theodore was a Byzantine martyr but, at the time of the arrival of the body of St Mark, no relics of Theodore's existed in the lagoon. Mark's body therefore proclaimed a new symbolic independence from Byzantium. Since Mark was not a Roman saint either, his presence in Venice also asserted a kind of symbolic independence from, or rivalry with, Rome. Just as the popes drew their authority from St Peter, now the Venetians could similarly claim that their authority came from Mark, whose body allowed them to link their past with the history of early Christianity. Mark's presence fed Venetian civic imagination and promoted the city, making it more prominent than its neighbours, both locally and around the Mediterranean. In one stroke, the theft of Mark's relics gave Venetians political and spiritual legitimacy.

The story of this robbery is also significant because it illuminates the expansion of Venetian trade around the Mediterranean in the early Middle Ages. The residents of Alexandria did not appear surprised to see Venetian merchants in their midst; if they were able to sneak Mark's body out of the city, this was in part because people were used to seeing Venetians in Mediterranean trade centres. By the ninth century and from 900–1100 in particular, Venetians had expanded their trade beyond the rivers of Northern Italy and turned outward into the Adriatic and the Mediterranean. Venice had always been Byzantium's main trading base in the northern Adriatic, but when Byzantine power began to recede, Venetian merchants began to extend

their networks in response. They increasingly travelled to the
East, to Constantinople, Alexandria and Aleppo to find exotic
goods, including silk and spices, that Greek traders had once
brought to them. By the ninth century, in addition to their usual
trade in fish and salt, Venetians began to bring these goods inland
to Northern Italy, especially to Lombard and Frankish courts.
One chronicle indicates that when Charlemagne's forces came to
do battle in Friuli, his courtiers appeared wearing luxurious
clothes and precious jewels bought from Venetian merchants in
Pavia. Venetians also began to transport timber (from groves in
Northern Italy, floated down the rivers into the lagoon) and
slaves (primarily from the Balkans) to Muslim Africa.

Not surprisingly the more the Venetians expanded their
sphere of influence, the more resistance they encountered, and
the more they became involved in conflicts and wars. For
instance, in 899 yet another barbarian tribe, the Magyars,
invaded and devastated much of north-eastern Italy and made
for Venice, anxious to conquer this city of growing wealth and
prestige. With no experience in naval warfare, the Magyars
were unable to defeat the Venetians on their own watery
terrain and, like Pepin's forces, were forced to withdraw.
Nevertheless, the Magyar came so close that the Venetians
promptly tightened their security within the lagoon. Doge
Pietro Tribuno (r. 888–912) ordered the fortification of the
Rialtine islands and the construction of a seaward wall on all of
the islands on the eastern side of the lagoon from the island of
Olivolo in Castello down to what is today the church of *Santa
Maria del Giglio*. A chain was also attached across the mouth
of the Grand Canal, crossing it near what is today the church of
San Gregorio in Dorsoduro, perhaps in imitation of the chain
the Byzantines used to protect the mouth of the Golden Horn
in Constantinople. No traces of the wall and chain remain
today, but they represented a fearful moment in Venetian
history when the city's inhabitants encased themselves in walls
like their mainland counterparts, fearing that the waters of the
lagoon might not be enough to protect them from invaders.

The biggest threats to Venetian survival and expansion, however, existed not so much in the form of invaders like the Magyars but more often in the form of commercial rivals in the Adriatic that threatened Venetian profits from trade. After subduing and subordinating its closest neighbours, such as Comacchio, the next major step in Venetian commercial expansion involved eliminating predatory pirates and raiders. Muslim Saracens had seized parts of Southern Italy in the early ninth century and threatened Venetian trade in the southern Adriatic, while Dalmatian pirates in the northern Adriatic raided Venetian ships during the ninth century. These Dalmatian or Narentine pirates had their base at the mouth of the Narenta River (now the Neretva River in Croatia); they infested the Adriatic and threatened mercantile convoys by stealing from Venetian traders and then retreating into the mouth of the river. On Ascension Day, 9 May 1000, Doge Pietro II Orseolo (r. 991–1009) sailed for the Dalmatian coast under a banner of the winged lion of St Mark to stop these thieves once and for all. His strategy was to blockade the pirates inside the river by seizing the islands of Curzola and Langosta (now Korchula and Lastovo) at the mouth of the river, and picking off their ships one by one when they tried to leave. Orseolo successfully defeated the pirates, though piracy continued to plague Venice until the last days of the republic. For the moment, however, the doge and his forces managed to eliminate one of the great threats to Venetian trade and, as a result, the city came to dominate the eastern coast of the Adriatic. This victory in the year 1000 represented the first major wave of Venetian territorial expansion, and the Venetian Empire was born with its domination of Dalmatia.

Doge Pietro II Orseolo was not only a great military commander but also an extremely successful diplomat and negotiator. In the interests of diplomacy he married his son Giovanni Orseolo to a Byzantine princess in 1005. She immediately created a stir upon her arrival in the lagoon city because she didn't eat with her hands; her servants cut up her food into small pieces which she ate with a tiny, golden fork, perhaps the first fork used, or at least documented, in the Western world. While forks did not become an overnight success by any means, they did begin to appear in Venetian and European wills and household inventories with regularity by the thirteenth century: a crucial component of western civilization that perhaps resulted from Venetian diplomacy. During his reign, Orseolo also released Venice from its annual obligation to pay a tribute of 50 pounds of silver a year to the Holy Roman Empire and additionally established tribute payments from the people and territories he had conquered in Dalmatia. The town of Veglia (now Krk), for instance, had to give Venice 35 marten and fox skins a year, and Pola (now Pula) 2,000 pounds of lamp oil for the lighting of *San Marco*. Latin and Slavic locals up and down the coasts of the eastern Adriatic, on the Istrian peninsula in the north and down the Dalmatian coast in the east, were forced to swear an oath of allegiance to the doge. The great significance of these victories, however, was not these tributes but the increased security they gave Venetian merchants. This safely allowed them to continue trading with Africa and the eastern Mediterranean without any interference from pirates. By the year 1000, in large part thanks to Doge Pietro II Orseolo, Venice had become the master of the northern Adriatic. It effectively monopolized all trade in this region.

As Venice expanded, its relationship to Byzantium became much more complicated. Venetian doges, traders and military men had to remember that technically the territory they conquered in Dalmatia was still part of the Byzantine Empire. Venetians needed to execute such conquests with great diplomatic tact. They offered the Byzantines their naval assistance whenever required, which made Venetian expansion more palatable. Venetian ships, for instance, helped the Byzantines defend their territories in Southern Italy when the Saracens attacked them in the tenth century. The Venetians were rewarded with their first 'Golden Bull' from the Byzantine

Empire in 992, which recognized Venetians as the preferred traders between Italy and Constantinople. This bull or 'letter of permission' gave Venetians a more favourable customs tariff than the one paid by other Mediterranean merchants from Amalfi or Bari. For many years, the Venetians assisted the Byzantines with their fleet and the Byzantines subsequently rewarded the Venetians with trading privileges. While this relationship worked well most of the time, the Venetians expected Byzantium to pay handsomely for their services, and the more the Venetians received, the greedier they became. The Venetians thought they were worth every privilege, but the Byzantines often found them demanding, arrogant and ungrateful. Consequently great disagreements often broke out between the two powers that eventually led to the slaughter of the Fourth Crusade.

A good early example of this symbiotic but tense relationship between Venice and Byzantium was illustrated when the Normans attacked parts of the Byzantine Empire in the second half of the eleventh century. Remember that while the Byzantine Empire maintained its capital in the eastern Mediterranean in Constantinople, it retained some territories in Southern Italy through much of the eleventh century. At this time an upstart family from Northern Europe, the Normans, came to Southern Italy in 1015 to work as mercenary fighters for the Lombards against the Byzantines. As they were paid for their services with land, the Normans slowly built up a large kingdom and eventually conquered Sicily and all of Southern Italy. They finally ousted the Byzantines from their Italian lands in 1071 when they conquered Bari, the last Byzantine stronghold in the south. Many thought that the Normans planned to extend their growing Mediterranean kingdom as far east as Constantinople, which would not have been that surprising since another branch of this family had recently conquered England in 1066.

After the Normans had ousted the Byzantines from Southern Italy, they then crossed the Adriatic and proceeded to attack and besiege the Byzantine city of Durazzo (now Durres, on the coast of modern Albania) in 1081 under the leadership of the Norman general Robert Guiscard. The Byzantine Emperor Alexius I Comnenus appealed to the Venetians for help. Durazzo represented an important strategic location for the Normans since it was at the beginning of a Roman road that ran through Greece and the Balkans directly to Constantinople. The capture of Durazzo would open up a direct route to Constantinople in the East. The Venetian response to this attack resulted in one of the great naval battles of Venetian history, and indeed the first Venetian naval battle for which we have any real description.

Doge Domenico Selvo (r. 1071–84) led this campaign and instructed Venetian forces to tie their ships together to form a type of floating harbour at sea that would effectively stop the Normans from leaving port. On top of this 'harbour' the Venetians constructed wooden towers around the boats' masts. Using ropes, they then hauled up smaller boats filled with armed men who, from this raised position, had a strategic advantage over the Normans.This great floating platform was the first of what would be many masterpieces of Venetian naval strategy. It allowed Venetian archers to catapult missiles from the top of the masts to sink the enemy and repulse Norman attacks. The Venetians hurled both stones and insults at the Normans; they threw bags of lime into their eyes and sprayed slippery soap on the Norman decks to upset their footing. The enemy eventually managed to advance towards Constantinople over land, but the Venetian naval forces beat them at Durazzo on the high seas.

Alexius I generously rewarded the Venetians with yet another Golden Bull in 1082 that greatly expanded the trading privileges the Venetians had already obtained in 992. This new charter included an exemption from tolls and tariffs in the Byzantine Empire, giving Venetian merchants a stunning competitive advantage over merchants from other cities. After 1082 Venetians could enter and leave all Byzantine ports between Venice and Constantinople without paying any taxes or tariffs. They could stop and transfer cargo free of charge in ports across the lower Adriatic and the Mediterranean, in strategic cities including Durazzo, Corfu, Modon, Coron, Athens and Thebes, and even the imperial capital. In Constantinople the Venetians gained permission to maintain commercial docks and warehouses in which Byzantine customs officials could not interfere. The Venetians still faced fierce competition from Provençal, Genoese, Pisan, Amalfitani and Pugliese traders in the wider Mediterranean but, as a result of the 1082 Golden Bull, Venice stood on the brink of a great commercial revolution. Its merchants and traders had suddenly gained a spectacular economic advantage.

The Crusades
While Venetians had often been successful in defending themselves and their Byzantine overlords against Normans, pirates and Saracens, a much larger threat was developing in Asia Minor (now Turkey): the Seljuk Turks. In 1071 Muslim Turks began attacking and colonizing Byzantine territory in the East, prompting the Byzantines to turn to Western Europe for help. By 1095 Pope Urban II had called on Europeans to come to the East's rescue and save the Holy Land, drumming up a fever for crusading among many European Christians. The Crusades, a period of European military and political involvement in the eastern Mediterranean, would last for several hundred years from 1095–1291. While thousands of crusading knights and their entourages began to make their way across Europe towards Jerusalem, Venetians found themselves in a precarious position. On the one hand, they had St Mark behind them and they too were devout Christians who supported the pope and their fellow Christians. On the other hand, war and crusading was not good for trade and Venetians were wary of disrupting their good mercantile relationships with their Muslim neighbours and markets around the Mediterranean. They watched their trading rivals of Pisa and Genoa slowly enrich their

coffers – in 1098, for instance, the Pisans conquered the Byzantine island of Corfu – and the Venetians eventually ended up using their fleet to prevent their rivals from gaining an upper hand. Venetian trade clearly benefited from peace and stability in the Byzantine Empire. It was in Venetian commercial interests to keep their Byzantine privileges intact. When peace was threatened by advancing Muslim forces Venice eventually decided to participate in a series of naval expeditions to the East.

At the very beginning of the crusading period, Venetians were most concerned with protecting the Byzantine Empire and had no particular interest in conquering land or gaining territory in Palestine or around the Holy Land. Active support against the Turks came first from Genoa and other European forces while the Venetians focused first on preventing their maritime rivals from gaining a trading advantage. So, in 1099, the Venetian fleet engaged the Pisans in a battle off the island of Rhodes, capturing 20 ships and 4,000 prisoners and essentially forcing the Pisans to promise to stay permanently out of eastern Mediterranean trade. The Venetians also used the early crusading period to continue the tradition they had established when they stole St Mark by looting and adding to their collection of relics and stolen trophies from around the Mediterranean. For some time Venetians had had their eyes on the relics of St Nicholas of Myra, the patron saint of seamen and merchants (and the same St Nicholas of Christmas and Santa Claus). They made their way to the coastal city of Myra in Asia Minor (near the modern Turkish city of Kas) only to find out that another raiding party from Bari had already stolen the body in 1100. As smart traders and shrewd inventors of their own sense of legitimacy, the Venetians responded by insisting that the seamen from Bari had made a mistake and that the true body of Nicholas was still there, which they then took. They returned with this body (though it was most likely someone else's), called it St Nicholas and lodged it in *San Nicolò* – the church of the sailors on the Lido – further empowering themselves with the divine protection of yet another significant saint. According to guidebooks, the body of St Nicholas of Myrastill lies in the church today. The Venetians demonstrated little initial interest in fighting the Muslims and their early crusading activities were dedicated primarily to peripheral forms of profit.

Within the first quarter of the twelfth century, however, Venetians began to realize the potential commercial gains to be made from engaging Muslim forces. In 1110 Venetians helped crusaders capture the city of Sidon (on the coast of modern Lebanon), and King Baldwin of Jerusalem rewarded them by giving them control over part of the port of Acre and trading privileges in the Kingdom of Jerusalem. In 1123, after the Egyptians had attacked the city of Jaffa (an ancient port just south of modern Tel Aviv), Doge Domenico Michiel (r. 1118–30) led Venetian forces in the attack on the Egyptian fleet in the Battle of Ascalon (off the modern coastal city of Ashkelon in Southern Israel). In this spectacular battle, the Venetians deceived the Egyptian fleet into believing that they were attacking a small caravan of cargo ships and pilgrims only to discover, too late, 40 Venetian galleys behind them. With the sea red with blood for miles around and the nearby beaches strewn with cadavers, the Venetians temporarily eliminated the presence of Muslim traders in the eastern Mediterranean. In addition, they captured several merchant vessels laden with gold, silver and spices. In 1124 they agreed to help the knights of the Kingdom of Jerusalem in their siege of the city of Tyre and were granted one-third of the city after its conquest.

The Venetian forces involved in crusading activities continued to aid their Byzantine allies as they always had. Defeating Muslims, after all, worked to fortify and protect the Byzantine Empire. Relations between Venice and Byzantium nevertheless continued to be volatile during the crusading period largely because Venetians just could not stop pillaging as they realized that fortunes could easily be made from theft. Returning from the Battle of Ascalon in 1124, the fleet of Domenico Michiel stole the body of St Donatus (still today in the church of his name on Murano) and repeatedly looted from the Greeks on their way home, sacking many additional Greek islands, coastal towns and ships. As a result, after Emperor Alexius I Comnenus died in 1118, his successors attempted to end Venetian trading privileges. In 1124 the Byzantine Emperor John Comnenus decided to revoke the favoured status that had been granted to Venetians in the bull of 1082. This favoured Pisan merchants and perhaps was aimed at generating increased competition between Venetians and Pisans, to the benefit of the Byzantines. This prompted Doge Domenico Michiel to capture even more Byzantine territory in retaliation, forcing the emperor to renew the Golden Bull. While Venetians preferred to be at peace with Byzantium to maintain the stability on which their trading privileges were based, they had no qualms about attacking the Byzantines when necessary. At one point, as tensions ran high between the two during the Venetian conquest of Corfu, Venetian sailors, surely drunk, attacked the dignity of the Byzantine Emperor Manuel Comnenus by placing a slave, dressed satirically in imperial robes, on the deck of a captured, imperial galley, insulting him before the Greek fleet.

The Byzantines needed Venetian allegiance as always to help them fight the Turks and the Normans, but they did not take Venetian attacks and insults lightly. In the spring of 1171, when relations with Byzantium had greatly deteriorated, this same Byzantine Emperor Manuel Comnenus, in a surprising move, suddenly called for the arrest of all the Venetians in the Byzantine Empire, seizing their property and holding about 10,000 Venetians hostage in Constantinople alone. Doge Vitale Michiel II (r. 1156–72), who would later become one of the more infamous doges in Venetian history, rallied Venetian forces for a large assault on Byzantine coasts and Con-stantinople, an assault that involved a massive reorganization of the city of Venice to fund this attack. Vitale ordered Venice to be arranged into six *sestieri*, or districts (the same six Venetian neighbourhoods that exist today), each of which was financially obliged to support a fleet of 120 ships. Concern for the lives of the Venetian hostages meant that the fleet could not act too aggressively. Doge Vitale tried unsuccessfully to negotiate with Byzantine officials but talks failed and, to make matters worse, an epidemic broke out in the Venetian fleet, killing thousands by the spring of 1172. The doge and his crew returned to Venice, humiliated.

Venetians at home were infuriated. Doge Vitale's failure left many Venetians' relatives in danger abroad and threatened the commercial existence of many clans. Fearing the wrath of many noble families, Vitale attempted to flee the Ducal Palace, aiming for the safety of the nearby convent of *San Zaccharia*. After crossing the *Ponte della Paglia* (the bridge from which to view the Bridge of Sighs), he turned left into the *Calle delle Rasse* and was stabbed. His murderer was caught and executed since crimes against patrician politicians were outlawed, no matter how horrific the doge's failure. And in order to underline the fact that violence against the political class was not permitted, the government declared that no stone building could ever be erected on the site of the murderer's house, located nearby. Builders followed this decree and erected only small and simple wooden buildings on this site until the construction of the new annex of the Danieli Hotel in 1948. The bad relationship between Venice and Byzantium, however, continued to sour. In an anti-Western riot in Constantinople in 1182, Byzantines once again seized Venetian property and imprisoned and eventually massacred many Venetians. These hostilities finally culminated in the dramatic events of the Fourth Crusade.

If Venetian ascendancy began with river trading in salt and fish, slowly enlarged into the Mediterranean and was promoted by Byzantine commercial advantages, the final event that solidified Venetian maritime supremacy was the Fourth Crusade. While Venetian participation in the early crusading period was somewhat minor, they finally became more committed. In 1203–4 as a result of growing tensions with Byzantium, the Venetians entered the fray of the crusades with full force. This

Crusade began in 1199 when Count Thibald of Champagne decided to try and retake Jerusalem from Muslim forces. He petitioned the Venetian navy to transport him and his knights to the Holy Land, and French crusaders arrived in Venice in the summer of 1202 to negotiate the terms of their passage. The Venetians agreed to ship 35,000 men to the Holy Land, with their horses and supplies, for nine months. In exchange they would receive a fee of 85,000 silver marks and half the loot. The crafty Venetians then talked them into hiring more ships than they needed, made all the worse when fewer crusaders than anticipated showed up. The Venetians – businessmen, well acquainted with failed contracts – agreed to take the crusaders to the Holy Land anyway in exchange for additional military assistance in subduing a series of cities that had recently rebelled against them in the Adriatic. The Dalmatian city of Zara had resisted Venetian control by placing itself under the protection of the King of Hungary in 1186. The Venetian fleet and the crusaders left for the Holy Land in October of 1202, stopping along the way so that the crusaders could sack and seize Zara, Durazzo and Corfu, thereby helping Venetians shore up their maritime control of the Adriatic.

Doge Enrico Dandolo (r. 1192–1205), who was over 80 years old at the time and either nearly or completely blind, accompanied the fleet and was so impressed with the subjugation of these cities that he craftily decided to use the crusaders to put the Byzantine Empire in its place for good. The Venetian fleet took a detour en route to Palestine and then sailed for Constantinople. Among the crusaders in the Venetian ships happened to be a man with a claim to the Byzantine throne, Prince Alexius Angelus. He wanted to capture the Byzantine Empire under his name, and in retrospect it seems hardly a coincidence that he was on board. On 26 June 1203 the crusaders arrived in Constantinople and attempted, essentially as a formality, to convince the Byzantines that Alexius was the lawful heir to the imperial throne. When this naturally failed, Enrico Dandolo led a brutal attack on the city.

The Venetians used incredibly creative tactics. Though seemingly impenetrable walls surrounded the city of Constantinople on its seaward side, the Venetians sidled their galleys right up against them. As in the battle of Durazzo against the Normans, they climbed the masts to build bridges from which to attack the walls. The Venetians managed to infiltrate and subdue the city and make Alexius the new emperor but he was slow to compensate the Venetians for their assistance. He was overthrown and murdered by another Byzantine faction in January 1204 and the next emperor to take his place, Alexius V Ducas, immediately defended Constantinople against the Venetians. Enrico Dandolo responded in April 1204 by completely sacking the city. Constantinople collapsed after four days of violence, murder and plunder, after which Dandolo announced that the Byzantine Empire had ended. It would henceforth be renamed the 'Latin Empire', with a Latin emperor to be chosen by Venetian and French electors. Enrico Dandolo, preferring to remain the Doge of Venice, declined the possibility of being elected, and Baldwin of Flanders was made the Latin Emperor of the East in May 1204.

The attack on Constantinople represented one of the most gruesome slaughters of the Middle Ages. In the history of Europe until the thirteenth century – a time of barbarian invasions, spiritual hatreds and even regular violence among European nobles – attacking, pillaging and killing was much the norm. But even in this culture of regularized violence, the sack of Constantinople was a shock to those who witnessed and heard about it. In one of the greatest ironies, mercenary crusaders who had set out to reclaim Jerusalem as the soldiers of Christ had slaughtered fellow Christians. Venetians and crusaders nearly emptied the city of all of its movable goods. They grabbed everything they could take, often destroying works of art to extract precious metals and gems. They stole relics, including a (supposed) fragment of the true cross, part of the head of St John the Baptist, the arm of St George and some of Jesus' blood which they typically justified as an empowering and honourable type of theft. As the Byzantine historian Nicetas Choniates famously recounted and exclaimed:

> How shall I begin to tell of the deeds wrought by these nefarious men! Alas, the images, which ought to have been adored, were trodden under foot! Alas, the relics of the holy martyrs were thrown into unclean places! Then was seen what one shudders to hear, namely, the divine body and blood of Christ was spilled upon the ground or thrown about. They snatched the precious reliquaries, thrust into their bosoms the ornaments which these contained, and used the broken remnants for pans and drinking cups... Nor can the violation of [Hagia Sophia] be listened to with equanimity. For the sacred altar, formed of all kinds of precious materials and admired by the whole world, was broken into bits and distributed among the soldiers, as was all the other sacred wealth of so great and infinite splendour.

The attackers brought horses and mules into the Byzantine church of Hagia Sophia to carry off their loot and, before leaving, in perhaps the most famous symbolic incident of the sack of the city, enthroned a whore in the patriarch's chair and left her dancing and singing obscene songs. Choniates concluded that 'no one was without a share in the grief. In the alleys, in the streets, in the temples, [one heard] complaints, weeping, lamentations, grief, the groaning of men, the shrieks of women, wounds, rape, captivity, [and] the separation of those most closely united.' The crusaders reckoned they had taken loot worth 400,000 silver marks: ten times the then annual income of the King of France.

The Venetians gained a formidable new degree of power in the Mediterranean. In the new distribution of political authority in the Latin Empire, the emperor received one-quarter of the empire and the rest was equally divided among the Venetians and crusading barons, giving Venice final sovereignty over nearly half the old Byzantine Empire and nearly half the city of Constantinople, including its most important harbours, docks and arsenal. In fact Venetians gained the section of the city with

Hagia Sophia, where Enrico Dandolo was buried in 1205. With the creation of this Latin Empire, Venice inherited a chain of naval bases from Constantinople to Venice, essentially the entire coast of Greece including the many strategically placed islands across the northern Mediterranean, including Corfu, Zante and Cephalonia. Overnight, the less than 80,000 inhabitants who lived scattered over a distant archipelago in the northern Adriatic found themselves in possession of a massive maritime empire that had once controlled them. The Venetians now eliminated Pisan and Genoese competition in the eastern Mediterranean, and Venice was transformed from being one of many maritime trading cities to a massive imperial power.

To sum up all of these complex events: between 800 and 1300, Venice went from being a city of fish and salt traders in Northern Italy to being the capital of a vast Mediterranean empire. In the process of this transformation, several key themes emerge that define the development of the city. Firstly, historians by now have long pointed out that Venice was interested in dominating the sea rather than gaining land or territory. While this has become somewhat of a commonplace in describing Venice, repeated more times than we need to hear, it nevertheless remains a platitude rooted in the truth. Unlike most other cities in Europe, Venice always negotiated to gain commercial rather than military advantages: to secure tax-exemption in ports on the richest trade routes rather than an empire made up of land and territorial possessions. Though it did gain quite a bit of territory after the sack and conquest of Constantinople, this territory was primarily in the form of coastal cities and in these cities, Venetians never built crusader castles of housed large armies. Secondly, in negotiating for business advantages rather then political or military advantages, we see how from the beginning, Venetians were practical businessmen and pragmatic traders, motivated to turn a profit above any and all other allegiances and motivations. They were happy to trade with Muslims, or to turn their backs on the Muslims and fight against them if securing Byzantine privileges so necessitated. Similarly, while the Venetians were often Byzantine allies, they were equally as happy to attack them when greater profits could be reaped from sacking their cities and stealing from them. Lastly, from the history of Venice in the Middle Ages, we can see that the Venetians were businessmen, but they were also great thieves, as the wealth and prestige of their city was derived from profitable trade as well as from pillage and plunder. The legitimacy of their state was built in part on their growing economic prestige, as well as on the protection given them by the relics of their stolen saints and protectors. Unlike for most other states, the greatness of Venice had little to do with Venetian military might but resulted instead from Venetian diplomatic skill, shrewd and exacting mercantile practices, and economic pragmatism.

Nautical and Commercial Revolution

Despite the fact that many commercial entrepots dotted the map of late medieval Europe, for good reason Shakespeare did not name his play *The Merchant of Florence* or *The Merchant of Antwerp*. Venice was *the* great commercial city of its time. The Venetians' ability to expand into the Mediterranean, establish a maritime trading empire that included the capture of Constantinople and bring home the wealth that they did was largely made possible because they were talented shipbuilders and sailors. Ships, rather than armies, were the real foundation of Venetian power. The conquest of Constantinople both encouraged, and was encouraged by, Venetian maritime trade. But how exactly did Venetians move about the Mediterranean, navigate its often dangerous seas, and manage and trade their goods? Where exactly did they trade, and what did they trade in? How did they maximize their profits, minimize their losses and finance their commercial ventures?

No one knows exactly when Venetian ships began to voyage east in great numbers. We know that the Venetians had established trade agreements with the Byzantine Empire by the mid-ninth century and were transporting silk from Constantinople to mainland Italy with some regularity by the tenth century. The galleys making these early voyages into the Mediterranean were most likely coasting galleys based on Roman models; they travelled close to the coasts, and only during daylight and in calm weather. Venetian ships slowly evolved, however, to include two principle types of craft: round ships for trade and carrying merchandise, and long ships or galleys for war.

A round ship was shaped like a walnut. It had sails on two masts and was usually about three times as long as it was wide. The ships were designed to transport light but bulky cargo, such as cotton and spices. They tended to weight about 200 tons, but the biggest of these ships, a *roccaforte*, weighed about 500 tons. Very few other ships weighed this much until the nineteenth century and the *Mayflower*, for instance, weighed about 180 tons. Galleys, in contrast, were warships designed to be easily and quickly manoeuvered in battle. They were flat-bottomed and long, with a length about eight times their width. Rowers propelled the boats, most of which were biremes, meaning they employed two men rowing side by side on each bench, each pulling a separate oar. Venetians eventually added sails to some galleys to increase their speed on the high seas. In general they carried little cargo and were used to assist and protect merchant ships. The government forbade Venetians to sell any ship to foreigners unless they were old or outdated; they did not want other powers to benefit from their knowledge of shipbuilding.

By the thirteenth and into the fourteenth century, Venetians protected their trading ships through two principal methods: by travelling in convoys and by sailing in particular seasons. Convoys typically included about 15–25 ships with from 10–20 small trading ships, a few large round ships and a handful of galleys for protection. One such convoy left in the spring and returned to Venice in the autumn, while another left in August, spent the winter overseas in the eastern Mediterranean and returned in the spring. These timed convoys were called the spring and fall *muda* and were used primarily to protect expensive and valuable cargo, such as spices. Less valuable (though not necessarily less profitable) cargoes, such as oil or cotton, often travelled alone and not necessarily on strictly prescribed routes. While this system was fairly effective, Venetians never wielded complete control over the whole of the Mediterranean. They could never stop their enemies from using the sea or make it completely safe for Venetian ships at all times, and in some cases sailing in groups merely provided a concentrated target for attackers. Nevertheless, to some degree, this system protected Venetian merchants and their cargoes by keeping ships off the high seas during periods of rough weather and by finding protection through safety in numbers.

The growth of the Venetian fleet was linked to the construction and growth of the Venetian arsenal or shipyard. The *arsenale* – a term of Arabic origins meaning 'house of industry' – was founded in 1104 in Castello in the eastern part of the city and was modelled on Byzantine examples. At first it was built to house arms, naval equipment and provisions for the navy, the aim being to store weapons, rigging and supplies in one warehouse. It was also used as a repair yard, but most new ships continued to be built elsewhere in the city. In the early 1300s, however, the government quadrupled the size of the arsenal to about 60 acres (with a circumference of about three miles) and began to use this fortified area as a construction site so that all the state's merchant galleys could be built within these walls under state supervision. Larger round ships were still built in private shipyards near the arsenal or on other islands in the lagoon.

After the enlargement of the arsenal, Venetian shipbuilders built almost the entire Venetian fleet here, mass-producing ships with a standard design, as in a modern factory. Labour was highly specialized in order to promote efficient production and easy repairs. The arsenal was organized into specialized components – carpentry, tarring, sail preparation, ropes, oars and the foundry for anchors and cannons – all of which were connected by canals and docks. Nearby on the quay, grain warehouses and bakeries prepared and supplied rations for state voyages. Perhaps most significantly, whereas Roman shipbuilders tended to build a ship's hull or main body first, Venetian shipbuilders perfected the technique of constructing the frame or keel first, which proved to be much faster and ultimately used less wood. The working conditions nevertheless remained grim: grim enough to prompt Dante to describe the arsenal as a pit in hell bubbling with black pitch and teeming with labourers. One of the ways that the state promoted productivity under such bleak working conditions was by supplying the arsenal workers with wine. Quite incredibly, wine purchases for the arsenal were second only to the purchase of timber, and the state spent more than two per cent of its yearly budget to supply its shipbuilders with drink.

This specialization of labour, including the use of standard and replaceable parts for all ships, meant that workers could construct a galley very quickly. In 1570, when the Turks attacked the Venetians on Cyprus, arsenal workers constructed around 100 galleys in approximately 60 days. At the height of its capacity in the fifteenth century, the arsenal employed over 16,000 workers – mostly carpenters – and the Venetian fleet numbered 3,300 ships: 3,000 for commercial travel and 300 galleys, almost all of which were constructed by arsenal workers. Today, while the lagoon quietly laps at its crenellated walls, its battlements enclose only office spaces and a wing of the Venice Biennale – the city's international art exhibition – but in the later Middle Ages the arsenal was a booming, bustling factory. It represented perhaps the largest and, as some have argued, first truly industrial centre in the world, employing a level of industrial production that would not be seen again until the industrial revolution.

When the arsenal was enlarged, a series of advances in navigation also occurred that, coupled with increased shipbuilding, allowed Venetian trade to become even more efficient. Venetians first began to use the nautical compass around 1250 and this, with the development of portolan navigational charts that plotted directions from one coastal landmark to another, enabled navigators to travel across the Mediterranean in the straightest routes possible. Ironically, the only place where navigation remained difficult was in entering and leaving the port of Venice itself and crossing the northern Adriatic to the Istrian peninsula. Especially during winter, Venetian pilots accompanied ships crossing to Parenzo in Istria and ships entering and leaving Venice to make sure they did not run aground on sand bars, or on shifting, shallow channels.

With the compass and new maps sailors could begin to cross the sea in winter since they could now navigate without seeing the sun or stars. These aids meant that navigators could plot their course through clouds and fog, and the state could therefore organize two convoys to depart and arrive within a year so that no convoy was required to winter overseas. As navigation advanced, so did shipbuilding as Venetians discovered the efficiency of one-masted cogs over two-masted round ships. Cogs were similar to round ships in design, but had square sails on one mast and were easier to manoeuver as a result, especially when changing directions. By the fourteenth century Venetians also began to use a fourth type of ship, the *galea grossa*, or 'great galley', a merchant galley built to carry high-value cargo. It was like a cross between a large sailing vessel and a low, fast warship with oars: a ship that had the solidity of a round ship and the speed of a galley. As trade increased, great galleys became incredibly useful because they could carry precious cargo under maximum security since their oarsmen also functioned as soldiers who fought to protect the goods on board.

Trade routes changed and evolved over the course of the Middle Ages but, for the most part, there existed two principle lines of Venetian trade that crossed the Mediterranean. One left Venice and sailed down to Modon or Coron and turned around the Peloponnesus to Negroponte and eventually up to Constantinople. The other main trade route also travelled south to Modon or Coron but then turned south to stop at

Candia on Crete, Rhodes and Cyprus, and eventually headed for ports in the Near East, such as Acre or Jaffa. Ships leaving Constantinople often followed the same route home, but ships leaving Acre or Jaffa often travelled further south to Alexandria and along the African coast before heading north for home. Venetian navigation formed a kind of triangle around the Mediterranean bordered by Byzantium in the north, Levantine ports in the east and Africa in the south.

Other routes emerged over time. After concluding a treaty with the Persian emperor in 1319, Venetian ships began to sail to Trebizond on the southern coast of the Black Sea as well as to Tana (now Azov) on the north coast at the mouth of the Don River. This arena of maritime trade as we shall see would become the source of much tension and a series of wars between Venice and its rival, Genoa. The Venetians also developed the Barbary route through the western Mediterranean along the coast of North Africa to Tripoli, Tunis and Algiers, etc., out of the straits of Gibraltar and up the coast of Spain to trade in Bruges and London. The route began around 1300 and became more popular by the fifteenth century. For much of the Middle Ages there was a covered archway at the foot of the Rialto Bridge where merchants met to consider these routes and plan their voyages using a world map painted on the wall.

It took about a month to sail from Venice to Crete through most of the Middle Ages, about eight weeks to Constantinople and three months to Tana or Trebizond, though these times lessened as ships improved in the sixteenth and seventeenth centuries. Trade in the opposite direction and cargo returning to Venice from the Mediterranean unloaded at the Rialto. The Rialto, of course, was the commercial and mercantile heart of the city where barges from the mainland met incoming cargo from the sea. Ships carrying as much as 200 tons of cargo could come up the Grand Canal to unload, and the Rialto was a wooden drawbridge that allowed ships to pass under it for much of the Middle Ages. Unloaded cargo then followed a series of overland European trade routes, up rivers or over the Alps, through passages in Friuli towards Vienna and Cracow or through the Brenner and Septimer passes towards Augsburg, Nuremberg and Ulm.

Venetians traded in a great variety of goods in different parts of the Mediterranean, but the bulk of their trade in the Middle Ages – and the greatest source of their profits – was in pepper, cinnamon, cloves, nutmeg and ginger, with spices being in high demand in Northern Europe. Even better, they were easily transported being light and not taking up too much space. They were incredibly valuable and relatively cheap to move. Furthermore, they did not spoil easily so merchants could keep them in warehouses or transport them over long distances without any risk of their rotting. They were the perfect cargo on which the Venetians could build a profitable empire. Though some of the spices came by overland routes from India, most of them were transported by ship into the Red Sea, to Jiddah, the port of Mecca on the Arabian peninsula, and then by camel to Damascus and Mediterranean ports including Acre and Jaffa. Alternatively, spices came via Egypt through the Red Sea port of Quseir and on to Alexandria. Pepper and ginger were the most in demand and the most profitable, and Venetians imported thousands of tons a year. By the middle of the fifteenth century Venetians were apparently importing as much as 5,000 tons of spices annually, and half of this was in pepper and ginger. The volume of Venetian merchandise grew to approximate 10–12,000 tons in the fifteenth century. While these figures may not appear so great in terms of weight, we must keep in mind that the spices sold for a high price. One chronicler claimed that by the beginning of the fifteenth century the value of the cargo of an entire convoy in any given direction was about 250,000 gold ducats and could even be double that depending on the cargo: a massive figure in the medieval economy when a salary of 15 or 20 ducats was enough for one family to live on rather well for a year.

It is nearly impossible to overemphasize the role of spices in the history of Venice. Indeed, when we think about the city in a tangible and physical way – the construction of its streets, waterways, homes and churches, the commissioning of its art and architecture, and even the sewing of the clothes worn by Venetian men and women – much of this material culture was fundamentally built up stone by stone or stitch by stitch from the income derived from spices. This is so much the case that when we walk in the city and gaze upon Venice's medieval palaces and churches today, we can imagine each stone slab, brick and marble arch as purchased with the profits turned from cloves of ginger or pepper. Spices were the 'black gold' of the Middle Ages.

Other goods were also in demand and proved profitable for Venetian traders. A dazzling array of merchandise, including dyes, silks, carpets, gems, incense and cotton, was transported in both directions during the Middle Ages. Many of these luxury goods commanded extremely high prices, allowing merchants to double their capital investment. In Trebizond and Tana, for instance, Venetians found Eastern products, such as spices, silk and, more importantly, hemp for rope making in the shipbuilding industry, that were popular in Western markets. In addition, they traded in the Black Sea for slaves. Technically there was ecclesiastic legislation against enslaving Christians, but both Venetian and Genoese merchants regularly turned a blind eye to such regulations and carried nominally Christian slaves – primarily Russians and Tartars – from the Black Sea to Muslim ports in the greater Mediterranean. According to one calculation, in the middle of the fifteenth century Italian traders brought over 2,000 slaves a year to Egypt to work as concubines, household servants or to be transported elsewhere, for instance to sugar plantations in Cyprus or Crete. (According to many accounts, the Venetian word for slave, *schiavon*, gave Italy the informal greeting *ciào*, from (s)*cia*(v)*o*, which loosely means 'at your disposition' and derives from 'I am your slave'.) Arab traders brought these goods by ship or overland caravan to the edge of the Christian world. Venetians met them there to exchange their cargo for European wares, usually metals, such as gold, silver, copper, tin, lead and mercury, and also woollens, furs, hats, amber and coral.

Venetians made their profits in three ways. They sold products, such as glass, salt and soap. They managed to create monopoly markets where suppliers were either forced or strongly encouraged to sell their products only in the city of Venice, thereby placing Venice in control of both the supply and demand of products, such as salt and grain. And, for the most part, they had the monopoly as middlemen between Europe and the East. In the Adriatic Sea in particular they had a monopoly on all exchanges and, by the eleventh century, trade between any two cities in the Adriatic was permitted only in Venetian ships. Foreign merchants and their ships did operate in the Adriatic, but Venetian patrols were powerful enough to force all merchants to unload their Adriatic cargo only in Venice. A Florentine ship, therefore, could not take cloth to Zara to do an exchange for spices; all exchanges had to take place in Venice where Venetians would be the middlemen and profit from the taxes on the buying and selling of all goods. To enforce their privileged position, strict Venetian maritime laws stated that merchandise coming to Venice either had to come on Venetian ships or on ships from the country where the wares originated. By the thirteenth century inspection points around the lagoon allowed officials to check ships and monitor that their cargoes were legitimate and covered by permits. Foreign merchants in Venice were prohibited from trading with each other in the city. Germans, for instance, could not trade directly with the Milanese, and Germans could only sell German goods in the city, not wares transported from France or England.

European states distant from the East or with little or no coastline often had little choice but to trade in Venice, and many luxury goods from the East could only be found in Venetian warehouses. Venice represented the most central point of trade and exchange in Europe in the Middle Ages because it existed at the crossroads of two great trading arteries: the sea route into the eastern Mediterranean and land routes over the Alps into Northern Europe. Playing all this to their greatest advantage, Venetians oversaw and policed every sale that took place in their city and ruthlessly made a profit from each one. The position of middleman was incredibly profitable in the Middle Ages. According to the figures made public by Doge Tomasso Mocenigo in 1423, an annual investment of ten million ducats in the spice trade yielded a profit of four million ducats. Spices earned Venetians the highest net profit among all their tradable goods. While the city itself produced very little, it profited from the riches, exchanges, needs and desires of others.

The Venetian trading economy, not surprisingly, was highly regulatory. As both a cause and result of the fact that trade enriched both individual merchants and the state, trade was organized and closely overseen by the state. The state built and owned the arsenal where it manufactured and maintained its fleet, and much civic regulation oversaw even the tiniest details of Venetian shipbuilding, including ships' rigging, ships' dimensions and the arms they carried. In addition, the republic of Venice precisely defined many aspects of Venetian commercial life. By the fourteenth century, the state regularly provided armed escorts for its convoys to the East and also began to build state-owned galleys that it auctioned and chartered to the highest bidders. The winning bidders agreed to operate these ships for one voyage in a convoy on a specific trade route under conditions designated by the state, including the length of the voyage, its exact itinerary and ports of call, and the exact fees to be paid by each travelling merchant. The winners of the auctions would hire a crew and organize the cargo, and the state would furnish each galley with enough rations for the journey. Convoys sailed under an admiral appointed by the doge, and ships leaving port had to post a bond that they would adhere strictly to the established itinerary and would not attack other friendly people.

Such state-organized convoys formed only part of the total fleet of ships trading out of Venice, and many merchants voyaged alone and unarmed throughout the Middle Ages. Typically, galley captains hired crews in the portico under the waterfront façade of the Ducal Palace or recruited them from various parishes around the city. Recalling many Hollywood images of Roman slaves rowing ships around the Mediterranean, it is often surprising to learn that the galley oarsmen were not slaves but free men, and the job of rowing on a galley in Venice during the Middle Ages was considered both honourable and profitable. There were usually more than enough applicants from the native population to fill Venetian convoys until the mid-sixteenth century. Especially with the advent of the great galleys used for commercial cargo, men were encouraged to sign up since they were allowed to trade individually and carry their own weapons. This meant that individual sailors could bring their own wares to trade and sell, duty-free, on state-owned galleys and would help defend their ships if attacked. Even such small-scale, individual trade could prove incredibly profitable. One pilgrim recounted that when a merchant galley arrived in Alexandria, local traders swarmed aboard to trade with the crew even before the ship's official cargo was unloaded. A saying existed in the Middle Ages that every Venetian sailor was worth four of his adversaries since he would fight so hard to protect his personal cargo and profit. By the thirteenth century, Venetian trade was tightly organized and controlled by the state, and by the fourteenth century great galleys manned by individual traders appeared invincible across the Mediterranean.

Venetian merchants originally tended to sail personally with their own goods and capital to trade in foreign lands, but a great variety of trading and investment patterns emerged over the course of the Middle Ages. Families, for instance, began to band together through marriage to form corporations in which one partner resided in Venice while the other lived and worked in foreign ports. Family partnerships then allowed other travelling merchants to invest either funding or goods to be traded in their vessels, so that a ship travelling to the East in the high Middle Ages might have 12 merchants aboard who represented the investments of more than 100 other people. The capital of both state-owned and private ships tended to be divided into 24 basic shares, each of which could then be further subdivided when necessary.

Travelling merchants originally obtained the funding for their voyages to pay for the ship and its services through loans, but by the twelfth century they tended to use a variety of different forms of financing. With an agreement called a *commenda*, a silent partner put up two-thirds of the voyage's capital and the active partner accompanied the goods abroad and oversaw transactions in foreign ports. The active partner put up the remaining third of the investment, and the partners would divide the profits accordingly at the end of the journey. Perhaps the most common form of financing was the *colleganza*. Under this arrangement, rather than promise a fixed percentage of returns on investments, the merchants who travelled to and from foreign ports promised to pay investors three-fourths of the overall profit from the voyage. In this way travelling merchants did not have to invest any funds initially but obtained them from their business partners. A trader could voyage to and from foreign ports and make a profit without putting up any of his own money, as investors contributed capital and the merchant contributed the labour.

The *colleganza* was an especially dynamic form of business arrangement because it enriched Venetians across the social spectrum. You did not have to be rich to enter into a *colleganza*; if you were talented and had a mind for business, you could do well by investing even small amounts of goods or capital. Other commercial arrangements included the joint venture, where investors pooled funds and paid in advance to make a large purchase from abroad, say wine or grain, and shared the profits when they returned. Some traded using commission agents who received a percentage of the value of the merchandise that they handled for investors, and earned a fee based on the volume of goods exchanged whether they ended up being prof-itable or not. Lastly, bills of exchange allowed merchants resident in Venice to send or receive funds from abroad and quickly receive the profits from a sale without having to wait for the bullion to travel, riskily, across the Mediterranean.

Furthermore, the development of marine insurance even-tually allowed investors to pay a premium in exchange for compensation for the loss due to shipwrecks or piracy, and Venetian knowledge about the practice of insurance became commonplace and widespread. In one colourful example, in 1587 the hospice of the *Convertite* – a convent on the island of the Giudecca – told the *Savi della Mercanzia* (an adminis-trative organization that oversaw trade) that it would pray for the successful voyage of Venetian ships in exchange for eight per cent of the insured capital: a proposal that was rejected for being 'too speculative'.

Innovative and forward-looking, Venetian banking tech-niques were another crucial factor supporting Venetian commercial life. Venetian bankers during much of the Middle Ages did not make loans so much as make payments on behalf of different clients. It was inconvenient and dangerous to carry coins so, instead, merchants used credit to pay for purchases with other merchants, orally instructing a Venetian banker to transfer money to the account of the person being paid. Such banks were established in the twelfth century as *banche del giro* or 'turning' banks because their main function was to 'rotate' or turn credit from one account to another. Four or five of these bankers typically sat under the portico of the church of *San Giacomo* or in the square at the Rialto. Money passed safely and easily between merchants, who often moved enormous sums of capital without the exchange of a single coin.

Venice was also at the centre of the cash economy. Enrico Dandolo minted the first Venetian coin, the silver penny or *grosso*, upon receiving payment in silver from the crusaders after the Fourth Crusade. In 1284 Venetians also began to mint the gold ducat, later known as the *zecchino*, that had same weight and economic importance as the Florentine florin. The ducat essentially became the medieval equivalent of the dollar or the euro. Because of its stable weight in gold, the ducat was considered one of the most stable currencies in the Mediterranean and around the world for hundreds of years, and was used until the fall of the republic. The bankers with their account books and money-changers with their ducats also sat at their desks at the base of the Rialto.

It is worth noting that in feudal states across the rest of medieval Europe, it was common for elite or noble families to hold land and wealth. In Venice, in contrast, where land-holding was not so valued (at least, not yet), all ranks of Venetian society took party in the expanding wealth of the city. A large part of the population of the city, both nobles and commoners alike, whether they worked for the arsenal, parti-cipated in *colleganze* or had family businesses in Venice and abroad, had a direct stake in the fortunes of the city and made money if Venice was successful. This widespread Venetian participation in trade and commerce is unique and fascinating in two principle ways. First, one of the hallmarks of Venetian life, and perhaps one of the reasons Venice saw remarkably less civic violence than many other cities, was that there was a greater distribution of wealth between nobles and non-nobles than in other states. The latter could make a good profit unlike their counterparts through the rest of Europe. Second, it was extremely unusual in the European Middle Ages for nobles to participate in commerce. In most of the medieval world, wealth was associated with landholding and rents. In fact ancient Roman law specifically prohibited nobles from parti-cipating in any type of commercial activity. This legacy of Roman law is made clear in a telling story related by the historian Robert Lopez. In 829 the Byzantine Emperor Theophilus saw a large commercial ship moving into the harbour of Constantinople. He inquired who owned this impressive ship, and when he discovered that it belonged to his wife, the empress, he was furious and ordered the ship and all its merchandise to be burned, exclaiming that 'God made me an emperor, and now, you, woman, want to make me a sea-captain!' According to Theophilus' Roman mentality, nobles made money by taxing plebian merchants, not by becoming merchants themselves. Venetians, however, clearly did not follow these rules.

European feudalism began with the Franks who rewarded their fighters with land in exchange for military service. When the Venetians defeated Frankish forces in 810 they took a significant step away from this traditional European social hierarchy based on the clergy, knights and workers. They declared themselves separate and distinct from the Romans and Byzantines since all Venice's social classes publicly engaged in, and profited from, the proceeds of maritime trade. Venetians purposefully created the conditions for good business. They established systems and institutions to support merchants and bankers separated by long distances or by different kinship orientations. A clear social hierarchy still existed in Venice, but it was much less rigid than in other European states. Doges, patricians and even Venetian bishops participated in commercial life, though perhaps not while in office.

Given the volume of international trade, many foreigners lived in Venice. In order to compete with other trading cities in Italy, Venice tried to attract foreign merchants by providing attractive lodgings and warehouse facilities in the city. Many warehouses sprung up around the city during the Middle Ages for different national groups; Venetians built the *Fondaco dei Tedeschi* (the 'German warehouse') in 1228, right by the Rialto Bridge (the *Fondaco* is now the city's central post office). Here, as in warehouses for other foreign communities, Northern Europeans could sell their goods in Venice and take home products from around the Mediterranean and the Far East. Similarly, many Venetians lived abroad, in various settlements around the Mediterranean; in the twelfth century and especially after the conquest of Constantinople, swarms of Venetian merchants moved about the Mediterranean, staying often several months or years in the Levant, selling their goods and buying new merchandise.

This Venetian presence around the Mediterranean raises a curious question. Historians typically argue that Venice was unique and different from other medieval nations in that it was not a feudal power. As we have seen, Venetians were not interested in gaining land or conquering vast swathes of territory but in gaining ports and trading privileges. Nevertheless, during the Crusades when Venetians were given one-third of every town they helped capture, and especially after the conquest of Constantinople in 1204, Venice became an empire as it gained foreign territories that fell under Venetian control. Why is it, then, that we do not tend to consider Venice a traditional colonial power, even in the middle of the thirteenth century at the height of the Venetian Colonial Empire?

Venice did indeed enjoy a network of trading posts around the Mediterranean that have long been called 'colonies', with seaports at the likes of Acre and Tana. Maintaining not only harbours but warehouses around the Mediterranean made trade much more profitable because if traders tried to unload an entire shipload of imported goods at once, this tended to depress local prices. Stockpiling goods and maintaining store-rooms and agents in foreign ports all-year round allowed Venetian merchants to wait and sell their goods when prices were highest. But because Venice had a relatively small population (approximately 50,000 in the thirteenth century), it never wanted to obtain or oversee and govern massive land-holdings. It did not have the capacity to do so. The Venetians may have reigned on the high seas, but they were not prepared to oversee the rough and mountainous terrain of inland Greece, for example. That's why the Venetian Empire was never colonial in the traditional sense; it did not seek to exploit local resources or labour. What interested the Venetians were ports and trade centres. This is not to say that Venetian populations living abroad were small. The Venetian colony in Constantinople, for instance, was so big that at times it rivalled the population of Venice in the thirteenth century. Venetian senators even had a formal debate in the wake of the conquest of Constantinople in 1204, to decide whether to shift the seat of Venetian government from Venice to Constantinople. Doge Pietro Ziani (r. 1205–29) apparently had his proposal defeated by only one vote.

The only places where Venetians tended to govern local populations in a more traditional colonial fashion – recreating their own native administrative and political structures away from home, developing a colonial aristocracy and exploiting local resources and labour – was on the island of Crete and, to a lesser degree, Cyprus. Venetians obtained Crete after the capture of Constantinople in 1204 and continued to hold it for more than four centuries. Like other territories it gained around the Mediterranean, Crete gave Venetians control over eastern Mediterranean trade routes. However, Crete was different from other colonial possessions because it was wealthy in timber and agriculture, especially grain, oil and wine. Venetians therefore sought to exploit its local resources. In doing so, they often found themselves in conflict with the local ancient feudal organization, controlled by wealthy landowners and peasants, which resisted Venetian rule, demanding a heavier ruling hand than most other outposts around the Mediterranean. Eventually Venetian Crete became a replica of Venice with its own Senate and Great Council. Otherwise, Venetian colonial occupation around the Mediterranean did not involve extensive landed territories, but more often only the key points on the tips of land masses: points like Durazzo, Modon, Coron and Negroponte, where colonies ranged from fortified military outposts to portions of coastal cities where Venetians governed the native populations of those towns. In addition, there were several examples of individual Venetian families who went to various Greek islands where they established themselves as colonial overlords, especially in the Aegean Sea. They did so by offering themselves as protectors against the Genoese and the Turks, which often delighted the locals. In this way a type of small, secondary colonial system arose during the crusading era when Venetian nobles declared themselves the feudal lords of various Greek islands.

During the period of Venetian expansion, a particular Venetian ritual developed that symbolized and captured the spirit of the age: the Venetian 'marriage to the sea', or the *Sensa*. This ritual began after Doge Pietro Orseolo first defeated the Dalmatian pirates in the year 1000. Venetians recalled his victories every Ascension Day when the Bishop of Venice and the doge blessed the sea in remembrance. This ritual blessing was elaborated when, as the story goes, on 25 February 1341 a Venetian fisherman was awakened by St Mark. He asked the fisherman to ferry him to the church of *San Giorgio Maggiore* where they were joined by St George. They then went to the Lido where they were joined by St Nicholas. Though a ship full of devils was sweeping a huge storm towards Venice, these three saints held it back and saved Venice from certain destruction. Mark then gave the fisherman a ring and told him to present it to the doge. With this ring, the *Sensa* eventually evolved to include the ritual marriage of the doge to the sea. Venetians rowed their doge out to the mouth of the Adriatic on the Bucintoro, the ceremonial galley of the doge, followed by a procession of vessels. There the doge dropped his ring into the water, declaring, 'We espouse thee, O sea, as a sign of true and perpetual dominion.' As a husband traditionally dominated his wife, so the doge made the sea his subject: a relationship that would define the city for hundreds of years to come.

If any architectural features in Venice symbolize this period of financial and maritime expansion, they are the two columns in the *Piazza San Marco*. Despite his tumultuous reign, Doge Vitale Michiel II left this incredibly important material legacy to his city: he brought these columns to the *Piazza San Marco* where they still stand today, topped with statues of St Mark and St Theodore. Vitale supposedly brought three classical columns back to Venice amidst much other loot from Constantinople, and perhaps used the heavy columns to ballast his ships on the way home. It is said that one column fell into the water as it was being unloaded, and was lost forever to the bottom of the lagoon where it may still lie today. As thanks for having donated these columns to the city, the republic permitted Vitale to add the honorific 'dalle Colonne', meaning 'of the Columns' to his last name and hand this title down through his family. An engineer from Lombardy, Nicolò Barattieri (who also designed the first pontoon Rialto bridge in 1178 and raised the campanile in *San Marco* in 1180), finally managed to raise the columns in place in 1172 using a system of ropes. Apparently his reward was the exclusive right to gamble between the two columns, but he was discouraged from doing so since public executions also took place on this spot. As the Venetian writer and bookseller Franco Filippi has astutely pointed out, for a city without walls or specifically delineated points of entry, these two columns neatly symbolize the perennially open door of the city, or the entrance to the city without doors.

3

LIFE AND POLITICS IN THE MEDIEVAL CITY

While the Venetian fleet, its sailors and merchants were building a maritime empire across the Mediterranean, the city of Venice was growing and changing. As the city and its commercial life developed, so did its government. During the course of the Middle Ages, Venetians expanded the offices and functions of their state to respond to the growing needs of their citizens and to further insure civic peace and stability. One of the most significant political changes that occurred in medieval Venice was the refinement of the office of the doge, who was elected with increasing scrutiny and was subject to increasing checks on his powers. Meanwhile, numerous other civic and religious organizations blossomed in the city, and complex networks of social and spiritual groups established a place in everyday Venetian life. How did Venetians govern their city? What did the city and its streets look like, and how did people experience daily life in the world of medieval Venice?

The Evolution of Venetian Political Life

As we have seen, the Doge or Duke of Venice was originally a Byzantine military figure who, over the course of late antiquity, began to gain more power and independence from Byzantium. The Venetian government in the early Middle Ages was technically a democracy since the doge was elected, and two tribunes oversaw his work to make sure that he did not abuse his powers. In addition, Venetians maintained a governing body called the *arengo*, a general assembly where people voted primarily on matters of state security. However, between the ninth and eleventh centuries the tribunes' powers became curtailed, *arenghi* were called less frequently and were increasingly dominated by several powerful families, and the doge became more like a prince. As a result, this period saw a succession of dynastic doges. Following the election of Doge Angelo Partecipazio (r. 811–27), the doge to whom the body of St Mark was given, the Partecipazio and two other families supplied Venice with 17 doges over the next 200 years. The Candiano family produced four doges and famously dominated this office in an almost hereditary fashion for much of the tenth century, and the Orseolo family had three doges in the tenth and eleventh centuries. Venetians, however, became uncomfortable with the idea of rulers or their families having close to unlimited powers and inheriting this office like a king. When the last of the Candiano doges, Pietro Candiano IV (r. 959–76), tried to introduce feudal reforms into the lagoon, including using state armies to protect his own personal land-holdings on the mainland, a riot erupted and a fire broke out in the Ducal Palace, forcing Pietro to flee. Angry crowds killed him and his infant son and dismembered both their bodies. After Otto Orseolo (r. 1008–26) was sent into exile as a result of overreaching his powers (by appointing his brothers, for instance, to become the Patriach of Grado and the Bishop of Torcello), another member of the Orseolo family, Domenico, engineered a coup to take over the government in his name, which he did for about 24 hours in 1031. In the wake of these

ambitions, Venetians became much more wary of dynasti-
cally-oriented doges and began to impose more limitations on
their power.

In the eleventh century Venetians slowly curtailed the
doges' powers with advisory councils, and the office of doge
was transformed from being like that of a king to more of a
symbol of the state and its authority. After Domenico Orseolo
was overthrown in 1032, Venetians began to elect two individuals – one from either side of the Grand Canal – to serve as
the doge's personal advisors. In addition they decided that the
doges could no longer nominate their successors, as had
become the norm. During the course of the eleventh century
and into the twelfth, the doge found himself increasingly
surrounded by groups of nobles who oversaw his work. While
the Michiel family had dominated Venetian politics for most of
the twelfth century after the reign of Doge Vitale Michiel II
(whose failed mission in Byzantium resulted in his brutal
murder outside the Ducal Palace in 1171), Venetians increased
the number of the doge's inner council from two to six advisors
(one from each *sestiere* or Venetian neighbourhood) to increase
surveillance of his activities. Thereafter the doge and his main
advisors formed a type of central cabinet called the *Signoria*,
and Venetians began to embrace the idea that the doge should
always act in accordance with his advisors. After 1172 a further
reform stated that future doges would be named by nominating committees, giving a committee the power to nominate
a doge who, it was believed, would respect his advisors.

At the end of the twelfth century, Venetians further curtailed
the power of doges by instituting the *Promesso Ducale* or the
'Ducal Promise'. As we shall see, one of the hallmarks of
Venetian politics was promoting the symbol of the unity of the
state above any other single individual or family. Venetians
were determined to stop family rivalries, and their state
survived for so long in large part because they were successful
in doing so. The *Promesso Ducale* restrained any sense of
family gain or glory that might result from becoming a doge.

Each new doge was required to swear a set of oaths or *promis-sioni* limiting his actions and, every time a doge died, a committee added new details to the oath before the next doge took office. The doge's heirs were even forced to compensate the state if the doge abused his powers or wrongly benefitted in any way.

The first doge to take these oaths was Enrico Dandolo in 1192. He promised to follow the laws of the state, not accept gifts or favours, not to have personal correspondence with the pope or other European rulers and to follow the directives of his advisors. The length of the *promissione* grew remarkably over the years: that of Doge Mariano Grimani, elected in 1595, ran to 108 pages and that of Lodovico Manin, the last doge, elected in 1789, was 301 pages. New limits on the doge's powers continued to be instituted until the last days of the republic in the eighteenth century.

Furthermore, in 1268, election procedures began to state that an elaborate system of votes and lotteries would be put in place to elect the doge. This incredibly complicated process required that,

> From the Great Council, there was chosen by lot 30 (out of anywhere from 1,000 to 2,000 members, depending on the year and size of the population); the 30 were reduced by lot to 9; the 9 named 40; the 40 were reduced by lot to 12; the 12 named 25; the 25 were reduced by lot to 9; the 9 named 45; the 45 were reduced by lot to 11; the 11 named 41; the 41 nominated the doge, for approval by the Assembly.

Lots were drawn in the Hall of the Great Council in the Ducal Palace when nobles filed past urns and drew copper ballot balls out of them; if they randomly chose a gilded or golden ball, they were allowed to remain in the chamber and participate in the nomination of the doge. Voting, by contrast, took place when ballot boys walked around the chamber and patricians dropped soft fabric balls into the bag for the person for whom they were voting. The balls were used to prevent others from hearing for whom you had voted. Though seemingly arcane, this lottery, nomination and voting procedure effectively prevented the rigging of elections. In all these ways, most dramatically in 1172 when nominating committees first began to choose the doge, doges lost their regal attributes and went from being monarchs to republican magistrates.

When we look carefully at the evolution of the office of doge over the centuries and all that being a doge required – especially in the evolution of the *promissione* – it appears surprising that anyone ever wanted to be doge at all. According to the writer Alvise Zorzi these many restrictions even meant that the doge could not receive any official state visitors without his advisors being present and he could not have any private audiences, he could not display his own coat of arms in public, he and his family could not give or receive gifts, he could not let anyone kiss his hand or kneel before him, he could not leave the palace at all except for official functions so that he could not go to the theatre, cafes or even into the streets, and that he could not have a holiday without state permission, and then only on medical grounds. Furthermore, the expenses of the office traditionally far exceeded the salary since doges paid hefty taxes. They also paid for civic festivities, their magnificent wardrobe and various expensive gifts to the church of *San Marco* and the city while, at the same time, they were forbidden from engaging in any commercial activities while in office. Many families surely cringed at the idea that one of their men might become doge, and it is a great testament to the honour and glory attached to this office that it was regularly filled, despite these enormous disadvantages.

In addition to all the ways that the powers of the doge were curtailed in the twelfth and thirteenth centuries, shifts also occurred in other important offices in the state. After the shock of the murder of Vitale Michiel, the *arengo* lost its powers to elect the doge and its authority was handed over to a new council called the *Maggior Consiglio*, or the 'Great Council', consisting of about 500 men. It included every Venetian patrician over the age of 25 and by the sixteenth century it had over 2,000 members. The *arengo* retained only the powers to acclaim a nominated doge and to approve the making of war or peace. Venetians also gave more power to another, more exclusive magistracy called the *Pregadi*, or the Senate, a group charged with receiving ambassadors and overseeing diplomacy and foreign policy especially when crucial to commercial life, such as drawing up trade contracts, gaining better tariff rates and introducing strategies aimed at defeating commercial competitors. All these changes swept through the Venetian state in the last quarter of the twelfth century and established how the state would function for hundreds of years to come.

Historians sometimes refer to a Venetian constitution, which is somewhat misleading since Venetians did not produce any one single document that codified its central body of laws. But the reason why historians use this term is because Venetians, like the British, generated a constitutional structure found in many different documents and sources, including the *Promissione Ducale*, civic statutes and various ancient customs. Historians have traditionally described the structure of the Venetian state as like a pyramid with the *arengo* – the general or popular assembly – at the base. While this popular assembly never ceased to exist, by the thirteenth century its powers were given to the next level up on the pyramid, the Great Council. This was the most central legislative organ and its primary purpose was to generate and approve laws. Since this council was rather large, ranging from 500 to over 2,000 men, more intense deliberation and debate occurred at the next level up, in the Forty or *Quarantia* (an appeals court at the apex of the state's judicial system, which also oversaw financial legislation), and in the Senate which oversaw international, military and economic matters. The Forty elected three heads or *capi*, who attended the meetings of the doge and his six advisors, and it was this group of ten men, the *Signoria*, that constituted the top of the pyramid and the most powerful executive council in the republic of Venice. The Signoria's responsibilities included tackling various state crises, naming the commanders of galleys and fleets and handing out justice at the highest level. At the very top of the political pyramid was the doge though, as we have seen, his position became increasingly symbolic.

The workings of the Venetian government were obviously much more complicated than this pyramid suggests. As the city and its overseas possessions and fortunes grew, so did various magistracies overseeing virtually every aspect of civic and commercial life. The Senate and the Great Council elected over 200 magistrates to oversee business, trade, crime, tax collection, customs duties, the food supply, price controls and flood control. City planning was particularly important in this city on water, and the state was quick to assert its authority over how the city grew and was organized. The doge and his magistrates took many initiatives to assure that the channels and canals remained clear and navigable. During the course of the thirteenth century, the government formed a magistracy to oversee the channels and a board to oversee communal property and issue building permits, and eventually formed the *Esecutori alle Acque*, or Water Commissioners, who, with other groups, oversaw flood control and the health of the lagoon. Eventually there were councils overseeing remarkably specific problems such as the organization and behaviour of nuns, corrupt voting practices, the salaries and behaviour of gondoliers, the eradication of blasphemy on the streets and the way people dressed in public, so that scores of administrative groups oversaw practically every aspect of daily life. In addition, each of the 70 or so city parishes had a chief, the *Capo di Contrada*, who oversaw tax collection, loans and naval service. The *capi* also doubled as neighbourhood policemen until the *Signori di Notte*, or Lords of the Nightwatch, became the civic police force in 1274.

At perhaps the very bottom of this administrative pile was an elaborate web of civil and criminal Venetian courts whose complex jurisdictions again covered even the most miniscule aspects of Venetian life, including who was and was not allowed to beg on certain bridges, the number of trees that could be felled in a certain area on the mainland and by what percentage retail fishmongers could price their fish above wholesale sellers. Well into the sixteenth and seventeenth centuries, offices and magistracies proliferated to meet the growing civic needs for organization, administration and justice. The Venetian government and its bureaucracy expanded well into the sixteenth and seventeenth centuries so that the state and its functionaries became like an octopus with infinite arms that extended into every aspect of daily life.

In general, however, while changes in state organization occurred from time to time, the way that the doge was elected, and how he operated in tandem with the Senate, the Great Council and a variety of smaller magistracies remained essentially unchanged until the arrival of Napoleon and the fall of the republic in 1797. In essence, during the course of the eleventh and twelfth centuries, Venice became a commune or a community with shared leadership that asserted its rule over the lagoon at large (the earliest Venetian document that mentions Venice as a commune dates from 1144).

It is important to note that from 1000–1250, political developments in Venice were much the same as they were in other parts of Northern Italy. Across the northern Italian plains, as citizens of various towns wrestled control away from the pope and the emperor, they too formed communes and placed political control in the hands of oligarchies of local nobles. The political scene in Venice differed, however, after 1250 when more and more communes fell victim to factionalism and family violence. On the mainland communes tended to collapse and become dukedoms or hereditary despotisms in cities where one powerful family was able to dominate its neighbours. Historians of Venice have long been fascinated by the fact that this never happened here. Though similar attempts were made, Venetians managed to generate and maintain a sense of loyalty to the commune as a whole and not become divided by family rivalries within the ruling class. The Venetian constitution was by no means perfect, but historians agree that it generally provided better government than elsewhere. The government, most unusually, tended to enjoy popular support among its inhabitants; the state rarely needed to maintain troops in the city, and the under-classes never attempted to overthrow the nobles.

People and Groups

As the state and its economy grew, so did its social life. People formed a great variety of social groups based on spiritual devotion, ethnic identities and different professions. These groups had an impact on both the physical development of Venice and its political life.

Different types of work and labour fundamentally influenced where people lived and the types of social organizations to which they belonged. Different parts of the city, which often meant separate, individual islands, were designated for different types of manufacture and work, often for safety reasons or to facilitate transport. Shipbuilding became concentrated in the eastern part of the city around the arsenal, the government transferred all glass-making activities (window panes and eyeglass lenses were manufactured as early as the twelfth century) to the island of Murano in 1292 to prevent fires spreading and destroying the city while the tannery was established on the island of the Giudecca to protect the city's water supply. Also, businessmen, traders, and wholesale and retail merchants of both food and more durable goods like spices set up their tables around the base of the Rialto bridge and the Grand Canal. In the Middle Ages people tended to live relatively close to where they worked, so that neighbourhoods of people who worked in similar crafts formed around their workshops and businesses. Shipbuilders tended to live near the arsenal and glassworkers on Murano. Different types of labour helped mould neighbourhood communities all over the city.

The street names told people then (and us, because the names haven't changed) where you could find different professions.

Calle del Forno indicates the street of a baker (there are 31 such streets in the city), *Calle del Magazen* was a street of shops (and there are 16 such streets in Venice), *Calle del Malvasia* had a wine merchant and *Calle dei Saoneri* was a street of soap makers. There are many craft names on the streets near *San Marco*: *Calle dei Fuseri* was a street of metal workers; *Calle dei Fabbri* of blacksmiths; *Calle del Fiubera* of buckle makers; the *Frezzaria* of arrow makers; *Calle dei Botteri* of coopers; and *delle Rasse* of the woolworkers who made gondola cabins. The streets and alleys around the Rialto identify the many different crafts and businesses that once existed (and, in many cases, continue to exist) there: the *Riva de L'Ogio* was the dock where oil for cooking and lighting was unloaded; the *Sotoportego del Banco Giro* was where the bankers worked; the *Campo de le Becarie* indicated butchers; the *Naranzeria* was the site of the orange market and warehouse; the *Ruga degli Orefici* was the street of the goldsmiths; the *Erberia* was where Venetians sold wholesale fruit and vegetables; and the *Campo della Pescaria* was the fish market. Unlike in any other city, the names of the streets, alleys and squares in Venice are written directly on the walls of buildings. These white signs, first painted in the early nineteenth century, are called *nizioleti/ninzioleti*, or 'little sheets' in Venetian dialect. Each one contains a story or a fragment of history, and reading them is one of the best ways of looking back into the complex social fabric of the Middle Ages in Venice.

Beside the names of the crafts and merchants, you can also see how the *nizioleti* record the presence of communities of foreigners in the lagoon. Good examples include *Calle dei Albanesi, dei Armeni, dei Greci, dei Tedeschi* and *dei Turchi*. If different professions were one of the organizing forces behind the different neighbourhoods and social groups in the city, so was nationality and ethnicity. As we have seen, Venice became the mercantile and trade centre of Europe in the Middle Ages and large communities of foreigners came to live here just as Venetian traders made their homes around the Mediterranean.

Venetians welcomed foreign merchants and traders, and often extended housing to communities of foreigners trading in the city. While the Romans coined the term *hospes* for 'guests' – a term that has the same roots as the word *hostis*, meaning 'hostility' – the Venetians adopted the slightly friendlier term *forestier* to mean all those who were not Venetian, probably originating in the idea of *da fuori*, meaning 'from outside'. Consequently foreigners from around Europe and the Mediterranean tended to live in concentrated communities in Venice, forming another significant part of social life in the lagoon. The government authorized foreigners to live in specific areas, allowing the state to monitor, to some degree, their commercial activities and keep track of the number of residents and their movements with the hope of reducing any possible tensions. The government allowed foreign communities to maintain their traditional cultural and religious practices but, by encouraging them to live in certain segregated areas, hoped to prevent them from mingling much with the native population. The Germans (i.e., all German-speaking people) were the largest foreign community and included Poles, Hungarians, Austrians and the Swiss. Greeks, Turks, Slavs and Egyptians also formed large communities in the medieval and early modern city. The Armenians were recorded in Venice as early as the second half of the twelfth century and maintained a hospice and a church close to *San Marco*. To this day a great variety of Venetian surnames, including *Schiavon*, *Tokazian*, *Turco*, *Del Turco*, *Turchetto*, *Moro* and *Moretto* indicate the historic presence of these foreign communities. The Greek and Armenian churches are still active today.

Throughout the Middle Ages, workers formed guilds in order to protect their economic interests in the competitive world of the market. Guilds were rather like modern labour unions, consisting of groups of craftsmen or labourers who drafted the rules governing their trade. The guilds regulated who was permitted to enter certain types of work and at what age, what training was required and how much money they could make depending on their age, experience and superiority. Perhaps most importantly guilds determined the prices for the goods they sold. They also tried to eliminate unfair competition, bad or inferior workmanship and excessive hours of work. In doing so they maintained standards and benefitted both individual workers and consumers.

Historians of Venice have long noted that guilds or *arte* were less powerful and significant here than in other mainland cities like Florence, and that guilds in the early Middle Ages, for instance, did not always represent the most significant professions in the city. This was in part because the central government of Venice was so well organized and its powers so well articulated that the state tended to oversee commercial life more than in other cities. In addition, to have both guilds and the state overseeing business life would have meant too much regulation. In 1173, for instance, Doge Sebastiano Ziani (r. 1172–78) created the magistracy of the *Giustizia Vecchia*: these three government officials regulated various aspects of the market in Venice, including the guilds themselves, as well as trades that did not form guilds. The *Giustizia* oversaw weights and measures, price controls and numerous other aspects of Venetian commercial life, and was the chief public institution overseeing the market until the fall of the republic. Quite simply, many crafts did not need a guild.

In addition, and perhaps most importantly, medieval people tended to form guilds to protect primarily manufacturers and labourers. However, the Venetian economy was based on commerce more than manufacture, and merchants in foreign trade – the mainstay of the Venetian economy – did not have guilds. Nevertheless, Venetians did form guilds in many industries, especially during the course of the thirteenth century when many groups found it necessary and useful to form organizations to protect their financial interests. The earliest groups to form guilds in the Middle Ages were tailors, jacket makers, goldsmiths, jewellers, physicians and surgeons. Various types of workers in the shipbuilding industries also formed guilds at this time, including the rope makers, oar makers, carpenters and caulkers. Fishmongers, oil vendors, sand suppliers (sand being used in well and water filtration) and various parts of the cloth and silk industries, to name a few, also formed guilds around 1250. By the middle of the thirteenth century, there were at least 100 guilds. This may sound like a lot but most guilds had less than 250 members.

Venetians also organized themselves into religious groups and formed societies, or brotherhoods, to provide aid and assistance to the needy. These groups were called confraternities or *scuole* (schools). *Scuole* were associations of laymen with communal and charitable goals that they tried to achieve through devotional practices, communal worship and philanthropy. If guilds were like labour unions, confraternities and *scuole* were like charities. It was common for groups of workers or guilds to form *scuole* to assist workers and their families in times of need. Their members included the rich and poor, all of who paid annual dues used to help those in need. Members met weekly to pray, sing hymns and hear a sermon. They also often participated in public, ritual festivals. These organizations had spiritual goals, but they were not religious *per se*: priests could not belong, and these organizations were places where lay people who did not become priests or monks could express their spirituality.

These fellowships each had a base in the city and a particular place of worship. The shoemakers' guilds, for instance, formed the *Scuola dei Calegheri*, or Shoemakers' Confraternity, in *Campo San Tomà*. Over the doorway of the house there is a relief of the Virgin protecting the members of the guild. Another relief here shows St Mark healing the shoemaker Aniano (connecting the cobblers to the city's saint), and around the lintel of the doorway are images of shoes. The largest and wealthiest of the *scuole* were the six *scuole grandi*, or 'big' confraternities, so-called because they admitted up to 600 members and often built extravagant houses for their members, such as the *Scuola di San Giovanni Evangelista*, founded in 1261 as a brotherhood of flagellants who physically beat themselves in imitation of Christ's suffering. Smaller *scuole* often maintained single chapels and altars in churches. The church of *San Giacomo* at the Rialto, for instance, has ten altars that were built by various *scuole* including the grain-winnowers' guild, the cheese-vendors' guild and the gold-smiths' guild. *Scuole*, in fact, became highly differentiated even within single professions. For example, though they were all carpenters, different *scuole* were created for the builders of houses, furniture and frames. Among the goldsmiths different *scuole* existed for those who spun gold and those who made gold leaf. Different national or ethnic groups, such as the Greek community, also began their own brotherhoods. The *scuole* would become particularly important in Venice – and particularly interesting to modern tourists – since these organizations commissioned so much of the city's art. Confraternity members used their pooled funds to purchase paintings from the leading artists of the day to decorate their chapels and altars, especially in the fifteenth and sixteenth centuries. The *Scuola Grande di San Rocco* founded at the end of the fifteenth century to assist the Venetians in times of plague, has more than 60 paintings by Tintoretto, one of the city's most important Renaissance painters. By 1200 there were at least 14 of these organizations in Venice; 200 were active by 1500 and hundreds still existed at the fall of the republic in 1797. *Scuole* were communities that integrated and embodied Venetian social, religious and civic life.

Many other groups and communities formed, and as we will see later in the cases of Jews and prostitutes, were forced to live together in designated parts of the city during the Middle Ages. This leaves us with one final group that played a prominent role in the early development of the city: the religious orders. Episcopal and parish churches were the first sites around which religious communities developed in the lagoon and, by the ninth and tenth centuries, monastic communities had also sprouted up. Monasticism, or the following of a set of rules governing community and spiritual life, first became popular in Europe in late antiquity, especially following the monastic rule developed by St Benedict in the sixth century. The Benedictines began to have a presence in Venice as early as the ninth century, followed by other orders such as the Clunaics and Cistercians. These early monasteries were virtually autonomous communities that often owned and oversaw their own fields, orchards, saltpans and water supplies. Indeed, the goal of early monastic communities was to be in this world but not of it, and to aid the surrounding community not by participating in it but by praying for it. By the mid-fifteenth century there existed some 50 monastic communities in the lagoon, representing more than 21 different orders of men and women, and new orders continued to arrive and grow throughout the history of the republic.

The most important of these groups were the mendicants who arrived in the thirteenth and fourteenth centuries. Whereas Benedictines led a quiet life of prayer and contemplation inside their monasteries, the mendicants, by contrast, emphasized poverty above all other values. In addition, their practices differed from the Benedictines since they preached in public and took their spiritual message out into the world instead of meditating and praying in cells by themselves. Historians have long argued that the development of the mendicants or friars – the Franciscans and the Dominicans – was the most powerful and important spiritual event of the Middle Ages. As European economies grew and prospered after the year 1000 – and Venice is a great example of this – the mendicants and their emphasis on poverty and charity offered a sense of spiritual relief to offset the Christian guilt associated with making money. The Franciscans (the followers of St Francis) settled in the city around 1227 and completed their magnificent church of the *Frari* in the western part of Venice around 1338. The Dominicans arrived around 1234 and finally finished and consecrated their church of *San Giovanni e Paolo* on the opposite side of town around 1430. If you visit almost any large Italian town that has its roots in the Middle Ages, it will almost always have two churches dating from the thirteenth century, built by the Dominicans and the Franciscans. In Florence there is *Santa Maria Novella* and *Santa Croce*. In Venice, if you climb any bell tower that offers a view over the city's roofs, the Franciscan and Dominican churches of the *Frari* and *San Giovanni e Paolo* immediately stick out being among the largest buildings: a testament to the prestige and power they wielded in the medieval city. By the mid-fourteenth century, the *Frari* was home to more than 1500 mendicants. Doges were buried in both churches. As historians have long pointed out, such social groups – religious communities, confraternities and workers – were so important in the medieval and early modern worlds since neighbourhood and community were among the most powerful forces giving individuals a sense of identity.

Political status

By the twelfth and thirteenth centuries, Venice had clearly become a bustling city and a powerful political and economic player in the world of the Christian Middle Ages. What marked out Venice as a truly legitimate political power, however, was the fact that it held a crucial summit in 1176 between the two greatest powers, Pope Alexander III (r. 1159–81) and the Holy Roman Emperor Frederick Barbarossa (r. 1155–90).

Frederick was one of the most powerful men of the European Middle Ages. A German king who was crowned emperor by the pope, he spent much of his life and career on military campaigns in Northern Italy, often in Tuscany and Lombardy near Milan where he attempted to conquer these territories and make them part of his empire. Various cities in Lombardy eventually banded together to resist his campaigns and formed the Lombard League in 1167. The pope supported this league since he did not like the German emperor interfering in Italian affairs. Frederick's campaigns eventually brought him into direct conflict with Pope Alexander III. Frederick went so far as to support an anti-pope, Calixtus III, to pressure Alexander III to give in to his (Frederick's) expanding power. Frederick's forces, however, suffered a tremendous defeat at the hands of the Lombard League at the Battle of Legnano in 1176, which finally broke Frederick's hold over Lombardy. Pope Alexander III was nevertheless afraid of being captured by German knights and, as a result, decided to flee to Venice for protection. Both the Venetians and the Lombard League forced Frederick to make a formal peace with the pope (though some accounts say that Frederick came willingly): the peace was arranged in Venice and overseen by Doge Sebastiano Ziani (r. 1172–78). On Ascension Day in 1177, Frederick came to Venice and kissed the foot of the pope in the church of *San Marco*, thereby reconciling their differences. Grateful for Venetian assistance, the pope gave the Venetians a series of gifts including, among other things, a gold ring. According to some, it was with this ring (and not the symbolic ring that St Mark gave the fisherman) that Venetian doges symbolically married the sea on each subsequent festival of the *Sensa*.

How much of the peace story is true? Not a lot. The pope supposedly came to Venice in disguise, and spent many nights hiding and sleeping in the doorways of various churches, including perhaps the church of *Sant'Aponal*, or the doorway of *San Salvador* or *Santa Maria della Carità*: all these churches claim this honour. A pilgrim apparently recognized him (by some accounts after six months in the city!) and alerted the doge to the pope's presence, and then accompanied the pope to the Ducal Palace. On the floor of the basilica of *San Marco*, a small lozenge-shaped stone in the atrium marks the spot where the emperor supposedly embraced the pope. We now know that much of this is fiction.

There were probably no episodes of disguise and recognition, and no ring. But as with much of Venetian history, the truth did not matter nearly as much as the symbolic meaning derived from whatever was exchanged between the emperor and the pope. Just as Mark legitimized the city, so did the fact that the pope fled here and that the doge was chosen to reconcile the pope and the emperor in Venice. The role of arbiter between the dominant forces of church and state in the Middle Ages gave Venice yet another degree of power and respectability, one that reinforced and heightened its simultaneously developing commercial, maritime and spiritual prestige.

Topography and Civic Space: Visualizing the Middle Ages

When we walk around Venice today, the historic centre of the city may at first appear incredibly well preserved, and in many ways it is. In truth, though, very little material or architectural remains still exist from Venice in the Middle Ages when Venice was at the height of its powers. If it were possible to visit Venice at this time, we would actually recognize very little. So what did the city look like, and how did it become a city? Few buildings survive from before the middle of the eleventh century. It took hundreds of years for Venice to begin to assume any aspects of a real city and, in order to understand this process, we need to return to the ninth and tenth centuries.

When the Venetians defeated the Franks and took their first steps towards political and economic independence, the city was not much more than a series of swampy islands and mudflats. Though the city now appears contiguous with integrated streets, at the start of the ninth century it rather resembled a series of lily-pads in a pond: separate, disconnected and entirely uninhabitable. Making Venice into a city, and eventually into a city that reflected the splendour of the capital of a Mediterranean empire, involved generations and generations of painstaking land reclamation.

The earliest structures in the lagoon were made of wood with thatched roofs since wood was plentiful, easy to transport into the lagoon and did not weigh heavily on its muddy foundations. The construction of anything more permanent eventually meant draining the land. First, Venetians would sink walls of wood or stone around the area where they wanted to build, usually a proposed plot for a building or a street. They would make these walls watertight and then pump out any water inside this enclosure and vertically sink in tightly packed groups of wood pilings, typically of varying lengths so that they would penetrate different levels of soil and create as much stability as possible. After filling in the rest of the area with dirt, debris and gravel, they would place planks and beams horizontally over the top to create a base platform, and then finally cover this raft of wood with slabs of stone, typically the hard, white stone that Venetians obtained from the peninsula of Istria. The wooden pilings beneath the water level would eventually petrify, making the area solid and safe for sustaining more lasting, permanent and heavy structures on top. It's thought that beneath the basilica of the church of *Santa Maria della Salute*, builders sunk more than 100,000 trees or pilings – literally an entire forest – to support this massive structure.

The investment of time and money in drainage paid off. The Venetians did an extraordinary job and many of today's buildings still stand on piles driven into the ground over 1,000 years ago. Through such land reclamation, slowly but surely, parts of the city began to spring up in solid form, usually as local families and religious orders built near one another. During the course of the Middle Ages the Franciscans worked on drainage projects in the area around *San Tomà* near their church of the *Frari*, and the ancient Badoer family drained land in that same area for their households and businesses. The Benedictines first reclaimed large tracts of land in part of the city that is now Dorsoduro, starting in the middle of the ninth century. Churches were often the first significant structures to appear on an island or stable tract of land, and houses and other buildings tended to appear around them. In this way, from 1000–1100, historians estimate that Venetians built approximately 50 churches on the islands of the lagoon.

Today, as we look at the *campo* or square around any Venetian church we can try to visualize how parts of the city came into being and functioned. With the construction of parish churches, bell towers chimed the hours of the day, calling people to work, to church or to arms in times of danger. A central square was established in front of each church: on one side of it a wharf or dock and boatyards, and on the other side workshops and a market. In times of war, the government set up public targets for archery practice in these squares and trained men to use crossbows.

Each island church had its own saint, identity and festivals. Gradually houses appeared, as did gardens, plots of vegetables and vineyards. The leading families who had endowed the local church had palaces, surrounded closely by the houses of workers and labourers clustered close together. Animals ran freely around the islands, including cows and especially pigs that thrived on the garbage people flung out their windows. Some believe the Venetians built mills powered by the ebb and flow of the tides. In areas of the islands that were left undeveloped, there would be mudflats and water creeping in at high tide, with pools where the inhabitants could fish. Though Venetians were not great horsemen, they nevertheless kept horses in the city right up to the nineteenth century, so stables also existed on various islands around the city. Medieval Venice differed most fundamentally from the modern city since there were fewer walkways, almost no real streets and many more canals. Streets were a precious expense but waterways were free. In most parts of the city streets were not much more than trampled muddy lanes but, by the eleventh century, some streets emerged between clusters of houses and buildings, and documents from that time already refer to them by the Venetian names of *calle* (street) and *fondamenta* (quay).

Just as the earliest structures built in the lagoon were made of wood, the primitive bridges that first connected these islands were also made of wood before stone bridges were built. Indeed, the first form of the Rialto Bridge consisted of boats lashed together. Fires were common and, with so much construction in wood, they occasionally destroyed entire quarters of the city. In an attempt at prevention, officials ordered all residents to extinguish fires and candles after the *terza ora della notte*, or three hours after sunset. For this reason Venice, in the Middle Ages, was unimaginably dark after nightfall and it was incredibly easy to fall into the water while walking or to be attacked by thieves. After a catastrophic flood and fire in 1106, however – a fire that became so large that chroniclers reported flames leaping across the Grand Canal – Venetians began to use more stone and brick for construction. In addition, in 1128 Doge Domenico Michiel (r. 1118–30, the commander of the fleet at the Battle of Ascalon) decreed that every night small lamps would be lit at shrines, gondola stops and intersections around the city at state expense. In order to shore up public safety, especially against night-time crime, Venice was the first European city to provide public street lighting.

It is important to note that despite increased building in stone during the course of the eleventh and twelfth centuries, Venetian expansion was largely based on one primary natural resource, wood. Besides water, wood – oak, beech, fir, larch and elm – was the main resource fuelling the city's growth and was increasingly in demand as the city grew, becoming a pressing problem in the city's environmental politics. The Venetians stripped bare the great forests in Istria near the sea and dramatically felled trees in Northern Italy to build their ships and houses, sink the foundations for their buildings and construct bridges to link the islands together. They tied felled trunks together in large rafts and floated them along the coast or down river from the foothills of the Alps into the lagoon's workshops and boat yards (hence the name for the *Zattere*, the long quay that faces the island of the Giudecca, where rafts loaded with wood first docked when they arrived from the mainland by river or canal). Some historians think that much of the Mediterranean basin, as far as Northern Africa and the Middle East, had become deforested by as early as the tenth century as a result of Venetian civic and commercial expansion. The supply of timber would always be an issue for the survival of the Venetian state and, by the fifteenth century, Venetians would have to confront the results of dramatic deforestation in the form of increased silting. Rivers that ran through deforested areas carried and deposited more silt in the lagoon that threatened the navigation of canals. This eventually forced the state to design environmental policies to try and conserve forests and protect their waterways.

The foundations of the ceremonial heart of the city hinge around the first church of *San Marco*, which was begun in the 830s. About the same time there was some kind of fortress for the doge in the area where the Ducal Palace is now, which is where the government of the lagoon was also sited. In fact, the name of this area of Venice, Castello, probably derives from a fortified castle erected in this area in the ninth or tenth centuries. We have only vague descriptions of the originals of these buildings, but they were most likely to include the first buildings in stone or brick. In the precarious times of the early Middle Ages, the Ducal Palace was most likely heavily fortified with battlements and towers, and may even have had a drawbridge. Right through much of the twelfth century, the *piazza* was still enclosed by the sea wall built at the end of the ninth century by Pietro Tribuno to protect the city from invaders. (According to John Julius Norwich, a few crumbling remains of the wall still survived in 1982 at the southern end of the *Rio dell'Arsenale*, but I have never been able to find them.) What is now the *piazzetta* (where the two columns stand today) formed a small harbour and bathing area, where water lapped the base of the bell tower and church. Much of the area that is now the *piazza* was, in the ninth and tenth centuries, grass and trees, and the orchard of the monastery of *San Zaccaria*.

By 1150 the bell tower in *San Marco* was lit at night to act as a beacon for ships and its bells, like other bell towers around the city, rang out the time. The *marangona*, the biggest bell, called labourers to work while other bells announced the meeting of the Senate or the Great Council and the bell called the *trottiera* rang to encourage patricians to rush or 'trot' their horses to the Ducal Palace. The smallest bell, the *renghiera*, announced the timing of executions. Many big ships moored themselves right up against the *piazza* and, well into the fourteenth century some of the largest shipyards existed right next to the Ducal Palace in what are now the public gardens.

There were also two churches that no longer exist today in the *piazza*. On the western side of the *piazza* was the church of *San Geminiano*, probably first built in the ninth century but destroyed on Napoleon's arrival. Its existence is still indicated by a plaque in the ground. There also would have been the little ninth-century church of *San Teodoro* – the patron saint of the city before the arrival of Mark – perhaps to the left of where the basilica of *San Marco* stands today. The *piazza* was often filled with the booths of craftsmen and officials who granted business permits or collected shipping fees. Looking out over the water, the *dogana* or promontory that sits at the mouth of the Grand Canal just across from the *piazza* was the site of a crenellated tower. The view around the *Piazza San Marco* during the early Middle Ages would have looked completely different from how it looks today.

By the twelfth century some aspects of the modern *Piazza San Marco* came into being. Most significantly, Doge Sebastiano Ziani (r. 1172–78) – the same doge who brokered the peace between the pope and the emperor, and also the first doge to be elected through the republic's new nominating procedure – supported public works programmes to enlarge the *Piazza San Marco*. Ziani had the old sea wall destroyed, had orchards in the area cut down and the entire area of the *piazza* paved for the first time. He also filled in a major canal, the *Rio Batario*, that once bisected the central part of the *piazza* just west of the Ducal Palace (you can still see signs of this canal by the bay, just under the sailing club as you head from the *piazza* to the public gardens). Some say this rearrangement was specifically so that the meeting of the pope and the emperor could take place, but it seems hard to imagine such big projects taking place at relatively short notice. Ziani was one of the wealthiest men in the history of Venice, and most likely he thought big and ordered this grand remodelling as a sign of growing pride and confidence in his blossoming city.

Though Ziani changed some aspects of the *piazza*, what we see today came into being primarily in the fifteenth and sixteenth centuries. So where can we still see medieval Venice in a city where remnants from the eleventh to the thirteenth centuries have long been erased? One of the few spaces that lets us experience the Venice of the Middle Ages is the courtyard where one of the more famous figures from Venetian history lived, Marco Polo. Polo's story is neatly woven into the grand events of the history of Venice. While the Venetians captured Constantinople in 1204, they lost it again in 1261 when the returning Byzantine Emperor Michael Paleologus retook the city. The Venetian fleet was away from Constantinople at the time and the best it could do was rescue Venetians from the city and take them to the Greek town of Negroponte. This was a tragic loss for Venice; it was impossible for the Venetians and the Latin West to retake the city and the Eastern empire and, in addition, it was no surprise that the new emperor found the Venetians untrustworthy and allowed a large number of Genoese to trade in Constantinople with the privileged trade status that the Venetians had always enjoyed. The emperor did allow the Venetians back into the city in 1268, but the Venetian dominance of trade around the Bosphorus was broken. The Genoese, as we will see in the following chapter, would become Venice's next greatest threat and challenge. Ironically the loss of Constantinople may have prompted the journeys of the Polo family, since the loss of Constantinople possibly encouraged Venetians like them to look for other routes to get spices.

In 1261 – the same year that the Venetians were ousted from Constantinople – two merchant brothers, Nicolò and Matteo Polo, set out to explore the lands beyond the Crimea to see what commercial possibilities existed beyond Constantinople where they were based. They travelled north into Russia to the town of Sarai but, according to some, did not attempt to return Constantinople since they had heard of the expulsion of the

Venetians. Instead, they travelled south to reach the wealthy city of Tabriz in Persia, but the roads were blocked as a result of local warfare among Mongol Khans. After about three years in the central Asian city of Bokhara, they went east with a caravan into China, over 3,000 miles to the Mongol capital of Peking and the court of the Great Kublai Khan. The Great Khan told the Polo brothers to ask the pope to send missionaries so that he could learn about Christianity. The brothers made it home overland through Persia to the Mediterranean port at Lajazzo (now Ayas on the southern coast of Turkey). They set out for China again in 1271 with two missionaries and Nicolò's son Marco, who was then 21. The missionaries turned back, but Marco made it to China to work in the service of the Mongol court where, for more than 20 years, he experienced a refined civilization that was quite different from that of the West.

According to legend, when Marco Polo returned home in 1295, no one in his household or neighbourhood recognized him or believed his stories until he slit open his pockets and pulled out handfuls of jewels and precious stones. While many were transfixed by Polo's stories, others, especially seasoned travellers (as Venetians often were), tired quickly of his tales. When Marco eventually wrote a book about his journeys, those who did not believe his wild stories supposedly called it 'Marco's Millions' in reference to his reliance on numerical superlatives when talking about his travels. Marco wrote his book in prison after he had been captured by the Genoese in 1298. He recounted his travels to a fellow prisoner, Rustichello of Pisa, who wrote them down and produced an almost instantaneous bestseller. Polo eventually returned to Venice where he died in 1324, allegedly claiming on his deathbed 'I did not write half of what I saw'. He was buried in the church of *San Lorenzo*, but his sarcophagus went mysteriously missing when the church was remodelled in 1592 and has never been found. The Polo family's travels are legendary for many reasons: they were most likely the first Latin Westerners to cross the Great Wall of China, and Marco's account is among the first in-depth,

anthropological and ethnological studies of the Far East from a
Western perspective. While some think that Marco Polo first
brought pasta from China to Italy and introduced Italians to
their national dish, this is unlikely, since forms of pasta were
probably first used by Etruscans, Romans or Greeks. Some
scholars think that pasta actually came via the Arabs who
invaded Sicily in the early Middle Ages.

The Polo family probably lived somewhere near the modern
Malibran Theatre, in one of the two courtyards nearby named
Corte del Million. These courtyards today are both picturesque and dingy. Off the beaten path, they can be dark and
gloomy on cloudy days and their façades reveal both delicate
medieval architecture as well as some decrepit and depressing
modern exterior plumbing. Modern windows, for instance, cut
abruptly into fragile medieval arches. Nevertheless, there is
something refreshing about the way that the past and the
present co-exist in this square since, unlike in other parts of the
city, restoration here has not been overdone. The remains of
these houses give us a real feel for the Venice of the thirteenth
century with their gothic windows, wooden roofs and various
spoglia or architectural fragments, such as Byzantine arches,
pilasters and *paterae*, fixed into the façades. In a quiet moment,
when the last Venetian talking into his or her cell phone disap-
pears under the archway and you are left alone in the square,
you can almost hear the clatter of Marco Polo counting out his
emeralds, rubies, sapphires, turquoise, opals and diamonds on
his kitchen table.

If not through the street names alluding to the medieval
activities or in the quiet courtyard surrounding what was (most
likely) Marco Polo's house, perhaps the only other site that part
survives from the Venetian Middle Ages – from the age of the
crusades and of Mediterranean trade and conquest – is the
façade of the basilica of *San Marco*. Today, with thousands of
visitors waiting in line to cram into the church, it is not at all
easy to imagine that this was a building of its time. But with a
little imagination and by focusing on some of its details, we can

get a sense of how this building embodied and symbolized Venetian majesty and cunning at the height of the city's power.

There is much debate about what the first church on this site looked like. Some say the first church consecrated in 832 was built to imitate the destroyed church in Alexandria from where the body of St Mark was stolen; others say its Greek cross plan derived from the great churches of Constantinople, including Justinian's sixth-century church of the Holy Apostles. A fire destroyed this first church in 976 and various doges restored and rebuilt it over the next century, so that the underlying structure of the church consecrated in 1094 is, for the most part, the one that exists today. While the basic structure dates from the late eleventh century, the history of *San Marco* and the material remains that adorn it span the ages. Its decoration has been altered greatly over time and any number of guide-books can point out the most significant features. Here, instead of repeating that I'll focus on the evolution and metamorphosis of the church during the high Middle Ages, especially after the Fourth Crusade. By focusing on the specific details that were added to the church in this period we get a sense of how Venetians became the imperial overlords of the Mediterranean and shamelessly displayed their power to the public.

The nineteenth-century art historian John Ruskin described the church of *San Marco* as 'a treasure heap', a telling phrase since it does not have an elegant spire that reaches effortlessly towards the heavens (like Chartres cathedral) or a simple, meditative space in which people commune directly with God and the universe (like the *Pazzi* Chapel built in Renaissance Florence). As Ruskin noted, it is essentially a pile of plunder, thieved from various sites around the Mediterranean, beginning with the body of the saint himself. (St Mark's relics could easily have been destroyed in the fire of 976 but, according to various legends, were lost and miraculously found several times over the ages and allegedly found again in 1811 when they was placed permanently under the high altar, but even this story is suspect.) Before the time of the Fourth

Crusade, the simple brick façade most likely already had some decorative elements. Mosaic decoration had begun as early as the eleventh century, and much of the church's decorative, geometric pavement was already in place. During the Fourth Crusade many of the church's great treasures first arrived and were literally stuck on, or in, the church as symbols of Venetian wealth and imperial domination. Rarely did a ship return from the eastern Mediterranean without a stolen column, capital or relief to fix on the basilica.

Most notably, the exterior on the ground floor or lower register of the basilica, especially in and around the portals or arches of the church, is covered with marble slabs and columns. These were added after the 1204 conquest of Constantinople when ships laden with precious eastern marbles, columns, capitals and reliefs arrived back from their voyages of conquest and crusade. These effects – Egyptian porphyry, Greek marble, Persian onyx and Syrian reliefs – are far from uniform, and their mix-and-match style clearly shows that they were stolen from around the Mediterranean and inserted here as decorative symbols of Venetian domination. On the right side of the cathedral, in the south-west corner, stands the *Pietra del Bando*, or 'announcement stone', a stump of porphyry column stolen from Acre and used for centuries to announce publicly the decrees of the Venetian government. Next to this red column, in front of the southern façade, stand two white pillars adorned with Syrian carvings from the fifth and sixth centuries. They were long thought to have been taken from Acre as well but are now believed to have been taken from Constantinople. Most famously, the four bronze horses that sit above the central doorway of the church also came from Constantinople. They might have once adorned the arch of Trajan in Rome, but were definitely displayed at the Hippodrome of Constantinople. In 1204 Doge Enrico Dandolo shipped them to Venice as part of the plunder from Constantinople in the Fourth Crusade. According to some stories, in order to bring them aboard the Venetians had to remove their heads and then make collars to hide the incisions. They were installed in 1254, and have now been replaced by replicas to protect the originals that are in the museum inside the basilica.

On the ground floor of the basilica to the far right, in the south-west corner close to the Ducal Palace, are the porphyry statues of the Tetrarchs, also stolen during the Fourth Crusade. The Tetrarchs were the four rulers charged with governing the Roman Empire during the reign of the Emperor Diocletian. While we do not know the precise origins of these statues, the missing foot of the figure on the far right was discovered in an excavation in Istanbul, suggesting once again they were stolen in the crusading era. Though small, humble and hidden around the side of the church, these statutes of the tetrarchs huddled together neatly display the visual process of generating the city's political legitimacy. Through the tetrarchs and other plunder pasted in and around the façade of *San Marco*, we see how Venetians savily used stolen property to generate political meaning. The tetrarchs are almost an afterthought in the corner, as if the Venetians simply pasted them in for a quick and easy fit. In fact much of the plunder from around the Mediterranean is displayed around Venice in precisely this way – a relief from Egypt is tacked up above a doorway here, a column plastered hastily into a façade there. What was most important to the Venetians was not the antiquity of their plunder but the political message. By unashamedly flouting such items in public in the very ceremonial heart of the city, Venetians clearly displayed to the world that they were the unrivalled masters of the Mediterranean.

There is plenty more plunder inside the church, and the altars and chapels shimmer with stolen artefacts, gems and stones. Tombs are studded with Byzantine fragments, and columns and capitals from around the Mediterranean are fixed all over the basilica. While guidebooks discuss the interior at length, one particular chapel highlights the nature of Venetian imperialism. On the eastern altar of the left transept of the church quietly sits the icon of the Madonna Nicopeia, shipped back from Constantinople by Enrico Dandolo after the Fourth Crusade. Called the 'bringer of victory', Byzantine emperors carried this icon at the head of their armies as they led their troops into battle since the start of the twelfth century. The theft and placement of this military icon in the church of the doge of Venice sent a clear political message about who was now in charge in the Mediterranean.

In and around the basilica of *San Marzo* Venetians brazenly asserted for all to see that they were equally or more powerful than the great ancient and modern empires, especially the Byzantines. Their treasures now decorated Venetian buildings. As official state representatives read the newly promulgated laws on top of a column stolen from Acre, in front of and surrounded by marbles thieved from around the Mediterranean, no one missed the message that the Venetians were now the masters of this world. No one questioned their power and authority; no one, that is, except the Genoese.

4

CRISIS AND CONSOLIDATION: VENICE IN THE FOURTEENTH CENTURY

The historian Barbara Tuchman once described Europe at the end of the Middle Ages as undergoing what she called 'the calamitous fourteenth century'. With war, spiritual unrest and disease this was indeed a bleak period in the history of the West. But it was not all bad news for Venice. On the one hand, as a result of advances in shipbuilding, seafaring, maritime conquest and economic expansion, the years from 1300–48 were among the most prosperous in Venetian history. Many historians believe that Venice was then at its most expansive and powerful. But on the other hand Venice certainly did experience its own version of Tuchman's calamitous fourteenth century, in part as a result of the plague, violence and political turmoil at home, but also as a result of a series of incredibly expensive and destructive wars with its maritime rival, Genoa. Venice also experienced a series of social and political transformations that made it a very different state in

1400 than it was in 1300. For this reason, this period merits special treatment. What events in the fourteenth century both threatened and stabilized the fortunes of the republic? Venice's wars with Genoa combined with threats at home had powerful and lasting effects on the city's social structure and political system, which came to be defined by a clear and more rigid sense of hierarchy by 1400. By the end of the fourteenth century, Venetians had developed very different ideas about the relationship between its social classes, as well as about the powers that the doge and its state possessed.

Venice and Genoa, 1257–99

As we have seen, Venice entered the crusades not out of religious zeal but to seize its fair share of plunder from the Middle East and to try and block its rivals from doing the same. By the middle of the thirteenth century, especially after the conquest of Constantinople, Venetian success in the crusading period had led to intense rivalry with several other maritime cities including Pisa, Amalfi and especially Genoa. The first war between Venice and Genoa erupted in 1257, but exactly who were the Genoese?

If Venice was the maritime outlet for north-eastern Italy, Genoa was its north-western counterpart, located in the northern Mediterranean on the western side of the Italian peninsula. While Venice was historically free and independent, Genoa was subject to the Holy Roman emperor though local families did wield considerable authority by occupying the office of consul, a high-ranking political position. And, as in Venice, shipbuilding, seafaring and trade were prominent in the city's culture and economy. Genoa also developed a formidable navy (indeed, the city would be the birthplace of Christopher Columbus) while its merchant and trading families possessed substantial political power. In addition, the Genoese founded trading colonies in the Middle East, the Aegean, North Africa and Sicily, and similarly made fortunes in the Near East. By the middle of the thirteenth century, the

Genoese were nearly as well rooted in Near Eastern cities, such as Acre and Tyre, as the Venetians. Though Genoa never had more than half the population of Venice, it too strove to control trade in its own geographic region of Liguria, aiming to create a trade monopoly in the Tyrrhenian Sea from the Rhone River down through Tuscany.

The rivalry between Venice and Genoa was initially over-shadowed when traders from Pisa threatened both Venice and Genoa, but Pisan power in the Eastern Mediterranean declined after 1250. As both the Venetians and the Genoese became increasingly aggressive commercial competitors, their interests began to clash in their struggle for the domination of various overseas markets, in particular those in Constantinople and Acre. Growing antagonism and war ensued; wars that on and off would last for more than a century.

With tensions between the two powers already running high, the spark that ignited the First Genoese War was the murder of a Genoese citizen by a Venetian in Acre. In response, the Genoese attacked the Venetian quarter of the city, causing the various factions in Acre to take sides with one group or the other. These attacks and tensions forced the then doge, Renier Zeno (r. 1253–68), to send a number of extra war galleys to provide protection for a trading fleet in 1257. The commander of the Venetian fleet and future doge Lorenzo Tiepolo broke through the Genoese chain blocking the harbour, burned a group of Genoese ships and eventually expelled the entire Genoese colony from Acre. The Genoese returned to try and retake the city in 1258 but, with reinforce-ments from Crete, Venice and the population of Acre (including locals who had come to hate the Genoese), the Venetians ultimately captured half the Genoese galleys. Their fleet defeated, and with over 1700 men dead or taken prisoner by the Venetians, many taken in chains back to Venice to be used as bargaining chips in peace negotiations, the Genoese fled to nearby Tyre. This victory fuelled the story that the Venetians uprooted and carried home the columns from the great tower in Acre and set them up on the south side of the church of *San Marco,* though recent research suggests these columns really came from Constantinople.

After this, the Venetians and the Genoese continued to spar with one another around the Mediterranean for many years – a period that is called The First Genoese War – until 1270. During this time various battles produced victories for both sides, with the Venetians generally getting the better of it. While they focused on keeping their trades routes safe and protecting their convoys in the face of Genoese aggression, the Genoese strategy was to try and lure Venetian galleys away from these convoys so that Venetian merchant vessels, unde-fended, could easily be raided. In this way the Genoese plun-dered Venetian ships and colonies, and the Venetians suffered financially from the cost of providing its merchant fleet with added protection. The Venetians tended to beat the Genoese when the fleets met on the high seas, as in the battle of Settepozzi in 1263, near what is now the island of Spetses off the eastern coast of the Peloponnese. But the Genoese were capable of outwitting and evading the Venetians, and tended to gain an advantage when they were able to raid Venetian convoys. Neither side, however, gained any decisive advantage over the Mediterranean Sea from such tactics, and the war came to a conclusion only because Louis IX, the King of France, threatened to confiscate Genoese properties in France if they did not make peace with the Venetians. Louis wanted to go on a crusade to Egypt and needed peace between the two warring factions to do so, producing in 1270 a temporary halt to the fighting.

This tentative peace was disrupted when Mamluk soldiers from Egypt retook various territories that had been conquered by the crusaders, namely Tyre, Tripoli and Acre. The fall of Acre to Muslim forces in 1291 meant that trading rights in the Black Sea became more valuable than ever before, and they were increasingly contested. Venetians and Genoese urgently tried to force each other out of this area to ensure their own exclusive access to spices, silk and slaves. In 1294 the Genoese caught the Venetian convoy making for Armenia off the coast of Lajazzo and spectacularly captured almost all the goods it carried, and possibly also Marco Polo. In doing so, the Genoese initiated their second war with Venice (1294–99). Emboldened by their success, the Genoese began to attack their Venetian rivals more than during the first war, most famously when the Genoese commander Lampa Doria forced a confrontation in 1298 off the island of Curzola (now Korcula in Croatia). This battle was the largest ever fought between Venice and Genoa, involving about 90 Venetian and 80 Genoese vessels. The Genoese were victorious, killing 9,000 and taking up to 5,000 Venetians prisoners, including the Venetian admiral Andrea Dandolo who was so disgraced by this loss that he committed suicide by beating his head against the hull of the ship that was taking him to prison.

Both sides were so depleted and exhausted that their respective commercial enterprises suffered heavily because they'd invested so many resources in the war. The Genoese had won a series of dazzling victories, reducing the Venetian mercantile fleet to an all-time low in the Mediterranean, but the Venetians were quick to recover. The two sides brokered a peace in 1299, but the outcome of the rivalry between Venice and Genoa was far from decided. Fifty years of calm followed the end of The Second Genoese War, but not because there was peace. Both sides were distracted, and in the case of Venice that meant political threats, social upheaval and the plague.

Threats, Conspiracy and Republican Resolve

While the Venetians battled the Genoese on the high seas, a revolutionary political transformation was occurring back in Venice. In both Venice and elsewhere in Italy, two main questions confronted most states: how to prevent factionalism and the fighting between families from disrupting civic peace, and how did one become, and what was, a noble? Many cities did not manage to stop factionalism, and their governments were

taken over by a single family that became dukedoms, as in
Milan, Ferrara and Mantua. Other cities developed complex
mechanisms to avoid this, such as the regular rotation of public
offices in Florence to prevent any one family from wielding
power for too long and creating jealousy and rivalries. All
cities also faced the question of what it meant to be noble. Was
nobility inherited exclusively through the family, or could you
become noble through marriage or economic advancement?
The question of who was a noble – which was important since
it conferred political rights and power – was particularly
pressing as more people came to live in Italian cities from the
countryside. These two issues – family violence and nobility –
defined politics for hundreds of years in medieval and early
modern Italy.

In Venice these concerns manifest themselves for several
reasons at the end of the thirteenth century in the Great
Council. This large body of magistrates elected other magistrates in the city and settled various political questions. It
consisted of about 500 men before 1300. Problems began to
arise, however, because the means of selecting its members was
fundamentally unclear. Traditionally, most members had held a
government office and were then, as a result, chosen by a
nominating committee to be on the Great Council. Most were
nobles but some were not, and tensions formed around the
question of who had a right to be on this council. For instance,
were immigrants to the city or wealthy families who had only
recently obtained their fortunes allowed to join? With Venice
having so much of a presence in Dalmatia and the East, would
foreigners who married into Venetian families, or their
children, be eligible? If so, would there still be room for traditional Venetian families? Would old Venetian families lose their
political clout if newcomers eclipsed them? Venetians were
forced to confront the question of how to select the members
of the Great Council and, in doing so, had to face the same
questions that other Italian cities did: who is noble, and how to
prevent families from arguing about it since this could easily

escalate into violence. Venetians needed to find a permanent solution that would prevent undesirable families from entering the council while not excluding old Venetian families.

Different ideas and different solutions for fixing this problem percolated towards the end of the thirteenth century, but in 1298 Doge Pietro Gradenigo (r. 1289–1311) finally passed the definitive rule that would answer this question once and for all. Gradenigo's reform stated that anyone who had been a member of the Great Council at any time during the last four years would be a member thereafter, as would his descendants. In addition, new members might be proposed, but only by the doge and his council and these families then had to be approved in the Council of Forty. With this ruling Gradenigo protected the political status of old families and also ennobled several common and foreign families by making them members of the Great Council, admitting them to the Venetian political order. After 1323 these reforms were finalized and membership in the Great Council effectively became fixed and hereditary. After this only these designated families were considered noble, and only these families could be elected to other offices in the state. These events became known as the closure or *serrata* of the Great Council.

In effect, Gradenigo closed the political class. He clearly drew the line between nobles (members of the Great Council) and non-nobles for the rest of the republic, though some new and foreign families did become nobles from 1298–1797. Some families were admitted to the noble class as a reward for their sacrifices during the War of Chioggia in 1382. Furthermore, when the government needed money it occasionally allowed new families to buy their way into the noble class for a tidy sum, as it would do in the eighteenth century. In general, however, after the closure of the Great Council it was no longer possible to become a noble; the title came only by inheritance. Venetians had answered the pressing social and political questions of the later Middle Ages in one fell swoop: nobility was hereditary, and if these nobles felt secure that their political power was stable, permanent and unthreatened this would prevent factionalism and family violence since no one family could oust another from its political position. For this reason the government of Venice is often oddly referred to as an 'aristocratic republic', a term that one might easily question. Venice's unique and singular political order from 1298–1797 stipulated that political decisions were made through voting and that magistrates had to be nominated and voted into their offices, but only nobles could vote or become officials.

One of the results of this reform was that the Great Council doubled in size, to well over 200 families and 1,000 men whose names were recorded in an official register called the *Libro d'Oro*. That's why this reform is also referred to as the enlargement of the Great Council. Though the city was now governed by a closed, hereditary class of nobles, this group of men was relatively large compared to the governing classes in other cities, perhaps generating less resentment from commoners because it was, in fact, so big. In addition, because of its size, it was more difficult for factional tensions to form among a group of so many people with diverse concerns. This political arrangement was strikingly different from the 'feudal pyramid' that existed in much of the rest of Europe. Whereas in England or France there were barons, counts, viscounts, marquises and any additional number of feudal titles in the pyramid of medieval nobility and authority, in Venice there were no distinctions in rank among nobles. All were technically equal. With this enlargement, the authority of the Great Council grew and its powers came to outweigh those of the ancient *arengo*, or General Assembly. This was significant because it meant that after the enlargement of the Great Council, the selection of doges was removed from the hands of the general populace and given to the nominating committees of patricians

While the closing of the Great Council clearly defined who had political representation and who did not, there existed one other significant social group that, though it could not vote, still played an important role in Venetian politics and culture: the citizen class or the *cittadini*. *Cittadini* existed one rung below the patricians, and one above the *popolani* or labourers, and formed and distinguished itself for the first time during the fourteenth century. The *cittadini* subdivided into the *cittadini originari* (native Venetians), *cittadini de intus* (immigrants who had lived in the city for ten years and were thus allowed trading rights in the city) and *cittadini de extra* (who obtained full citizenship rights, enabling them to trade as other native Venetians on the international market after 25 years). While *cittadini* could not vote and did not rank as high as patricians, their class was still extremely exclusive. Its members formed about five to eight per cent of the population of the city. Membership came either by birth or by application with proof that the applicant and his father and grandfather had not earned their livings though manual labour. The *cittadini* were small business owners – innkeepers, publishers, artisans and often merchants like their noble counterparts – and a large subset of this class, primarily the *cittadini originari*, also worked in the Venetian civil service as the secretaries, lawyers and notaries who staffed the bureaucracy of the Venetian state. *Cittadini* formed a large portion of Venetian confraternities and were the ruling group in the *scuole grandi* or the largest confraternity in the city. They were also highly influential patrons of the arts since rich *cittadini* commissioned art and architecture to increase their cultural capital.

From 1298–1323 when these social shifts were occurring, a series of calamitous events shocked the lagoon and contributed to fundamental social and political change in the city. Between 1309 and 1313 Pope Clement V placed an interdict on Venice and excommunicated the city for failing to come into line with his demands that Venetians withdraw from the mainland city of Ferrara. Ferrara had long been economically dependent on Venice, and during a dispute about political succession in the city the Venetians occupied it until a member of the local Este family effectively ceded Ferrara to Venice. The pope, however, had longstanding claims to rule Ferrara and his interdict freed European Christians from their treaties and oaths to Venice so that Venetian goods could be plundered with no legal or spiritual punishments. The many enemies of Venice immediately took advantage of the War of Ferrara to seize Venetian merchandise. However, an additional crusade launched against Venice by the pope and his allies resulted in the loss of Ferrara. The Venetians eventually managed to force the pope to lift his interdict by threatening to cut a canal above Ferrara that would link the Po and Adige Rivers and ruin the economy of Ferrara by cutting it off from trade. Nevertheless, Venice had to pay a large indemnity to Pope Clement V – 100,000 ducats, or one-tenth of the public debt – and the loss of money, goods and men made this war one of the worst in the city's history. The Genoese Wars and the War of Ferrara clearly demonstrated that while Venice had become a world power, Venetians were not invincible.

Not surprisingly, between the closure of the Great Council and the devastating War of Ferrara, many Venetians thought the government was on the wrong track. After the Great Council had been enlarged, many old, aristocratic families continued to worry that the government of Venice was being overrun with undignified 'upstarts'. Not everyone approved of Doge Gradenigo's reforms. In addition, many of these same families argued that Ferrara should have been abandoned rather than pursued, disputing Gradenigo's opinion that it was crucial to control this mainland city. Indeed, Gradenigo was unpopular, if not one of the most hated doges of all time. Many oppositional families rallied around the patrician Tiepolo family. They had clamoured for the election of Giacomo Tiepolo – a decorated admiral whose father and grandfather had both been doges – when Pietro Gradenigo was elected in 1289. Giacomo's son Bajamonte and his father-in-law Marco Querini now began to hatch a plot to overthrow the doge.

The Querinis and the Tiepolos were old Venetian families who resented the fact that Gradenigo's reforms were diluting their families' political power. They therefore had the support of similar longstanding patrician lines, as well as the support of many non-nobles who long ago had wanted Giacomo Tiepolo as doge rather than Pietro Gradenigo. The rebels prepared their plan of attack, fixing the date for 15 June 1310. The Querini and Tiepolo families each planned to lead their allies along two different routes – the long alleyways of the *Merceria* and *Calle dei Fabbri* – to meet up in the *Piazza San Marco*. Badoero Badoer, the leader of another old Venetian family, and his forces would approach the *piazza* by water. The three would attack from all sides but the doge had been warned of the plot days earlier by an informer named Marco Donato and was prepared for the attack.

When the rebel families and their forces arrived in the *piazza*, the doge's forces (backed by workers from the arsenal) immediately overwhelmed them while a storm and rough seas prevented Badoer from landing. The leading members of the Querini family were killed and their allies defeated. In one of the more famous anecdotes in the history of the city, the Tiepolo forces were also defeated as they approached the *piazza* in the *calle* known as the *Merceria*. Under the now-famous *Sottoportego del Cappello*, a woman named Giustina Rossi dropped either a flowerpot or a piece of mortar on to the crowd below. Though the object missed Bajamonte, it immediately killed his standard-bearer and the Tiepolo flag fell into the mud. Confused, and surely unable to see in the narrow and crowded street, the rebels turned and fled back across the Rialto to the neighbourhood of the Tiepolo palace near *San Stin* on the other side of the city. When the dust settled, Badoer was executed and Bajamonte went into exile across the Adriatic in Dalmatia. The palaces of the Querini and Tiepolo families were demolished. Rewards, by contrast, were handed out to those who had helped defend the doge. Giustina Rossi, when asked how she would like to be honoured, asked to be allowed to fly the banner of *San Marco* from her window on saints' days and to be promised that her rent would never be raised (her house was owned by the state), a promise that was kept for 150 years, and perhaps longer. The informer Marco Donato was admitted to the Venetian patrician class and became a member of the Great Council, and his abbreviated Venetian name, Donà, came to mark a particularly illustrious Venetian noble clan. History has read Bajamonte Tiepolo on the one hand as the hero of the people and a champion of democracy during the rule of a tyrannical doge. On the other hand, historians have also depicted him as a disgruntled noble who only sought to do what princes up and down the Italian peninsula were doing at the time: namely, establish himself as the despotic and singular ruler of Venice. Regardless interpretation, however, the Querini-Tiepolo conspiracy laid bare the fact that while Venetians had already taken great strides towards eliminating factionalism and violence among families by enlarging the Great Council, additional measures to prevent the growth of factionalism and individual ambition were still necessary.

Developing a better way to monitor potential cases of treason, rebellion and violence against the state happened somewhat by chance. When Bajamonte Tiepolo and his followers were exiled, the Venetian state created a council to keep track of his activities abroad. Exile was a common form of punishment in Europe in the later Middle Ages, and it was also common for those in exile to plot their return to their native cities, either by waiting for an overthrow of the government or by secretly plotting a revolution from afar, sometimes over many years. In order to prevent the Tiepolo faction from attempting something like this, the Venetian government created a special council of ten men for a period of several months, called the *Dieci*, or the 'Council of Ten', to keep track of these hostile families in exile. This council proved to be so useful and effective that in 1334 the republic voted to make it permanent.

At first the Council of Ten focused primarily on checking that exiled families were serving their sentences as ordered. It tracked the exiles if and when they moved, lessened their penalties if they behaved well and ordered them to be executed if they did not. Many of the exiled conspirators left Dalmatia soon after they were exiled there and began to plot their return from nearby Padua. In order to combat this threat, the Council of Ten hired a network of spies, informers and assassins. After the immediate danger of the Querini-Tiepolo conspiracy had passed, the Ten continued to oversee urgent and secret matters that affected the security of the state.

Venetians remained shocked for decades by the Querini-Tiepolo conspiracy since it was both unexpected and could easily have succeeded. They had to make sure it could not happen again. The Council of Ten was particularly well designed to combat secret plots since its small membership meant it could make quick decisions and keep them secret, unlike the larger bodies of the Senate and the Great Council. The Council of Ten was like a medieval version of the American FBI or British Secret Service and began to check possible plans for armed uprisings or threats. The Ten even made it its business to know if, and when, families solicited votes from one another in the Great Council to avoid factionalism. In order to keep this council itself free from factionalism, its members were elected for just one year, could not come from the same family and were not immediately eligible for re-election. In addition they took all their decisions with the doge and his six councillors. The Council of Ten quickly became the most feared tribunal in the city and merely catching a glimpse of one of its members surely sent a chill down Venetian spines.

The Council of Ten came to occupy a specific place in the workings of the Venetian government. It had absolute powers to do what it wished and when it wished, but these powers only applied to cases of treason or threats to the state. Even though it operated within the law, descriptions of its practices have long been exaggerated and romanticized. For instance the Council of Ten accepted secret and anonymous denunciations in boxes shaped like lions' mouths all over the city. The Ten were famous for torturing those named in these denunciations to extract information. They did not hesitate to extinguish a potential threat, sometimes by poisoning or drowning, and supposedly executed criminals who threatened the state in a tiny, dark alley called the *Calle della Morte*, or the 'Street of Death', not far from *San Marco*. The reality was that while it did accept anonymous denunciations, it scrutinized them carefully before acting. It had extraordinary powers and was much more severe and extreme in its operations than any other judicial authority in the city and, as we will see, its powers grew so much over the course of the republic that many questioned whether it had gone too far. By the nineteenth century, looking back, the Council of Ten had become a fundamental part of decadent descriptions of Venice as dark and despotic. Nevertheless, dank prisons and torture were common across Europe in the Middle Ages, and the practices of the Ten were most likely extreme only in that it seemed to have been particularly effective at doing its job.

The council certainly helped prevent the second and probably final attempt by one man – doge Marino Falier (r. 1354–55) – to take over the government of Venice. Falier had served the republic of Venice as a distinguished military commander, diplomat and, ironically, had several times been a member of the Council of Ten. There are several stories behind Falier's attempt at a *coup d'etat*; according to one, a young Venetian noble fell in love with Falier's young and beautiful wife (who would have been about 45 to Falier's 70), and when love notes and drawings were discovered in the Ducal Palace, Falier supposedly became so enraged that he irrationally began to formulate a way to make himself the despotic ruler of Venice to weaken the power of other patricians. According to another more likely story, Falier became aware of the growing popular resentment against nobles at this time and hoped to use it in his favour to become the ruler of Venice, as in nearly every other Italian city republican states gave way to despots in the fourteenth century. The story claims that the noble paymaster of the navy, Giovanni Dandolo, hit a galley officer, Bertuccio Isarello, when Isarello refused to follow some of Dandolo's orders. Isarello quickly formed a gang on the waterfront that stood in wait to strike back at Dandolo. Dandolo complained to Doge Falier who publicly chastened Isarello, but then later that evening secretly recalled Isarello and invited him and other middle class men to join a plot to oust the ruling nobles of Venice and put Falier in charge of the city. They did not plan their attack very carefully however and the Council of Ten soon discovered the plot.

Falier was dramatically and publicly beheaded on the stairway in the courtyard of the Ducal Palace, where he had not long before sworn his allegiance to the laws of the city. As Frederick Lane describes, when his head had been cut off the chief of the Council of Ten held up the bloody sword and announced to the crowd, 'Note well, justice has been done to the traitor.' His main co-conspirators were hanged from the upper story of the Ducal Palace with bits stuffed in their mouths to prevent them from crying out to the crowd below. In the following days, as the Council of Ten found more traitors, they hanged them along the loggia of the palace until there were 11 dangling bodies, sending a powerful message to the inhabitants of the city. The unity of the state came before individual honour and ambition.

The Myth of Venice in the Middle Ages

When we look back at Venetian history so far, it is remarkable that through the fourteenth century – indeed, up until the fall of the republic in 1797 – the city of Venice did not experience any significant revolts or civic unrest. A handful of doges attempted to enact some aspects of sovereign rule, the Querini-Tiepolo conspiracy aimed to oust Doge Gradenigo and Falier tried to take over the government in his own name. However, not only did none of these attempts succeed, but none of them appealed to the broad base of society and all were quickly suppressed. This noteworthy degree of peace in Venice is additionally surprising when we consider that in the fourteenth century revolts and rebellions were commonplace in Europe, especially revolts of the disenfranchised lower classes against nobles, kings and those who had political representation. These uprisings included peasants' revolts in Flanders in the 1320s, the Jacquerie in France in 1358, the Ciompi revolt in Florence in 1378 and the English peasants' revolt under Wat Tyler in 1381. Historians have long marvelled at, and wondered about, the comparable degree of civic peace in Venetian history. But how can we explain the Venetians' successes in keeping political ferment and popular revolt at bay in a world where insurrection was the norm? How did large concentrations of manual labourers, such as arsenal workers and fishermen, live and work in the city without ever threatening or challenging the patrician class?

One of the main arguments has been that commoners must have been relatively content and felt included in the political culture even if they had no official political voice. If they had not been, they would have played a much greater role in the few plots against the governing class. The *scuole*, or confraternities certainly gave everyday Venetians a sense of political importance and civic participation even if they could not vote in the Great Council. The middle and lower classes, historians argue, used these organizations to assert their prerogatives and develop a sense of political community. Furthermore, the state awarded many such organizations specific privileges that may well have offered the common people a sense of political prestige. The confraternity of shoemakers, for instance, had the honour of giving the doge's wife a pair of shoes every year on the festival of the *Sensa*. Similarly, arsenal workers rowed the doge out to sea on the day of the *Sensa*, carried the doge around the *Piazza San Marco* immediately after his coronation and carried his casket to be buried. Through such ritualistic relationships with different groups of workers, the republic made them feel important and they felt less inclined to revolt. And while the *serrata*, or closure, of the Great Council and its connected reforms in the first quarter of the fourteenth century excluded most commoners, it did also ennoble some of them, which was the unusual in European politics at this time.

Some argue that the reason why Venice enjoyed such remarkable civic stability had more to do with the city's economic practices and class structure. In most of medieval Europe, class structure was both rigid and extremely unbalanced, with a relatively small number of highly visible, wealthy, landowning nobles in charge of huge numbers of disenfranchised commoners who did not own land. You were either one or the other, and there was no way across the divide, and that generated plenty of friction and violence against the ruling class. In Venice, by contrast, there existed a large middle class of merchants and traders. And though they were not nobles they often became even wealthier than the nobles through trade. In addition, most nobles made their profits from Mediterranean trade, so the two classes shared the same business practices and economic interests.

A third possible reason for Venice's lack of civil unrest is rooted in the Venetian emphasis on civic unity and allegiance to the state rather than to individuals or families. The fact that there were so many different offices and councils, and that representation was always for brief periods of time, having been nominated by lot and election, meant that no one person or family could develop any type of hereditary power or rule. Power was distributed broadly and this encouraged patricians to subordinate their individual interests to the interests of the republic. The subordination of the individual to the state is evident in many ways, including street names that infrequently record individual or family names, and art that did not emphasize individual portraiture to the extent that it did in courtly cities; when individual doges are represented in Venetian painting, they are often part of a larger, allegorical scene and are not the main focus.

Others argue that civic peace in the lagoon city was the result of effective Venetian justice. Venice maintained a large number of courts to serve a wide variety of litigation needs ranging from cases of deflowering a virgin before marriage to merchants overcharging their customers or customers not paying their bills. Voluminous archival records testify to the fact that many people from a wide swathe of society – from commoners of the lowest ranks to the richest patricians – used the Venetian courts. This argument claims that Venetians felt content with their lot because they felt that justice protected their interests and livelihood. Venetian law extended power, respect and protection to the lower classes and this, in tandem with the constitution and laws of the state, did much to promote internal harmony. By contrast, a darker interpretation of Venetian stability suggests that if Venice was so peaceful, it was not because Venetians felt empowered by their system of courts and justice, but because they were terrified of the repressive powers that governed them. According to this argument, the patrician class clearly wanted to protect the political order that they had established: the order that represented their political interests. Instilling fear into the hearts of the city's inhabitants through a series of repressive forces – namely the Council of Ten and other policing bodies – kept the inhabitants in line and stifled any possibility of rebellion and revolt.

It must be stressed that Venice was not perfect. Factionalism was common in the tenth and eleventh centuries in particular, and Venetian patricians were far from selfless and self-serving, and were by no means immune to corruption. Many attempted, by manipulation and guile, to seek prestigious or lucrative offices and to avoid offices that entailed heavy expenses, such as ambassadorships. When nobles picked lots some occasionally stuffed balls up the wide sleeves of their gowns so that when they reached down into the urn this hidden ball would fall into their hands, and they'd stand a (fractionally) better chance of getting a place on an important committee. Sometimes patricians moved to Murano to avoid being present for nominations to offices that they did not want to hold. Venetians clearly had their rivalries and their political interests, and quite ironically patricians as individuals were always the biggest threat to the patrician class as a whole.

In addition, murder, theft, assault and rape were as commonplace in medieval Venice as elsewhere, and insurrections did happen from time to time. Seamen were often badly paid, and sailors and galley crews sometimes demonstrated or rioted in the city, as they did in 1437 when they looted shops to protest about the government delaying their pay. Nevertheless, the political interests of individuals and the violent outbursts of workers only very rarely became serious threats, and crime and violence never escalated into the more widespread form of class violence that was then common through much of the rest of Europe. Venetians simply found more effective means of quelling violent impulses, and the reasons for this are surely found in a mixture of these various theories.

We can get a sense of Venice's unique and relatively peaceful political environment simply by looking at the city's architecture. It is no accident that in mainland cities rulers lived in castles with walls and ramparts. The Medici, the fifteenth-century republican rulers of Florence who lived in a palace on a street in the centre of their city, for instance, had a ground floor built from large, sturdy stones with small windows to protect those living inside. Venetian palaces, by contrast, betray little or no fear of rebellion. Their delicate tracery, abundance of arches and windows, and relatively open architecture, even on the ground floor, seem confidently assured that no attacks would occur. Far from the bulky, stone fortresses that most Europeans used to protect themselves from warring neighbours or protesting workers, Venetian palaces, such as the *Palazzo Corner Loredan* (built in 1362, now the city's Town Hall) and the *Ca' D'Oro* (built 1420–34), though imposing and monumental remain light and airy compared to the impenetrable strongholds of their Italian neighbours.

Plague, War and Political Resolution

Fourteenth-century Venice was relatively rich and peaceful, and remained independent from foreign powers. With a population of about 120,000 in the city and 160,000 around the lagoon in 1300, Venice was one of the largest European cities in the Middle Ages – when cities of more than 10–20,000 were considered large. It was rivalled only by other Italian cities including Milan, Florence, Naples and Palermo, and abroad by Paris with a population of about 100,000. Nevertheless, the second half of the fourteenth century in Venice witnessed a series of highly destructive events. Venice is built on a seismic zone and, in 1348, the city experienced an earthquake so powerful that chroniclers claimed it emptied the Grand Canal and left it dry for more than two weeks. Also, Venice's thorny relationship with the Genoese remained unresolved in the middle of the fourteenth century, and as in much of Europe Venice was hit hard by plague, in 1348.

Though the Venetians and the Genoese were technically in a period of truce in the 1340s, tensions between the two trading cities ran high as a result of their continuing trade rivalry in the Black Sea. In 1344 the Tartars attacked the Genoese trading city of Caffa on the northern rim of the Black Sea. While the Tartar threat to Western traders was so great that the Venetians and Genoese temporarily considered an alliance against them, the Tartars suddenly broke off their siege in 1346 to the great surprise of both powers. The Tartars were struck by a mysterious illness and, according to some sources, hurled dead bodies into Caffa to infect Western forces before withdrawing. As the Venetians and Genoese picked over what remained of Tartar camps around the Crimea, they came into contact with the black rats that carried the disease which had killed the Tartars and which, until then, had been found in South-east Asia. The Mongols had brought it across Central Asia to the Tartars and then, to the Europeans. Venetian and Genoese ships returned from the Crimea to Venice in January 1348, and together they both shared the horrific fate of introducing the whole of Europe to the Black Death. It was carried by the fleas that infested the onboard rats which scuttled among the spices and furs bound for Europe.

By the summer of 1348, historians estimate that 500–600 people a day died of the plague in Venice. The plague spread in two different ways: through the lungs in its pneumonic form, transmitted from one person to another, and by fleas in its bubonic form, which caused the glands to become black and swollen. In a world unfamiliar with microbes and bacteria, traditional medicine had little to offer. According to the historian Horatio Brown, cemeteries overflowed and the dead had to be sent to new islands in the lagoon, such as San Marco in Boccalama, an island that no longer exists but which became a mass grave for thousands of plague victims. The government was forced to assist the collection of the dead and did so by organizing death boats that passed down the canals yelling '*corpi morti*' ('dead bodies'). By the time the plague finished sweeping through the city, 55 patrician families had died out and the city had lost close to half its population. With recurring bouts of the plague, the city would not return to its pre-plague population of 120,000 for several hundred years.

Shortly after the arrival of the plague in Venice, the city once again resumed its battles with Genoa. The Venetians had broken an agreement they had made with the Genoese to boycott travel to Tana (now Azov), a trade outpost in the northern reaches of the Black Sea at the mouth of the Don River. Ignoring their shared defense against the Khan of the Golden Horde, the local ruler around the Black Sea, the Genoese began to attack Venetian ships and war between the two broke out in 1300. In the Third Genoese War, the Venetian fleet faced an entirely new challenge: conscription. Since the Black Death had decimated the population of the lagoon, there simply were not enough men to produce a citizen navy. In addition, one of the primary economic effects of the plague was that with less labour available, wages went up. Many Venetians felt that they could make more money by staying and working instead of serving on a galley, and those who were drafted often hired others to go in their place. The city was therefore forced to hire allies from Catalan and Greece, and recruit crews from Dalmatia and Venice's own Greek colonies, though they were not as well trained or as disciplined as the Venetian rowers.

As a result, the Venetians did not do that well in the Third Genoese War (1350–55).Their fleet won some battles against the Genoese, for example at the Battle of Alghero in 1353, off the coast of Sardinia, but famously lost others, such as at the Battle of Porto Longo, near Modon, in 1354. In this devastating battle Genoese galleys managed to slip past the guarded entrance of the port and attack Venetian vessels that were tied up and unprepared for battle. The Genoese commander Paganino Doria successfully captured every last Venetian ship from the Venetian commander Nicolò Pisani who, with most of his men, was taken prisoner. The Venetians were spared a punitive peace only because the Visconti family from Milan had been governing the city of Genoa and, unlike the Genoese, it wanted to negotiate a serious and lasting peace with Venice.

The Third Genoese War had a powerful impact on social and political life in the lagoon since it placed many strains on the Venetians, and not just with conscription. Such strains often dramatically increased tensions between social classes, and that certainly happened after the Venetians' devastating defeat at the Battle of Porto Longo. Seamen were discontent and often proved troublesome. We must remember that it was precisely at this time in 1355 that Marin Falier attempted to take over the government by tapping into this discontent, supposedly in the name of 'democracy' and the common people, in defiance of the haughtiness and self-interest of nobles. Many people expressed anger and hatred for the incompetent nobles who commanded the fleet, and the state, after this massive defeat. Such tensions were momentarily quelled as Falier and his allies were defeated, but they nevertheless demonstrate the ways in which wars abroad tested the unity of the state and society at home. Though Venetians had taken many steps to insure the solidity of their government and prevent factionalism and ensure peace, The Third Genoese War tried the cohesion of Venetian society and tested its political institutions.

The entire fourteenth century, so much of it taken up with war with Genoa, came to a close with a fourth and final war, often called the War of Chioggia (1378–81). It was caused by tensions between Venice and Genoa over control of trade in the Black Sea and the island of Tenedos, a small island in the Aegean – strategically located at the mouth of the Dardanelles and claimed by both Venice and Genoa.

The Fourth War involved two famous patrician commanders from Venice: Vettor Pisani who patrolled the Adriatic Sea against the incursions of the Genoese and attacked them in their own waters on the west coast of Italy, and Carlo Zeno whose fleet attacked the Genoese, and their colonies and commerce in the eastern Mediterranean. Pisani at first won a victory against Genoa off the town of Anzio in 1378, near the mouth of the Tiber River, but then was soundly defeated in the spring of 1379 when he was lured into an ambush at Pola (now Pula in Croatia) and, as a result, he was thrown into prison in Venice.

The summer of 1379 was one of the bleakest in the history of Venice as the city came closer to being taken over than at any other time between the attacks of the Carolingians in 810 and the arrival of Napoleon in 1797. Pisani's defeat at Pola dangerously gave the Genoese full access to the northern Adriatic. The enemy fleet received reinforcements and began to attack Venetian ships within sight of the lagoon. The Genoese set fire to towns on the island of the Lido, and the Venetians began to fortify outposts, including the monastery of *San Nicolò*, near the mouth of the lagoon. They barricaded the central entrance to the lagoon by chaining large ships together. As in their historic engagement with Pepin, they removed all the channel markers in the lagoon so that invaders could not navigate through it. While they undertook these precautionary measures, the Genoese took the city of Chioggia on the southern end of the lagoon in August 1379. That meant the Genoese commanded the northern Adriatic and one of the mouths of the lagoon, so that by the middle of August Venice was encircled and blockaded. Though the Venetians tried to negotiate, the Genoese replied that they wanted only 'to bit and bridle the horses of St Mark'.

The Venetians managed to raise large sums of money by forcing loans from various families, and used this to finance the war and especially to man the forts around the lagoon. The state then rallied popular support by releasing Vettor Pisani from prison. Though he had suffered a huge defeat at Pola he was nevertheless adored by workers and seamen, and his release and new command over six galleys dramatically prompted new conscription. Pisani and his forces began to employ the same strategy that the Venetians had used against Pepin hundreds of years earlier: they sank ships weighted with stones in the channels of the lagoon to separate the Genoese at Chioggia from the rest of their fleet while the Venetians waited for Carlo Zeno and the rest of the Venetian fleet to return.

While the Genoese were besieging Venice the city ran dangerously low on food and supplies, but at the same time the Venetians succeeded in blockading the Genoese inside the lagoon. Zeno returned to help the blockade of Chioggia on 1 January 1380; deprived of food and gunpowder, the Genoese surrendered in June 1380. In the ensuing peace between the two powers, Venice accepted some harsh conditions: it gave up the island of Tenedos, the right to trade at Tana for two years and recognized Genoese sovereignty on Cyprus, among other terms. Nevertheless, the control of the Adriatic returned to the Venetians so that the city maintained its monopoly over trade in the Adriatic that was so essential to its economic survival. For Venice, the War of Chioggia was both a defeat and a victory. As the Black Sea would become increasingly less commercially important in the fifteenth century, antagonism between Venice and Genoa declined and the two powers never fought again.

The War of Chioggia or the Fourth Genoese War represents an important marker in the history of Venice partly because it was a time of both profound danger and remarkable patriotism. The city had never been in greater danger and the Venetians had never come together so solidly against all odds. Artisans left their workshops to learn naval maneuvers and patrician women sold their jewels to support the war effort and help defeat the Genoese in an incredible reversal of fortune. In addition, like the Third Genoese War, it also had significant political implications in Venetian political life because the republic dramatically decided to admit 30 'popular' families to the noble class as a reward for their war sacrifices and contributions. In September 1381 these new families were admitted to the Great Council, resulting in a decisive and fundamental shift in the structure of the Venetian ruling class by giving power to new families at the expense of the older ones.

Older families, also called the *longhi* or *case vecchie* (literally, 'old houses'), claimed they descended from the tribunes who had governed the lagoon when it was first inhabited. These 24 families included names such as Badoer, Contarini, Dandolo, Falier, Gradenigo, Michiel, Morsini, Querini, Tiepolo and Zen, names that had long held the most important offices in the republic, being commanders, ambassadors and doges. After the acceptance of these 30 new families, or *curti*, no old family would produce a doge for several hundred years; after 1382 doges tended to come from these newer families.

By the end of the fourteenth century, all these events and changes that resulted from wars and political re-arrangements meant that Venetian society became rigid, fixed and stratified in a fairly permanent way. Venetian society would never represent the complex and hierarchical feudal pyramid that defined much of the rest of Europe but, by 1400, there were now nobles and non-nobles in Venice, and mobility between the two was essentially impossible. The noble and political class became impenetrable and, at any given time in the history of the republic, it represented about four per cent of the city's population. In the fourteenth century Venetian political and social life became fundamentally fixed until the arrival of Napoleon.

While there is no one place or site in the city from which to get a sense of the tumultuous fourteenth century, a handful of small but significant details around the city mark the curious and crucial events from this period. For instance, in every mask shop in the city you can find replicas of the bizarre and macabre masks used by doctors in the plague. They are clearly discernable with their strange, curved beaks into which doctors inserted a mixture of herbs thought to protect the air they breathed. In the Ducal Palace there is an especially sombre reflection on the deeds of Marino Falier. While Falier's burial was unremarkable, his plans are powerfully remembered here in the frieze of doges that encircles the walls of the Hall of the Great Council. Among the faces of all the other doges of the city, a black curtain hangs where his portrait should be, on top of which is written, 'This space is reserved for Marino Falier, beheaded for his crimes.' His family palace, where he lived before he became doge, is currently a posh hotel overlooking the *Campo Santi Apostoli*. Leaving the *Piazza San Marco* under the clock tower and entering the *Merceria*, you can look up to the left and see on the second floor an unobtrusive and muted plaque noting the spot where Giustina Rossi momentously dropped her flowerpot on the head of a conspiratorial standard bearer, thereby preventing the Querini-Tiepolo revolt from overthrowing the republic.

It is on the other side of town, however, that we can catch a less touristed but perhaps much more profound glimpse into both the drama of fourteenth-century Venice as well as into the deeply stratified layers of history. The families involved in the Querini-Tiepolo conspiracy lived on this side of town, away from the *Piazza San Marco*; they burned the wooden drawbridge of the Rialto, destroying it completely in their wake, to prevent ducal forces from following them back to their neighbourhood when their insurrection failed. Leaving *San Marco* behind, crossing the Rialto Bridge and passing west through the market we soon come to the placid and now peaceful *Campo Santa Maria Mater Domini*. Standing with your back to the bridge that bears the square's name, on the left there is the thirteenth-century palace of the Zane family, complete (like the *Corte del Million* of Marco Polo) with early gothic windows and an inlaid Byzantine relief of a chain of crosses above them.

Straight ahead, on the opposite side of the square, is the façade of the *Palazzo Viaro-Zane*. The gothic second floor of this family palace dates from the fourteenth century, and the upper floors from later in the fifteenth or sixteenth centuries judging by their classical Roman arched windows. Stepping closer and looking carefully at the remains of the relief between the ground floor and the second floor, in the segment directly over the front door in the centre of the building, are the markings of what was once a flying lion that had been placed on this façade. This once indicated that the state had confiscated the personal goods of the family because it participated in the Querini-Tiepolo conspiracy. The relief was later chiselled out under Napoleon as an unseemly reminder of the aristocratic Venetian state that his new and enlightened regime had come to stamp out.

Gazing upon the shattered remains of this piece of stone with a bit of imagination, we can construct some of the tumultuous events that happened in this *campo*: the rioting crowds and failed and terrified conspirators beating a hasty retreat to their family homes and locking their doors behind them: the officers of state following rapidly on their heels to haul them out of hiding and into exile across the Adriatic in Dalmatia or to be hanged in the *Piazza San Marco*: the republican bureaucrats accompanied by stone masons who systematically marked various sites around the city with stone reliefs to shame the families who had dared threaten the unity of the republic: the thousands of passers-by who, for hundreds of years, would gaze upon such markers with pride or fear; and the renegade general, Napoleon, who crossed the Alps from the grey and cold of the North to enlighten the backward peoples of Southern Europe by imposing his own liberal but megalomaniac and imperial order.

We can visualize the agents of Napoleon's bureaucracy, one dragging a wagon behind him and the other carrying a checklist, followed by a morose and impoverished local stone mason dressed in rags. They systematically tread the winding streets of the city with the agent in charge indicating with a pointed finger the markers, plaques, blazons, shields and sculptures to be removed. The mason then tiredly does their bidding, chiselling out the plaque and placing the stone carefully in the cart to be taken to Paris. Napoleon's men sought to erase the signs of a thousand years of history while simultaneously enriching the general's coffers with precious art and artefacts. Here, we get ahead of our story, but still we must note: all this we can make out in this tiny patch of stone in this otherwise quiet corner of the city.

5

VENICE IN THE EARLY MODERN WORLD: 1400–1600

The Renaissance – when Europeans rediscovered the world of classical antiquity, the cultural remains of ancient Greece and Rome – marks the Western shift from the Middle Ages to the modern world. Italian humanists and artists, such as Petrarch and Ghiberti – primarily Florentines at first – unearthed and studied ancient texts and art that spawned a host of transformations in Europe, especially in science, technology and geography.

The defining events of this age were the discovery of the New World, the invention of the printing press, the Scientific Revolution and the Protestant Reformation, and they all profoundly affected the city of Venice. These events were all closely linked to the rediscovery of classical culture, but their influence and effects also spread far beyond the elite worlds of art and literature. For these reasons, historians often use the term 'early modern' to label this period in European history: a term that denotes this period of sweeping changes as linked but not limited to the 'Renaissance' or rediscovery of classical culture. While Venetians became fascinated with ancient Greece and Rome, they did not embrace classical culture as quickly or in the same manner as the Florentines or Romans. That is why historians often refer to early modern rather than Renaissance Venice.

In addition to changes wrought by the Age of Discovery, the advent of print, the Copernican challenge and Martin Luther's defiance of the pope in Rome, early modern Venetians also grappled with complex challenges related to a growing mainland empire and a dramatically altered relationship with the eastern Mediterranean as the Ottoman Turks advanced. Women and Jews also came to play more significant cultural and political roles in the city at this time. So while early modern Venetians gradually became classicists like their Florentine and Roman counterparts, becoming fascinated with classical Latin and Greek texts and Roman architecture, they experienced an additional host of changes from 1400–1600 that went far beyond the rediscovery of the ancient world.

Changes in and Challenges to Venetian Rule

In the fifteenth century Venetians began to conquer and rule subject cities on the mainland to the west of Venice. For a city that had always built its fortunes on the sea, this was quite a shift in the state's political interests. Some historians think that after the Greek reconquest of Constantinople in 1261, Venetians began to pay more attention to the nearby mainland, or *terraferma*. Though Venice had long focused almost exclusively on the extension, development and protection of its maritime empire, there were now good reasons for looking towards the land. First, Venetians wanted to protect their trade routes. They also needed more secure and local access to food and other supplies, especially raw materials for developing manufacturing industries, so securing mainland territory for cultivation, wood, water and other resources was important.

Second, a territorial buffer zone on the mainland would help protect Venice against military threats by land. And third, Venetian nobles in search of state incomes quickly came to understand that they could obtain lucrative and prestigious positions, becoming local governors or commanders in or near mainland cities as a result of expansion.

The Venetians had conquered Treviso on the mainland as early as 1339, and then in 1403, following a war against the Carrara family in Padua, the Venetian state acquired political control over the mainland cities of Vicenza, Feltre, Bassan and Belluno, followed a few years later by Verona and Padua. By 1420 its territories included Friuli and Udine, thereby protecting most of Venice's trade routes into the rest of Europe. Patrician administrators and bureaucrats left the lagoon to oversee the government, justice and tax collection on the mainland as, slowly, one by one, town after town in north-east Italy came under Venetian rule. As the Venetians scored one military victory after another on the mainland, many Venetians became deeply concerned about the direction the state was taking. For an economy and a government that had flourished by looking east towards the sea, did increased involvement in mainland affairs risk jeopardizing Venetian security and prosperity? Doge Tommaso Mocenigo (r. 1414–23) argued that maintaining the traditional Venetian commitment to a maritime empire was the best way to preserve state stability. War on the mainland was costly and it was better for Venice to maintain its eastern focus. He warned Venetians as much from his deathbed. But the head-strong and reckless doge who succeeded him, Francesco Foscari (r. 1423–62), insisted that Venice did have the resources to maintain a maritime empire and simultaneously expand its mainland territories.

After the election of Foscari, the Venetian state pushed its boundaries even further west and fought a war against Milan that would last 19 years. Despite much public disagreement, Foscari pushed ahead. With no standing army of its own, the Venetians hired mercenary captains, or *condottieri*, to continue their conquests, men who were expert tacticians and commanders but whose loyalty was often in question. The commander Carmagnola won Brescia (in 1426) and Bergamo (1427) for Venice (though he was later beheaded for negotiating with the Milanese), and armies under the leadership of the mercenaries Gattamelata and Bartolomeo Colleoni later reinforced these conquests. By the middle of the fifteenth century, with the Venetian mainland empire at its largest, the Venetian patrician Bernardo Giustiniani proclaimed the three greatest powers of the world to be the Holy Roman emperor, the pope and the doge. However, the price of these wars in Lombardy was exceedingly high. The Venetians went to incredible expense, and even transported an entire fleet overland by oxen to fight the Milanese on Lake Garda in 1438. Acquiring and maintaining these mainland territories was so costly that they bankrupted members of the nobility – including Foscari's own father-in-law – and the state had to initiate direct taxes on Venetian subjects for the first time in its history since financing war from the public debt was no longer sufficient. The Peace of Lodi in 1454 put an end to these wars for the time being by establishing a boundary between Venice and Milan along the River Adda in Northern Italy. The Venetians held their mainland territories, but the cost was extraordinarily high.

Two other events between 1450 and 1500 dramatically challenged Venice's position in the world, and according to some this meant that Venice would never again be a world power. First, in 1453, the city of Constantinople fell to the advancing Ottoman Turks, marking the end of the Byzantine Roman Empire in the East. The Ottoman Empire formed around 1300 and slowly extended its rule over the Balkans and Asia Minor (now Turkey). The collapse of Byzantine Constantinople cemented the Ottomans as a great imperial power. Though the Venetians had no political power in Byzantine Constantinople, the city was still the most crucial hub of Venetian trade in the East. After several months of siege, Sultan Mehmed II and his troops rushed the gates of Constantinople and, as the city fell into Turkish hands, Italians and Europeans alike believed the collapse of the Venetian economy would soon follow. When Constantinople fell, the Venetians suddenly became everyday traders in the Mediterranean, no different from anyone else. While the Venetians established trade agreements with the Ottomans they no longer had a special or privileged trading status with this powerful empire. The Ottomans were happy to trade with the Venetians, but only on terms that benefitted the Ottomans.

After Constantinople, the Turks continued their advance and other Venetian trade outposts in the Mediterranean fell soon after. In 1470 Mehmed's forces seized the important island of Negroponte (now Euboea). In the battle for the city of Chalkis on Negroponte, Venetians and Turks fought street by street and house by house to hold the city. On the morning of 12 July 1470, the *bailo*, or Venetian ambassador to the city, was sawed in half alive and all the remaining Venetians had their throats cut when the Turks finally won. The Ottomans advanced to capture the towns of Modon and Coron in 1499 on the southern Peloponnesus, towns that had been crucial strategic outposts for the Venetians since 1204. According to chroniclers, the Turks advanced so far into Venetian territory that when they sacked towns in Friuli, just north of Venice, Venetians could see the smoke on the mainland from the bell tower of *San Marco*. By 1503 the Ottomans had conquered almost the entire Venetian maritime empire and the Venetians, longing for peace, surrendered their outposts in Greece and Albania, maintaining their hold only in Dalmatia, Crete and Cyprus. Venice had arranged a strategic marriage between Caterina Cornaro – a young Venetian noblewoman – and King James of Cyprus in 1468 to help secure control of the island. After the early death of her husband and child just two years after her marriage, Queen Catherine was forced to hand over Cyprus to the Venetian state in 1489 and in 1570 the island fell to the Ottomans.

The second crucial event concerned the enormous discoveries being made in maritime exploration. The Venetians had always been intrepid explorers and continued this tradition into the fifteenth century. Under the patronage of Prince Henry the Navigator, the Venetian Alvise Ca' da Mosto (1432–88) was among the first to explore the west coast of Africa and appears to have been the first European to reach the Cape Verde islands in 1456, resulting in one of the earliest known descriptions of Western Africa. In 1497 Henry VII of England authorized the Venetian John Cabot (or Giovanni Caboto) and his son Sebastian to sail west across the Atlantic in search of islands. They landed off the coast of Labrador, which Cabot marked with both English and Venetian flags. However, Portuguese ships were the first to sail directly from Europe to India when Vasco de Gama returned to Portugal in the summer of 1499 and announced to the world the opening of a direct sea route to the spices of India.

When reports of this discovery reached Venice in the following months, many Venetians were aghast. The Venetian chronicler Girolamo Priuli reported that such a discovery would allow the Portuguese to obtain spices, the mainstay of the Venetian economy, at a fraction of the cost paid by Venetians. Venice, he feared, would be ruined. Shocked and worried, in 1504 Venetian nobles went so far as to debate a massive engineering project that would involve cutting the isthmus of Suez to connect the Mediterranean to the Red Sea, a forerunner of the Suez Canal, to allow Venetians to continue to compete in the spice trade, but the project was soon abandoned because of its complexity and expense. In the end, Venetian trade with the East would not be seriously damaged until the Dutch formed the powerful East India Companies that more effectively excluded Venice from the spice trade in the seventeenth century. The Venetian economy in the sixteenth century was diversified and healthy enough to weather the Portuguese discovery. It is nevertheless interesting to note that when word of the Columbian discoveries began to spread from Spain in the summer of 1493, no Venetian ambassador ever considered Columbus' activities worthy of mention in any their reports. It was the symbolic meaning of the new Portuguese route to India that grabbed their attention.

Despite these setbacks in the world of Eastern trade – or perhaps because of them – the Venetians continued to add territories to their mainland empire. Even at a time when much of the rest of Italy was in turmoil – the King of France swept into Italy in 1494 and seized vast Italian lands, at times unopposed – the Venetians occupied Cremona in 1499 and won a series of victories in Friuli in 1508. By this time other European powers began to question seriously Venetian goals and motives as Venice appeared poised to extend its sovereignty even further. Fearful of Venetian ambitions, Pope Julius II (the same pope who commissioned Michelangelo to paint the ceiling of the Sistine Chapel) organized a defensive league to prevent the Venetians from gaining further ground. The League of Cambrai – so called because it was formed in Cambrai, France, in 1509 – included France, the Holy Roman Empire, Spain and most other Italian states. It aimed to deprive Venice of its mainland possessions and to stop Venetian imperialist ambitions once and for all. At the Battle of Agnadello on 14 May 1509, French forces routed Venetian cavalry in the territory between Milan and Bergamo, dealing a crushing blow to Venetian forces. In one city after another, from Brescia to the shores of the lagoon, mainland nobles declared their allegiance to France and Germany (since local nobles had long resented the Venetian presence in their cities) and the armies of the League continued to push their forces up to the lagoon, effectively eliminating the Venetian presence on the mainland. The humanist and statesman Nicolò Machiavelli observed this advance from the headquarters of the Holy Roman emperor in Verona, and he described, in Chapter 12 of *The Prince* how, in one day, the Venetians 'lost what it had taken them eight hundred years' to conquer.

The defeat was crushing but not lasting. By 1516 Venice regained much of its lost mainland territory up to the Adda River, and continued to hold it until the arrival of Napoleon in 1797. Nevertheless, this war and the dramatic defeat of

Venetian forces at Agnadello in many ways changed Venice forever; the symbolic trauma of the loss endured long after these lands had been regained. For many historians of the Republic of Venice, Agnadello represents the most significant date in Venetian history since it marked the beginning of Venetian decline though it is now thought that the Venetian state and its economy remained vibrant to the end of the sixteenth century. However, the combined events of the fall of Constantinople, the Portuguese arrival in Calcutta and Goa, and the Battle of Agnadello, all signalled a change in Venetian mentality. Venetian merchants, entrepreneurs and industrialists still made a profit in the sixteenth century but, after 1509, Venice could no longer claim to be the greatest European power. This was especially true as Spain and other countries in Northern Europe began to exploit the emerging economy of the Atlantic World in ways that the Venetians never would.

Science, Industry and Entrepreneurialism

While many events implied the potential beginnings of Venetian decline, they were offset by a number of trends in Venice that promoted a sense of optimism and vitality in the sixteenth century. Venetian industries and manufacturing took off as never before and, in addition, the Scientific Revolution unfolded in Venice in ways no one could have predicted. In these and other ways, Venice was part of the cultural movement of the Renaissance, and shared the conscious sensation of being a part of a new and forward-looking age.

Up until now, Venetians made most of their money as the middlemen between Europe and the East, transporting spices and luxury goods back and forth between Venice and the eastern Mediterranean. However, in the sixteenth century Venetians began to produce and manufacture more of their own wares. The production of woollen cloth became common in the city, and the silk industry boomed as Venetian mills began to spin more and more silk and export finished cloth to France and the Low Countries. The soap, glass and shipbuilding industries also thrived in the sixteenth century. The industry that blossomed most dramatically of all, however, was the printing business.

The technology of moveable type did not originate in Venice but China, and in Europe it was Johannes Gutenberg who first unveiled the mechanical printing press in Mainz around 1440. The printing press changed the world forever. It promoted literacy by making texts cheaper and more accessible to those outside the nobility; it encouraged new stirrings of nationalism as people became increasingly aware of the greater world around them through print; and it changed the way memory functioned because now people did not need to remember as much information since it existed on the printed page. The effects of the printing press – cultural, social, political and economical – were huge, but what is important here is that Venice became the print capital of the early modern world.

Paper was cheap and readily available in Venice, and the culture of the city was relatively liberal and open to new and controversial ideas often found in books. Venetians had no problem in defying Roman censorship. The print industry began in 1469 and, by 1500, there were approximately 150 presses in the city. In the sixteenth century Venetian printers produced some 17,500 editions, nearly half the books printed in Italy during that time. Scores of print houses popped up around the city and in particular lined the streets around the Rialto, the area near *San Salvador*, and along the streets of the *Merceria* and the *Frezzeria* leading towards *San Marco*. Printing houses under the names of Giunta, Giolito, Marcolini, Zanetti and Gardano hung distinctive signs outside their shops and printed them on the frontispieces of their books, sending the Venetian *imprimatur* around the world wherever Venetian books were bought and sold. The Venetian presses published in every field and for every audience, producing books on science, music, theatre, religion, language, politics and spirituality. A great variety of people worked together in the print houses to produce books, ranging from printers to editors, humanists, playwrights, poets, linguists, translators and clerics, creating a great nexus for the exchange of ideas and information. If fourteenth-century Venetian businessmen made their profits primarily through commerce and trade with the East, the fifteenth and sixteenth centuries witnessed the growth of this new entrepreneurial arena, the print house.

The press of one particular Venetian, however, most profoundly affected the world of books: that of Aldus Manutius. He was first and foremost a scholar and humanist, being well read in classical Latin and Greek. The Fall of Constantinople in 1453 drove many Greeks to Europe and Venice in particular, and by 1500 there was a Greek community of about 5,000 in Venice alone. As the Greek world was crumbling in the East, Manutius strove to preserve Greek literature by committing its chief masterpieces to type in his printing house that he opened in 1490. Manutius gathered Greek scholars and workers around him in his Venice workshop to collate pages, read drafts and develop models of Greek print to be set into type. From 1495–98 he issued a five-volume edition of the works of Aristotle, the first published by the Western press. Through the first decade of the sixteenth century he went on to publish the works of Aristophanes, Thucydides, Sophocles, Herodotus, Euripides, Plato and others, including a host of other texts in Latin. Prior to these Aldine publications, Greek literature existed haphazardly only in manuscript volumes in monastic libraries. By the time of his death, only the Greek works of Aeschylus remained to be printed. Manutius gave Greek literature and philosophy to the Western world, one of the most significant Venetian contributions to the West.

In addition, and perhaps even more importantly, the Aldine press produced for the first time, and popularized, a new and more modern type of volume, a portable, hand-held book, about 15 × 23 cm (6 × 9 inches) big, that readers could take with them anywhere, rather like a modern paperback. Manutius was not simply an elitist intellectual, he was also an entrepreneur who was interested in producing highly marketable texts. He was the first to use italic print, not for emphasis (as today) but because the slanting letters meant you could pack in more words to the page. The small size and reasonable price meant that anyone from the roaming scholar to the upwardly mobile merchant could easily load his saddlebag with these portable Greek and Latin classics.

It is interesting to note how Venetians both absorbed, and did not absorb, the culture of the Renaissance. The Renaissance was largely a Florentine phenomenon, with humanists such as Poggio Bracciolini and Coluccio Salutati for instance reading and editing ancient Roman texts and using them as guides for interpreting the modern world. But Venice was not interested in the ancient world in the same way. As a curious example of this so-called 'bibliophobic' tendency, Petrarch promised his own library of about 200 codices and even more individual titles to the Venetian republic in 1362 in exchange for housing in the *Palazzo Molina* on the *Riva degli Schiavoni*. As the story goes, Petrarch would keep his library until his death, but living in Venice he discovered that Venetians were not that interested in his library and work as a humanist, and so he moved to Padua. After his death, his library remained neglected for centuries at the *Palazzo Molina*, crumbling to powder, petrifying and decaying into unrecognizable forms. In 1468 the Byzantine humanist Cardinal Bessarion similarly made a bequest of over 1000 codices, manuscripts and books to the Venetian state, but it was more than 50 years before the Venetian Senate began to make plans to erect an official state library to house the collections of (what remained of) Petrarch and Bessarion.

Based on these stories and other evidence, some have argued that Renaissance Venice was not a literary city. Venice did not produce humanists to rival Petrarch or Lorenzo Valla who plumbed the depths of the classical past and used their knowledge of classical Latin or Roman history to feed arguments about contemporary politics. Nor did Venice have equivalents to great Florentine humanists, such as Marsilio Ficino, and nor could it rival the Florentine Platonic Academy, dedicated to translating Plato's works into Latin. But why should it? Venetians did not have a Roman past and were not that interested in rediscovering it. They were interested in classical texts, but primarily as a means to support and glorify the Venetian government. Venetian humanists, including Giovanni Caldiera and Francesco Sansovino, looked to the classical past but with the almost exclusive purpose of finding evidence that would support the Venetian ideology of patrician rule, portray the impartial nature of Venetian justice and help describe the grandeur of their city. Men with a humanist education did not become lecturers or philosophers in Venice; they became ambassadors, diplomats and bureaucrats who staffed the offices of the Venetian state or entrepreneurs (like Manutius) who sold the printed word and used it simply to make money.

The Scientific Revolution also affected Venice in specific ways. One of the defining transformations of the early modern period happened when Nicolaus Copernicus and Galileo revolutionized how Europeans understood their place in the universe. We went from being at the centre of an orderly, geocentric and finite universe, as described by Aristotle, to having no clear place in a seemingly endless and changing heliocentric universe. These ideas did not concur with the teachings of the bible or the authority of the pope and generated great cultural and spiritual controversy.

Venice played a role in the Scientific Revolution since Galileo worked as a mathematics professor at the University of Padua from 1592–1610, when he also gave private lessons in Venice. Since Padua was then under Venetian rule, the Venetian authorities oversaw the workings of the university. Galileo was also a frequent visitor to the Venetian arsenal where he indulged his fascination in mechanical devices, and it was during his time in Padua and Venice that he invented the telescope. His good friend the cleric Paolo Sarpi obtained an audience with the Venetian Senate for Galileo and, in front of a group of Venetian patricians, he first demonstrated the use of his telescope on 25 August 1609, according to some accounts on the top of the *campanile* in the *Piazza San Marco*. It was also during his time in the Veneto that he wrote his famous *Starry Messenger* announcing his discoveries; the book that eventually got him into trouble with the Church demonstrated that the universe was constantly changing, and most likely heliocentric. Galileo's contribution to the Scientific Revolution is traditionally most closely associated with Florence since it was there that he was tried, and it is in the Museum of Science in Florence that Galileo's telescope and his [middle] finger are preserved. Historians of science have long speculated that if he had he stayed in Venice his fate would have been very different. Instead of being forced to recant his ideas and being placed under house arrest for most of the rest of his life, in Venice, his theories may have found support, and a cultural and political setting in which to flourish. With its long tradition of being politically and culturally separate and distinct from Rome, and its tradition of bucking Roman authority – especially, as we shall see, with the likes of the writings of his friend Paolo Sarpi – it is quite possible that the republic might have been able to protect him.

The Scientific Revolution in Venice was more than just a revolution in astronomy and physics; it was also a revolution in scientific curiosity. Medieval, Christian ideas about scientific investigation were somewhat negative. St Augustine (d. 430) famously considered curiosity a form of lust and pride since curious people lacked humility. Now curiosity changed everything. The University of Padua became the centre for European research on anatomy where Andreas Vesalius, his teachers and students dissected the human body, demonstrating a new obsession with understanding how it was put together, and how ancient Greek and Roman doctors were wrong about its construction. The Venetian Senate funded annual anatomy demonstrations suggesting that advances in this branch of science were a point of civic pride that enhanced the city's stature in the scientific community. In addition, the concept of 'curiosity' became a positive, not a negative, force in part as a result of the exposure to so many new and curious things arriving from the New World. With a new array of specimens of flora and fauna at healers' fingertips, the world of medicine and healing expanded apace. The sixteenth-century Venetian marketplace was a true emporium of 'curiosities' from around the world. Venice had numerous pharmacies that sold a variety of herbs and new medical potions, many of which hailed from the New World as well as from traditional Eastern trade routes. By the middle of the sixteenth century, the city had more than 50 apothecaries. The street name *calle del spezier* still indicates their presence in the city. In addition charlatans, such as the medical man Leonardo Fioravanti, hawked their wares around the city, often on portable stages erected in various public squares including the *Piazza San Marco*, trying to make a quick profit by selling their curiosities and magical healing potions to passers-by. Pharmacists and charlatans alike marketed a wide variety of pharmaceuticals for the early modern market: crocodile skins, holy mud, distilled serums and elixirs from exotic plants and animals, and even Egyptian mummies, widely reputed to cure many ailments. Both Renaissance humanism and the Scientific Revolution in Venice encouraged varieties of entrepreneurship and industry. Venetians were interested in Renaissance literature and scientific discovery especially where a profit could be turned, true to the longstanding, pragmatic spirit of the city.

Social Change in the Early Modern City

The early modern period in European history is marked by what were shocking and often strident challenges to traditional forms of authority. Columbus' discoveries challenged the ancients' understanding that there were only three continents; Copernicus and his followers challenged everyone's understanding of the structure of the universe; and Martin Luther – a monk and professor of theology at the University of Wittenberg – challenged the authority of the pope and the power of the Catholic church. Luther sent a powerful and defiant message to the church in 1517 when he attached his Ninety-five Theses to the door of the Wittenberg Castle church. These questioned papal authority and many of the traditional practices of the church – such as the sale of indulgences (buying people out of purgatory), the veneration of saints, pilgrimages, the act of confession and the way the popes solicited and spent great sums of money recklessly – that Luther viewed as corrupt or a corruption of what the bible intended. Luther essentially argued for a return to what the bible said, and he wanted to ban a great variety of Christian practices that he felt had no basis in the book. The Ninety-five Theses were quickly translated into many languages and printed widely. They called upon the church to answer to centuries of corruption and abuses, thereby generating the Protestant Reformation. While the crusading age had witnessed an unprecedented unification of all Europeans under the shared umbrella of Christianity, after Luther's challenge Christianity became permanently fragmented into the camps of Catholic and Reformed Christians, and would never again have the same shared meaning that it did for people in the Middle Ages.

Some Venetians, such as the cardinal Gasparo Contarini, were strongly in favour of trying to reform the traditions and practices of the Catholic church from within to reconcile Catholics and Protestants and preserve the unity of the Christian church. But they were unsuccessful and the differences between Catholics and Protestants hardened and became permanent with the Council of Trent, a series of meetings of churchmen from 1545–63 that denied the legitimacy of Luther's arguments. Trent embodied the ideas of the Counter-Reformation, or the Catholic reaction to Luther's challenge. The Counter-Reformation reaffirmed the Christian tradition (the power of the pope and the legitimacy of saints, etc.) while simultaneously calling for the reform of Christian practices and behaviour on many different fronts to shore up Catholicism in areas where its respectability had waned, for example demanding that bishops must live in their bishoprics and nuns must be kept in convents. Luther's challenge and the Roman reaction to it had powerful effects on the city of Venice as they filtered down to the residents of the lagoon.

Most dramatically, in 1542 Pope Paul III revived the workings of the Holy Office, otherwise known as the Roman Inquisition, which came to Venice in 1547 and would remain until the arrival of Napoleon. Since Venice was close to the Alps, Protestant ideas appeared in the lagoon soon after Luther's challenge and spread quickly, often in and around the print houses that employed workers from the north and became hotbeds for discussion and the exchange of ideas. We can easily imagine print houses hiring German workers to set their type and collate their pages: workers who casually questioned their Italian colleagues about why they could not eat meat on Fridays and how the pope had acquired so much money and power. In the early years inquisitors focused their energies on cases of heresy, especially Venetians who dappled in Lutheranism and Anabaptism. As the years passed and heresy ran less rampant, the Inquisition became more interested in a wider range of heretical practices that threatened civic piety, such as witchcraft, magic and superstition. As a mandate from Rome, the Holy Office was accompanied by the printing of the *Index Librorum Prohibitorum* (*Index of Prohibited Books*) in 1543, which forbade the publication and possession of a list of texts considered heretical, immoral or generally unwholesome or offensive. They included the writings of Nicolò Machiavelli, Johannes Kepler and, of course, Martin Luther. Compared to the Spanish Inquisition introduced by Ferdinand and Isabella, the Venetian Inquisition was relatively mild. Only a handful of people were put to death over the several hundred years of the existence of this office, and those who were punished often received only gentle punishments, for example having to recite specific prayers a certain number of times a day.

Nevertheless, the arrival of the Counter-Reformation in Venice produced an atmosphere of fear and it changed the energy and tenor of city life. As this wave of social and cultural conservatism descended upon the city, the inhabitants of Venice, its artists, writers, printers, churchmen, fishmongers and shipbuilders, felt the tightening of the screws. Public behaviour was more closely scrutinized, blasphemy was harshly punished and sumptuary laws enforced rules requiring more modest dress and quieter parties. As the freedom of the press that had encouraged so many printers and writers to work in the city was overshadowed by the fear of the Inquisition, books about literature and science became more scarce. The influential publisher Gabriel Giolito, for instance, was forced to appear before the Inquisition and several Venetian texts with anticlerical or ribald passages were added to the *Index of Prohibited Books*. In addition, a plague from 1575–76 devastated the city's population, wiping out nearly one-third of its inhabitants and bringing much of the city's cultural production to a halt. However, this era of caution and contraction saw some surprising social turns and openings.

In the sixteenth century more Jews came to live in Venice. They had frequented the city with some regularity since the end of the fourteenth century when, in its state of financial desperation after the War of Chioggia, the government began to court the services of Jewish moneylenders as an alternative to Christian usury. The Jews not only paid taxes but also lent money to the state and the urban poor at a reasonable rate of return. They were allowed to come and work in the city by day, and the state increasingly extended their rights to stay in Venice over the course of the fourteenth century, to the point where they could remain in the city for up to 15 days. During the war of Cambrai, Jews offered their financial resources to help defend the city and, in return, the state allowed them to settle permanently in the lagoon in 1516.

Jews lived in the city under strict rules and regulations. They had to wear clothing in public that distinguished them as Jews – typically a circular yellow badge or hat – and were forbidden to own property or to marry Christians or have sexual relations with them. They were only allowed to practice certain professions, namely to work as doctors, money-lenders and vendors of used goods, and were kept physically separate from Christians on the island of the Ghetto. (The Ghetto was so called because it had previously been the site of an iron foundry, *getar* meaning 'to cast'.) The word 'ghetto', now used to mean any area of ethnic or racial confinement, represents a unique Venetian linguistic contribution to the history of violence and persecution in the West. Jews were required to return to the Ghetto at night where they were enclosed by a series of doors and drawbridges. Some claim that the windows on the first floor along the canals were even walled up to prevent night-time escapes. Others argue that since the growing number of Jews could not move to other islands, they were forced to build upwards and construct buildings much taller than those found elsewhere in the city, often with their synagogues on top, which are still visible today. The Jewish population reached its height in 1630 with over 2,400 people living on this small island, which must have been extremely crowded. They lived under such cramped conditions until the end of the eighteenth century when Napoleon's forces threw open the Ghetto gates and allowed the Jews to live elsewhere in the city.

The early modern period also witnessed the new growing influence of women as they began to take on different social roles and often became increasingly empowered. Somewhat ironically, while the two figures that symbolized the city of Venice were both female – Venus (born from the sea like Venice) and the Virgin (like Venice, never conquered) – Venetian women possessed no official political power. Besides the ceremonial role played by the *dogaressa*, the wife of the doge, Venetian women could not vote or participate in political debate. Nevertheless, Venetian women came into positions of power and influence outside the halls of government in a variety of ways. The historian Stanley Chojnacki has demonstrated how Venetian noblewomen wielded a unique amount of economic power compared to their mainland counterparts.

Around the turn of the fifteenth century, as lucrative state offices became more coveted, patricians jealously guarded admittance to the Venetian noble class and required that applicants should have both a father *and* mother of noble pedigree. This raised the status of patrician women and subsequently caused a dramatic rise in the price of their dowries. Since Venetian women retained their dowries after the death of their husband, they often used their substantial dowries to make large capital investments. They also passed them on to their daughters, and they maintained a fair amount of social leverage over males who regarded them with increased respect since they had so much money.

It is also now clear that more Venetian women headed their own households and worked to support themselves, and their families, than was previously believed. The wills, leases and business proposals in the Venetian archives show that non-noble women, like their noble counterparts, were also an independent financial force, with one-third of all tax declarations in the early modern city being filed by women. They also had a wide variety of jobs, being landlords, property managers, writers, bead stringers, seamstresses and writers. The second half of the sixteenth century saw the publication of Moderata Fonte's *The Worth of Women* (1600) and Lucrezia Marinella's colourfully entitled *The Nobility and Excellence of Women and the Defects and Vices of Men* (1600).

Perhaps most notoriously, Venetian women worked as prostitutes and courtesans. Venice was famous for prostitution, and chroniclers in the fifteenth and sixteenth centuries regularly cite their large numbers in the city. The chronicler Marin Sanudo put their number at close to 50,000 at the beginning of the sixteenth century, a clear exaggeration but a sign of their ubiquitous presence. Venetian law had regulated the work of prostitutes since 1358 by opening a state-sponsored bordello (as did many other late medieval European cities) in the *Castelletto* region near the Rialto Bridge. Prostitutes frequented a variety of houses, inns and taverns in this area and, like the Jews, were required to return to their quarters at night, usually before 10 pm, when the doors were closed. Prostitutes did not always obey the city's rules and eventually settled in various areas around the city. Nevertheless, it is interesting to note the degree to which the city viewed Jews and prostitutes alike: their presence was an unfortunate but necessary evil that the state tolerated and controlled by confinement on an island. Look for a narrow canal in the neighbourhood of *San Cassiano* with the *Ponte delle Tette*, or 'Bridge of Breasts' where prostitutes paraded topless both to attract clients and to discourage Venetian men from the practice of sodomy.

The sixteenth century was the golden age of Venetian courtesans. In addition to selling sex, they were in high demand and charged high fees for their spectacular beauty, manners, education, exquisite dress and ability to sing and play instruments, recite poetry and converse on philosophy and literature with ease. They entertained their elite clientele, including the *crème* of the Venetian aristocracy, in luxurious settings. One of the most famous courtesans was the poet and humanist Veronica Franco. Many sixteenth-century writers and tourists came to Venice to meet these women, and when Henry III, the future king of France, visited Venice in 1574 he specifically requested a meeting with Veronica Franco who composed two sonnets for him.

If early modern Venetian women became increasingly visible and powerful in these ways, more attention was also paid to women and the vices associated with them as a result of the Counter-Reformation. Along with the arrival of the Inquisition came a wave of reforms in Venice that sought to establish ways to assist and protect potentially wayward girls and women, and to eliminate sexual promiscuity. This resulted in the dramatic growth of charitable houses for women in the sixteenth century. Among others, the *Convertite* ('of the converted', now a women's prison) was opened in 1530 in an attempt to convert women from prostitution, the *Zitelle* opened in 1559 to protect young girls from falling into prostitution and the *Casa del*

Soccorso (literally, 'House of Rescue') opened in 1577 to protect adult women and retired prostitutes. On the one hand these houses were founded to control women, their movements in the city and their potential to turn to a life of vice but, on the other hand, they were were also typically staffed and run by women and, as a result, they were new and uniquely female communities that supported women and the challenges they faced.

In addition, the early modern period witnessed the dramatic growth of convents in the lagoon. Nuns came primarily from the Venetian nobility and like Jews, prostitutes and foreign communities in the city, they were restricted to enclosed areas, in this case convents. As the price of dowries rose, patrician families typically could not afford to marry off more than one of their daughters and the rest were often deposited in convents. By 1650 there were 33 nunneries in the city and 17 more around the rest of the lagoon, housing more than 3,000 nuns in all. Like houses of charity and the asylums, convents offered their inhabitants both attractive and unattractive living conditions. They were bastions of prayer and chastity as well as of vice and rebellion; they were places where women could escape the drudgeries of housework and domesticity and the dangers of childbirth, but where they were confined under lock and key, often against their will, for their entire lives. In practice most nuns managed to maintain a great degree of contact with the outside world. They often owned their own animals, dressed in fashionable clothes and maintained their own supplies of wine and fine food. The richest and rowdiest of Venetian convents, like the convent of *San Zaccaria*, held parties and dances, and even put on plays for the public. The early modern era witnessed the great growth of convents across the lagoon, presenting the growing number of Venetian nuns with both a protective female community and a life of enclosure and imprisonment.

Venice and the East
Since people first settled on the islands of the lagoon, Venetians maintained a dynamic relationship with the Byzantine East,

and Byzantine politics and culture defined life in the lagoon from the start. In the Middle Ages Venice acquired a vast maritime empire that extended across the Mediterranean, but by the beginning of the sixteenth century it had lost most of these territories to the Ottoman Turks. By 1500 Crete and Cyprus were the only places where Venetians maintained substantial colonies and the Turks, unlike the Byzantines, did not offer the Venetians any favourable trade status. In the fifteenth and sixteenth centuries, Venice's relationship with the eastern Mediterranean became more complex than ever before. In a period when much of Europe was focused on the New World and the economy of the Atlantic, Venetians continued to look to the East. The Venetians may have lost a lot of territory to the Ottomans, but they continued to benefit from their cultural and political contacts with them.

Venetian diplomats and merchants maintained a continuous presence in the main cities of the Islamic East, including Pera, Aleppo, Damascus, Acre and Alexandria, and there was a *bailo* or permanent ambassador to Constantinople. Mamluk and Ottoman officials also frequently visited Venice on diplomatic missions, bringing gifts to exchange and fostering a diplomatic relationship between Venice and the East that distinguished Venice from the rest of Europe. The Venetians even opened the *Fondaco dei Turchi* on the Grand Canal, a permanent hostel and warehouse for the Turks, as well as a mosque and *hammam* or bath for Turkish envoys in 1621 to provide the Turks with safe lodging and to facilitate good relations.

Such regular and consistent political contact also meant that the Venetians had a deep knowledge of the Islamic world. Islamic customs and culture held less mystery for Venetians than other Europeans, and this encouraged cultural exchange. In many ways the Venetians' cultural connection to the East became even more profound in the early modern world as a great new variety of cultural and material exchanges began to take place between Venice and the Ottoman Empire. Perhaps most famously, in September 1479 the Venetian Senate sent the painter Gentile Bellini to Constantinople as a kind of cultural ambassador, in particular because Sultan Mehmed II expressed an interest in Italian art. Bellini stayed at Mehmed's court for two years and painted a portrait of the sultan, now in the National Gallery in London. Easterners also admired Venetian glass and the Ottomans became huge consumers of Italian luxury textiles and copied Italian patterns and styles. In fact over 50 per cent of the recorded commercial transactions between Venice and the Islamic world were in textiles, and chroniclers claimed that when Ottoman envoys and their retinues arrived in Venice, Venetian merchants displayed their best textiles and, not surprisingly, textile prices went up at the Rialto during their stay.

Venetians similarly admired Islamic culture and sought out Ottoman goods. Expensive eastern carpets were in incredibly high demand in both Venice and Italy during the early modern period, and were a sign of wealth and prosperity. The *Scuola di San Rocco* acquired and perhaps even commissioned carpets from the Eastern Mediterranean to cover the large tables at which their members held their meetings, and Eastern carpets are at the centre of many Venetian paintings from this period. In addition, during the late fifteenth and sixteenth centuries, many Venetian confraternities commissioned painters to decorate their halls with large, narrative canvases depicting the lives of their patron saints, many of whom came from the East, so that Islamic figures and architecture regularly appear in the paintings of Renaissance Venice. Representations of the Islamic world can also be found Vittore Carpaccio's paintings – among the finest in Venetian art – in the *Scuola di San Giorgio degli Schiavoni* depicting the life of St George.

St George, the patron saint of this confraternity, came from Cappadocia in Turkey, and in Carpaccio's paintings recounting his life and trials, he depicts scenes peopled with the turbaned heads of a world far to the east of Venice. Venetian and Italian industries also produced imitations of Eastern glass, textiles, ceramics, book bindings and metalwork. Perhaps most notably

Venetian architecture seems to be deeply rooted in oriental models. Though it remains unclear exactly how such architectural knowledge and forms were transmitted, the art historian Deborah Howard has demonstrated how a variety of Venetian architectural details, including the rooftop terraces and stone screens that adorn Venetian palaces, echo and emulate Eastern forms and designs. Venetians were so interested in Islamic culture that the bishop's throne in the church of *San Pietro di Castello* has a carved quotation from the Koran on the seat's back plate.

At the time of the crusades, the Venetians often preferred to fight the Pisans or the Byzantines rather than the Muslims, and helped to sack Constantinople rather than the Turkish stronghold in Jerusalem. The Venetians clearly had a pragmatic, rational relationship with the Ottomans, with whom they tried to maintain a good economic and political rapport. Indeed, Venice was perhaps the European city whose inhabitants best understood and appreciated Islamic culture. As the nineteenth-century art historian John Ruskin wrote, 'the Venetians deserve a special note as the only European people who appear to have sympathized to the full with the great instinct of the Eastern races.'

However, it is important to remember that Venice's relationship with the East was not always rosy, and the city often found itself in ferocious and brutal battles with the Turks in order to protect its own economic survival. After conquering most of what had remained of Venetian territories, the Turks went on to conquer Syria and Egypt in 1517, Rhodes in 1522 and Algeria in 1529, at which point the Ottoman Empire encircled much of the Mediterranean Sea. Many diplomatic and military crises occurred between Venice and the Ottomans during this period of aggressive Ottoman expansion. To try and put a stop to the endless march of Turkish expansion through the Mediterranean, the Venetians joined forces with the Spanish and other members of a Holy League to prevent the Ottomans from advancing into Western Europe. In what is often described as one of the most decisive battles in the history of the West, the Holy League, half of whose galleys came from Venice, defeated the Turkish fleet off the coast of Western Greece in the Battle of Lepanto on 7 October 1571. This was one of the first battles where guns and cannons gave the Christians a decisive advantage, allowing them to prevent the Ottomans from expanding further to the West. (Some claim had the West lost, it might now speak Turkish.)

Perhaps the most horrific example of hatred and violence between Venetian Christians and Ottoman Turks concerns Marcantonio Bragadin. Bragadin was the local patrician governor on the island of Cyprus, which the Venetian republic had seized in 1489. Ottomans frequently raided the island during the period when Venetians ruled it, and Venetian control collapsed when the Ottomans attacked the island with more than 60,000 troops in 1571. In Famagusta, one of the main towns on the island, where Bragadin was resident, Venetian defenders were left without a grain of wheat or a drop of water by the time they finally gave in to the Turks, in August 1571, after a year's siege. Though a peaceful pact of surrender had been made, the Turks immediately betrayed it and brutally massacred Venetian soldiers, ripping their bodies to pieces and feeding them to famished dogs. Turkish troops mounted the heads of 350 of their victims in front of the tent of the Turkish general, Lala Mustafa. Bragadin was singled out for even more spectacular treatment. While accounts vary, they describe how the Turks cut off his nose and ears and dug out his eyes, dragged him around the city and then skinned him alive. According to some reports he did not die until they reached his waist. They stuffed his skin with straw, tied it to the back of a cow, sent it on a mock procession through the streets of Famagusta and then tied this stuffed body to the mast of a ship for all to see as they paraded it around the Mediterranean. Afterwards, Bragadin's skin was taken back to Constantinople and offered to Sultan Selim II, though Venetians later managed to get it back and, according to legend, it is now in an urn in the church of *San Giovanni e Paolo*. Today, both a street on the Lido and a *vaporetto* bear his name.

Bragadin was not the only one brutally punished by the Turks. The diplomat Giovanni Soranzo was dragged through the streets of Istanbul in chains and publicly ridiculed, and his interpreter was murdered in a moment of political tension between the Venetians and Turks in 1648. The Turks imprisoned and tortured the ambassador Giovanni Cappello, who died of starvation in the Castle of Adrianople in 1652. These, and many other tales of violence and brutality, remind us that the relationship between Venice and the Ottomans was dicey and characterized by harmony and hatred during the hundreds of years when these two powers shared the Mediterranean. As throughout their history, the Venetians were great pragmatists who focused on filling their coffers which they did primarily though amicable exchange, though at times they were forced to defend with the cannon and the sword. Unlike many other European powers, Venetians were unique since they could comfortably be both a friend and an enemy at the same time, especially if by maintaining such a contradictory and complex relationship they still managed to generate a profit.

Venice and The Renaissance

Initially, as we have seen, Venetians were not nearly as fascinated by ancient Greek and Roman art and literature as were their Florentine counterparts. One of the characteristics of the Renaissance in Venice was that classicism came to the Venetian lagoon comparatively late. When the Florentine sculptor Ghiberti first unveiled his classicizing relief of *The Sacrifice of Isaac* for the doors of the Florentine baptistery in 1401, or when Brunelleschi first began to employ the techniques of ancient Roman engineering to construct the dome of the Florentine cathedral in the 1420s, the work of Venetian artists continued to remain heavily indebted to medieval and Byzantine artistic traditions, emphasizing rich surface ornament and gilded mosaics rather than the classical harmony and proportion of the Roman world. This is not surprising since Venice had never been a Roman city, had no distinct Roman history or Roman roots, and typically sought to distinguish itself culturally and politically from Rome. In the early modern period Venetian culture was invigorated and enlivened more by its vibrant cultural exchange with the East than by classical antiquity.

Nevertheless, Venetians did become interested in the art and ideas of the Renaissance. They began to admire the ancient Romans and emulate their models of order and proportion in their architecture and painting. Art historians typically point to the southern gateway of the arsenal, constructed in 1460 and attributed to the local architect Antonio Gambello, as the first example of Renaissance architecture in the lagoon. With its Roman arch, this doorway clearly expresses the triumphal significance of the Venetian shipyards by using ancient Roman forms. By the sixteenth century Venetian art and architecture in particular became even more dominated by classicism with columns, pilasters, coffered ceilings and Roman arches arranged in the orders and proportions suggested by classical design. We can see the full-blown arrival of the classical tradition in Venice perhaps most clearly in the *Piazza San Marco.* During the course of the early modern period, the *piazza* came to look much the way it does today. The Ducal Palace was completed in the fifteenth and sixteenth centuries. Doge Andrea Gritti (r. 1523–38) enacted numerous architectural and civic reforms to clean up the city, and make it respectable in the wake of the disaster of Agnadello. In the early sixteenth century the *Piazza San Marco* had been cluttered with money-changing booths, food stalls, hostels and latrines. Gritti hired the renowned Renaissance architect Jacopo Sansovino to remove the sordid and dilapidated wooden stalls that had infested the *Piazza San Marco* and replace them with new ones to present a more civilized, classical face to the outside world. In the 1530s Sansovino designed the *Loggetta,* the base of the bell tower in *San Marco,* as well as the nearby Mint and Marciana Library, all in a classical style. With the work of Sansovino and other Renaissance archi-tects, Venice as 'a new Rome' emerged out of the dark years following the League of Cambrai, and similar civic and archi-tectural reforms continued throughout the sixteenth century. (Gritti similarly attempted to introduce Roman law to Venice during his rule.)

The architect Andrea Palladio, arguably the most copied architect in the history of architecture, also turned the façades of Christian churches around the city into classical temples, and following the demands imposed by the Counter-Reformation and the Council of Trent, produced churches such as *San Giorgio Maggiore* that represented a 'purified' Catholicism, 'cleansed' of medieval clutter and superstition. Unlike the medieval church of *San Marco*, the pure white walls and exteriors of his Renaissance churches were 'cleaned up' and devoid of sculptural ornamentation or decorative elabo-ration. Giovanni Bellini and Titian in particular brought a clas-sical, Renaissance style to Venetian painting.

Historians and art historians regularly refer to the period from 1400–1600 as the time when Venice 'turned West'. Venetians built up a mainland empire and discovered the clas-sical traditions of the Western Roman world. Venetian elites also increasingly sought to connect their family lineages to those of ancient Roman families who lived on the mainland before the conquest of the lagoon, and the *terraferma* to the west of Venice saw a veritable building boom as patricians built villas on their mainland estates in dramatic numbers. This increase in development resulted in the construction of more than 250 mainland villas by the end of the sixteenth century. These villas allowed Venetian nobles to display their fabulous wealth for all to see and embrace classical architecture.

Nevertheless, Venice's 'turn to the West' was never complete or comprehensive. The city and its artists and artisans always maintained a particularly Venetian artistic vision, even after the arrival of Renaissance classicism. While hosts of art historians over the ages have described the story of Venetian art and the contributions of the city's artists, it is worth making six points here about the unique nature of Venetian art and visual culture.

First, Venetian architecture has a long history of imported pastiche or collage. Buildings and their façades regularly included inserted pieces of sculpture, tracery, carved window trim and borrowed or stolen elements, many of which defy classification. This tradition began with the *altinelle* first brought to the lagoon from Altino when immigrants fled marauding barbarians on the mainland. Such fragments are often fixed seemingly randomly on to buildings with no attempt to integrate them in any coherent way. These bits and fragments are visible around the city, around doors and windows or simply plastered into façades. The church of *San Marco* is one of the best examples of this tradition. (Sculpture in Venice was primarily a surface ornament, and there was never any formative school of Renaissance sculpture in Venice.) This tradition of what might be called 'stick and go' is significant because it runs contrary to the classical tradition. If Roman and classical visual culture was proportional, orderly, graceful and often symmetrical – just think of the Pantheon – Venetian visual culture was much more idiosyncratic, irregular and asymmetrical. The *Piazza San Marco* is not a square but a trapezoid, bridges often cross canals at sharp angles and architects often placed palace doors and windows to one side of a façade rather in the centre.

Second, Venetian painters came to appreciate classicism but they also consistently emphasized surface patterns as much as modelled forms, creating the illusion of three dimensions. For example, Venetian painters were familiar with the mosaics of *San Marco* and their brilliant optical effects, and often included such details in their works. Giovanni Bellini, for instance, incorporated a detailed painted mosaic in his 1505 *San Zaccaria* altarpiece, with a strong nod to Byzantine art. The lozenge pattern on the façade of the Ducal Palace is another good example as it appears to emulate the surface detail of Eastern and Islamic models.

Third, Venetian paintings often emphasized narratives and the details that underlay them. The art historian Patricia Brown has shown how painters, such as Vittore Carpaccio (for example, in *The Miracle of the True Cross* series in the Accademia Galleries), recorded the bustling daily life of the city and delighted in *minutiae* like Venetian chimneys, dogs, the presence of Africans and everyday Venetians talking on the street. While many Italian Renaissance painters in Florence, for instance, began to produce canvases that emphasized the majesty, emotions and graceful gestures of a handful of figures in scenes of classical serenity and simplicity, Venetian painters, in contrast, often employed what Brown calls an 'eyewitness' style. This packs in as many of the details in a scene as possible, generating panoramic, busy images, and emphasizing the cosmopolitan dynamism of the city.

Fourth, Venetian art was significantly employed in the service of political power, not so much in dynastic portraits of important individuals as in allegorical depictions used to exalt the Venetian state. For example, paintings by Palma il Giovane (*Allegory of the War of the League of Cambrai*, 1582) and Veronese, many of which are in the Ducal Palace, depict important events in Venetian history and the foundation myths of the republic and, in so doing, glorify the mythical republic as a whole and the citizens who serve the state.

Fifth, compared to its mainland counterparts, Venice is for the most part far from any greenery. The city is surrounded primarily by brick and stone and, especially on foggy winter days, the city's walls, air and water form a decidedly grey world. For this reason it is somewhat surprising that Venetian painting in the Renaissance emphasized landscape, light and colour, although this tradition may have been inspired by the very elements that Venice lacked. In any case, Venetian painters were landscape painters of pastoral scenes: one of the more prominent strains in Renaissance painting in the city. And while there is much debate about this, art historians – beginning with the first art historian, Giorgio Vasari – have long argued that

Venetian painters, such as Giorgione and Titian, emphasized light and colour where their Florentine counterparts emphasized design and hard contours.

And sixth, while frescoes were the medium of choice for the star painters of Florence and Rome, Venetian artists quickly learned that frescoes soon fell apart in the humid climate of the lagoon. For this reason, Venetian painters pioneered and established the practice of painting in oil on canvas.

Considering even this brief synopsis of Venetian art and architecture, it is easy to see that there are many sites around the city that reveal the spirit of the age. As with the fourteenth century, though, there exists no one place that singularly or sufficiently embodies the myriad changes that took place in early modern Venice. The *Ca' D'Oro* on the Grand Canal, built between 1420–34, reveals the complexity of Venetian visual culture. One of the most ornate and beautiful palaces in Venice, it is at once asymmetrical, gothic, classical, Islamic (especially in its attention to surface decoration), substantial and light, with delicate tracery covering the façade. Later in the sixteenth century, the Rialto Bridge, finally completed in stone in 1591, and Jacopo Sansovino's classical buildings around the *Piazza San Marco* give a sense of the Renaissance tradition in the city. So does a walk along the islands of the Giudecca and San Giorgio where a series of classical façades by the Renaissance architect Palladio neatly stand in a line along the water.

What was once the site of Aldus Manutius' printing house, now a bank, is marked by a plaque on the northern end of *Campo Manin*. Some pharmacies around the city still show the signs of the early modern medical emporia that they once were: behind the counter and under the modern cardboard advertisements promoting self-tanning lotions and body-firming creams often stand the dusty majolica jars that once held cures for syphilis, gout and the curses of witches. And in the *sottoporteghi* or underpasses that lead into the square of the Ghetto, we can still see the remains of the iron hinges on which the doors once hung to enclose the Jews: a haunting reminder that the early modern age was one of both expansive discovery and violent persecution.

Finally, a trip around the mainland of the Veneto reveals the winged lion of St Mark, often placed on top of a tall column as Venetians systematically branded the central *piazza* of each town that came under Venetian control with this symbol of their dominance. In the countryside between these towns, Venetians built their majestic but now eerily quiet and darkened villas. Often closed and frequently gated, their long and stately driveways lead up to the imposing mansions that once held the extravagant summer parties of patricians and their guests seeking relief from the summer heat of the lagoon. In the sixteenth century nobles' bank accounts still over-flowed, allowing them to build these extravagant villas and throw lavish parties that spilled out on to the surrounding porches and gardens. Such a world of wealth, security, laughter and luxury however was slowly slipping away as insidious forces began to chip away at Venetian fortunes around the turn of the seventeenth century.

6

CASANOVA, CARNIVAL AND COFFEE: VENICE IN THE BAROQUE AGE, 1600–1797

By 1600 the Venetian republic had prospered for almost 800 years, no small feat in a world where disease, warfare and expanding states like the Hapsburg and Ottoman Empires were a constant threat. The Venetian economy had survived the Portuguese discovery of the overseas spice route, and Venetians had rebuilt most of their mainland empire even after the League of Cambrai beat the Venetians back to the shores of the lagoon in 1509. In the sixteenth century, in fact, Venetian fortunes even grew as a result of thriving new industries. Around 1600, however, things began to change. There was no one decisive event or single blow but, after 1600, the economic and political centre of Europe began to shift from the Mediterranean to the North, to England, France and the Netherlands as the power and momentum of these states grew. The Venetian economy began to shrink while those states involved in the dynamic market of the Atlantic grew. In addition, Venetians were very resistant to new political ideas and political change. For the most part, they turned their backs on the powerful new ideas emanating from Enlightenment France, preferring to maintain their age-old government and *modus operandi*. In the realm of both economics and politics, Venice became antiquated and marginalized.

However, despite the fact that Venice slowly began to slip from the economic and political forefront of Europe, from 1600–1797 the city became a cultural mecca, the centre of fashionable Europe where everyone flocked to spend money and enjoy themselves. Venice was a world of scarlet silk mantles and masks bordered with pearls, powdered wigs and penciled-on moles, casinos and theatres, and coffee and conversation, all of which took place under a government of old men that lay only half awake as it was carried along by the currents of history that Venetians would soon be powerless to oppose. It is not an accident that the Venetian who was most representative of this period was not a doge, a sea captain, nor even a great merchant, but a devious and wily playboy – Casanova – who spent his days gambling and running from the law. But why did the Venetian economy decline? How and why were Venetians resistant to new political ideas? And how did the city remain the cultural centre of Europe?

Economic Downturn

The Venetian economy in the sixteenth century remained relatively healthy in large part because of its great diversity and complexity. Portuguese and Habsburg (or Spanish and German) expansion created some difficulties for Venetian traders but it was not devastatingly detrimental. The Portuguese had discovered how to go around the Cape of Good Hope to get spices directly from Calcutta and Goa, but Venetian spice routes between India and Alexandria continued, partly because this Mediterranean route was still shorter and safer than the voyage around Africa. While the Ottomans had taken over most of the trading outposts once overseen by the Venetians, the Venetians were resilient. Ottoman Constantinople was still a huge market for Venetian goods, and a large population of Venetians and Venetian traders remained in Constantinople to the end of the sixteenth century.

According to some historians, there were more round ships (cargo-carrying vessels) in Venice in 1560 then there had ever been before, and the overall tonnage carried by the Venetian fleet may have even reached its peak around this time. The Venetian population probably also peaked around 1575 at 180,000, the highest it would be until the 1950s. Furthermore Venice was still a great emporium and a manufacturing centre of silk, glass, mirrors and books. Even if international trade slightly declined in the sixteenth century, markets on the Italian mainland near the city grew and Venice became the port of its own mainland. At the end of the sixteenth century the patrician Nicolò Contarini even boasted that 'Venice is perhaps greater than it ever was before'.

Nevertheless, the economy was clearly changing. The loss of Cyprus to the Turks in 1571 was crushing to the Venetians. The bout of plague that followed from 1575–77 was also devastating and profoundly disrupted much of Venetian economic and cultural life. In addition, timber had slowly become harder to obtain in Venice. It was more abundant in Northern Europe where ships were consequently cheaper to build and had better rigging than the Venetian kind, making them faster and able to carry heavier arms. The cheaper cost of ship construction combined with a revolution in shipbuilding in Holland meant that while Venice remained a flourishing port, foreign ship-builders outpaced the Venetians after 1600. It was no accident that Peter the Great went to Holland to study shipbuilding in 1697 rather than Venice.

The late sixteenth and early seventeenth century also saw a dramatic rise in piracy, and the Adriatic became more infested with Uskok and Barbary or African pirates than it had been since the tenth century. Piracy became so bad that Venetians began to dock their ships in Albanian ports and take their merchandise overland in caravans to the Ottoman East in order to bypass the seas altogether. In addition, while the Venetian and then later Dalmatian, Cretan and Greek oarsmen who rowed Venetian ships had traditionally been free sailors who were paid a wage, during the course of the sixteenth century, it became so difficult to hire them that the Venetian fleet had to rely on forced conscription, on criminals who were chained to their benches. In fact by 1580 Venice's fleet of galleys that patrolled the Adriatic was populated almost entirely by convicts. Also, merchants were increasingly unwilling to incur the expenses and run the risks of maritime trade. Venetian nobles, once the main participants in the making of the Venetian commercial empire, preferred to stay safely ensconced in their mainland villas where they instead made their money through farming, rents and holding office.

The real demise of the Venetian economy began, however, when English and Dutch ships began to swarm the Mediterranean in growing numbers. The English and the Dutch asked the Venetians if they could dock and ship goods north from the lagoon. The Venetians denied this request and maintained their age-old requirement that foreigners could only buy and sell goods through Venetians, thereby destroying the possibility of potentially reinvigorating their port with new traffic. Not surprisingly, Northern traders took their business elsewhere and rival ports, such as Trieste, Ancona and Livorno, got their business. When these cheaper, faster and more heavily armed Northern ships started using other ports that the Venetian economic downturn began. In addition, when the Dutch East India Company formed in 1602 it effectively cut off the flow of spices to all other traders, including the Venetians. These two factors resulted in a 40 per cent decline in Venetian trade around 1600. By the 1630s Mediterranean trade was almost exclusively in the hands of the English and the Dutch, and Venetians eventually had to send merchants to London and Amsterdam when they wanted cinnamon, cloves and pepper.

Venetian merchants and traders suddenly found themselves pushed to the periphery of Mediterranean and European trade.

Increasingly Hemmed In by the Papacy, Ottomans and Hapsburgs

Around 1600 events on the Venetian mainland brought the city into conflict with the papacy. In 1604 the republic announced that no religious buildings or structures could be built on the mainland without the permission of the Venetian state. In 1605 the government also forbade Venetian subjects from donating any land to the church. Both measures were meant to prevent the growth of Roman power and income on the Venetian mainland. When government officials arrested two clerics (one of them, the canon Scipione Saraceno, had smeared the house of a noblewoman with excrement because she had rejected his sexual advances) on the mainland in March 1605 and brought them before the Council of Ten, Pope Paul V (r. 1605–21) objected, arguing that such arrests violated papal jurisdiction. The church in Venice had long been subservient to the state: the cathedral of Venice was far removed from the city centre, St Mark was given to the city's doge and not its bishop, and Venetians insisted that when the Inquisition came to Venice they be allowed to maintain three Venetian judges on its court. Paul V decided that enough was enough and that the Venetians needed to learn who was boss in the realm of spirituality. He excommunicated the city and its empire in 1606. This effectively meant that sacraments could no longer be administered to the inhabitants of Venice and the Veneto, which was no small punishment for all those deprived of baptism for their children or last rites for dying family members.

The papal interdict generated heated controversy in Venice since it demanded that people state where their loyalties lay. The doge at the time, Leonardo Donà (r. 1606–12), ordered the Venetian clergy to ignore the interdict and to continue administering the sacraments or face death. The Jesuits – the order of the church charged with purifying and empowering Catholicism in the wake of the Protestant Reformation – refused to comply, and the Senate banished them with several other orders that would not observe the state's ruling. The Jesuits left the city in a dramatic procession, wearing crosses as if they were removing spirituality from the city itself. Crowds of Venetians flanked them on the streets as they departed, yelling 'go to hell!' in one great chorus. The Venetians hired the polemical cleric and writer Paolo Sarpi to advise the government in canon law and defend their position. Sarpi published a series of pamphlets that attracted worldwide attention, especially from Protestants, by arguing that the state could indeed forbid people from donating lands to religious houses since states had a right to organize their own resources for their own good. The controversy was ultimately resolved in 1607. While the Venetians kept their property laws on the mainland they effectively agreed not to enforce them in order to receive papal absolution. The Venetians emerged from the interdict neither defeated nor victorious. They had thwarted this challenge from the pope, though Paolo Sarpi's life was threatened several times by papal plots and attacks.

Soon after this threat from Rome, Venetians faced additional diplomatic challenges from other European states. The economic changes facing the city around 1600 were mainly caused by the size of the states that surrounded Venice. Venice was simply less able to compete militarily and economically with states that were becoming so big and so powerful that they dwarfed the island city. By 1600 not only had the Ottomans conquered most of the eastern Mediterranean but the Spanish Hapsburgs had also taken over most of the Italian peninsula. The Austrian Hapsburgs lay just to the north and were also seeking to expand their territory. Seventeenth-century Europe is marked by the growth of large states with their enormous armies and their extravagant displays of wealth and power. Most early modern people came to live under the umbrella of one empire or another: the Spanish or Austrian Hapsburgs, the Ottomans or the Bourbon dynasty in France. This was the age of Louis XIV, the Sun King, and his elaborate and wealthy court at Versailles. It became increasingly difficult for Venice to compete in this international context. Over the course of the seventeenth and eighteenth centuries these massive states crowded around the tiny lagoon city, directly challenging Venetian independence and its neutrality.

Venetians faced many political, diplomatic and military threats as these surrounding empires confronted and bullied them. From 1613–17 the Venetians entered into the War of Gradisca against Uzkok pirates. Venetians attacked Uzkok ships in the Adriatic after pirates captured the Venetian captain Cristoforo Venier and flayed him alive. But since the Uzkoks worked for the Austrian Hapsburgs as defenders of the borders of their empire, fighting the Uzkoks brought the Venetians into direct conflict with the Hapsburgs to the north. After several years of fighting, the Austrians forced the Uzkoks to resettle further into the interior of the Habsburg Empire, temporarily resolving the conflict between Venice and the Austrian Hapsburgs.

The Spanish branch of the Hapsburg family, however, represented an even greater political threat to Venice. The Spanish ruled most of Italy by 1600 and tried to overthrow the Venetian state when the Spanish Viceroy of Naples, the Duke of Ossuna, sent a fleet to the Adriatic to break Venetian control of that region. In the War of Ossuna (1617–18). Venetians used hired help to drive this fleet out, but the Duke of Ossuna went on to hatch an incredible plot to overthrow the Venetian government from within. Working through the Spanish ambassador to Venice, the Marquis of Bedmar, the Spanish mounted a plot to seize the Ducal Palace and flood the city with Spanish forces. The Council of Ten discovered these plans and about 300 people were executed for their involvement. This plot was confused and ill-organized but it had involved large numbers who were prepared to overthrow the Venetian state.

Then, in 1622, several years after the expulsion of the Marquis of Bedmar, the prominent nobleman Antonio Forscarini was arrested for treason. Foscarini came from an old

patrician family and had been the republic's loyal ambassador
to England and France. He was tried for selling state secrets to
foreign powers and for spying on behalf of Spain, and was
strangled to death in prison and hung by one leg between the
two columns of *San Marco* in 1622. However, the Council of
Ten later discovered that Forscarini had been framed and was
innocent. His body was disinterred and he was reburied with
state honours, but the incident painfully revealed both the
arrogance of some of the city's most powerful families who
were able to frame him in this way, and the ways in which
larger diplomatic and imperial forces had managed once again
to infiltrate Venetian politics since he had been accused of
selling secrets to the Spanish.

The advances and threats posed by the Ottoman Empire
were even more dramatic than those from Europe. Though the
Venetians had controlled the island of Crete for 450 years, the
island fell to Ottoman forces after the War of Candia. After
years of diplomatic tensions, the Ottomans attacked Crete in
1645 and placed the island under siege by 1648. The siege
continued, unbelievably, for almost 22 long years – arguably the
longest siege in history – reducing the island's inhabitants to
skeletons cloaked in rags. The Venetian commander Francesco
Morosini finally capitulated in 1669 but, to this day, the
memory of this expensive, drawn-out and disastrous war lives
on. In contemporary dialect to say '*sémo in Candia*' or '*séco
incandio*' means 'you are as thin as a Candiote', or someone
who has not eaten in years.

The Venetians took their last stand against the Ottomans in
the 1680s. By then Francesco Morosini, the commander at
Candia, miraculously led Venetian forces to make quite a
comeback by retaking most of Morea or the Peloponnese
Peninsula of Southern Greece from 1685–88. Then, in 1687,
Morosini and his forces stormed Athens. In a moment not
unlike the sack of Constantinople in 1204, a Venetian cannon
hit and almost destroyed the Parthenon and Morosini co-
ordinated the looting of the temple. He pillaged the sculptures

of two lions and brought them back to Venice as symbols of his victory, sculptures that stand to this day at the gate of the arsenal. He was made doge in 1688, and the Treaty of Karlowitz in 1699 temporarily ended fighting between the Venetians and the Turks. The Morea, however, was eventually lost. Venetian rule in Greece at this time was incredibly unpopular and the Ottomans regained this territory once and for all by 1714. The Congress of Passarowitz, a meeting between the Austrians, Turks and Venetians in 1718, reduced Venetian territories abroad to virtually nothing but a handful of territories in Istria, Dalmatia and the Ionian Sea. Venice had permanently lost its maritime empire. The last significant Venetian admiral, Angelo Emo, launched several successful military excursions against Barbary pirates and corsairs from Northern Africa in the second half of the eighteenth century and he encouraged the arsenal to produce more modern ships of war but, by the end of the eighteenth century, there were fewer interested patricians and there was less money for pursuing war with any seriousness.

One might well wonder, if the economy was suffering and Venetians were broke, how exactly did they pay for their wars, and especially these long drawn out and extremely gruelling battles against the Turks in the second half of the seventeenth century? Venetians obtained money using perhaps the one trick they had left: they sold titles of nobility to anyone willing to pay. A total of 67 families were ennobled in 1646 to support the War of Candia and 47 more in 1685 to support Morosini's campaigns in Greece. These families each paid 100,000 ducats – a sum close to 10 million dollars in modern currency – to have their names added to the Golden Book of Venetian noble families. Additional families were allowed to become nobles as late as 1770, again as a result of urgent financial need. Many of these families were not only from outside Venice and the Veneto but also from outside Italy, and though wealthy many actually came from humble and lowly origins. The picturesque *Campiello Widmann*, for instance, in the northern part of the city, refers to the Widmann family from North Europe that purchased its Venetian nobility. Lodovico Manin, the last doge of Venice, also came from a family in Friuli to the north of Venice that bought its way into the noble class at this time. Venice's larger role in the Mediterranean was over, but this last infusion of cash that came from those who wanted to become Venetian nobles helped finance Morosini's spectacular campaigns. Thanks to him, for one final moment in their history at the end of the seventeenth century, the Venetians once again briefly held an empire in the eastern Mediterranean, permitting a last chance to experience a glimmer of the city's past greatness.

The Extravagant Baroque

Even as the city entered an economic downturn and found itself increasingly squeezed between aggressive and expansionist neighbours, Venice in the seventeenth and eighteenth centuries was the playground of Europe and one of the great cultural centres of the world. The eighteenth century was the era of the Grand Tour when English families in particular espoused the idea that foreign travel improved a gentleman's education and imparted political expertise, enabling their sons to become effective members of ruling class. Men like Edward Gibbon and Francis Drake toured Italy in their twenties, and visitors from around Europe flocked to see Venice and enjoy its earthly delights. Historians typically describe Venice in this period as decadent and frivolous: a city of gamblers, opera-goers and fan-fluttering ladies who pursued their various pleasures and frittered away their time and money while the city and its economy were slowly but surely collapsing. While the culture of extravagance was also common to many other European cities, Venice's unique location on water drew extra attention to its endless parties, lavish entertainment and reckless spending.

Venice also had a lively theatre scene. Its first commercial theatre opened in 1565 and, by the end of the seventeenth century, there were close to 20 theatres in the city. The *commedia dell'arte* was incredibly popular: a type of theatre based on largely unscripted works that included pantomime, improvisation and slapstick humour. In the eighteenth century the plays of Carlo Goldoni and Carlo Gozzi often depicted and ridiculed middle-class life in Venice and were wildly popular. In addition the seventeenth and eighteenth centuries saw the rise of opera in the city. Opera was originally performed for private aristocratic audiences but, in 1637, Venice opened the first public opera house in Europe, the *Teatro San Cassiano*, and became the centre of opera in the West after Claudio Monteverdi was appointed choirmaster of *San Marco*. The city opened as many as seven opera houses in the seventeenth century, putting on close to 400 different operas from 1637–1700. Historians sometimes attribute this development to the fact that the severe and puritanical Jesuits had been expelled from the city at precisely this time allowing for a more liberal cultural atmosphere in the lagoon.

The city's reputation as a centre of opera and baroque music was further enhanced in the eighteenth century by the Venetian Antonio Vivaldi who composed 44 popular operas in his lifetime. In May 1792, as the riots and massacres of the French Revolution took place in Paris and events in the North unfolded that would have implications far beyond what any Venetian could imagine, the city opened the *Teatro la Fenice*, or 'Phoenix' opera house. One of the most sumptuous and fashionable opera houses in the world even today, it was financed by selling subscriptions to wealthy patricians who purchased boxes and then passed them down through their families. Eventually, the opera house sold all the box to the city, which came to own *Teatro la Fenice* after the First World War. But as the Tuilleries were being stormed and the guillotines crashed, Venetians turned a blind eye, happy to wave their lace handkerchiefs and gossip behind raised fans while they took in the works of Monteverdi, Scarlatti and Vivaldi.

Gambling was also an incredibly popular pastime in the city and drew thousands of foreigners to the lagoon every year. Like opera performances, gambling houses in the city initially tended to be in private halls owned by Venetian nobles, and the word *casinò* (pronounced cah-zeen-OH) originally meant a small house where Italians met for exclusive social occasions. These informal pavilions were often set in secluded gardens that were ideal for gambling. We can still see a surviving example of such architecture in the *Casinò degli Spiriti* that juts out into the lagoon on the remote northern edge of the city. While most popular casino games were eventually invented in France, Venice officially opened the first public gambling house in 1638, the *Ridotto*, to better control gambling in the city and earn a profit while doing so. The *Ridotto* was located near *San Moisè*, just west of *San Marco*, and offered different rooms housing various games as well as food and drink. Gamblers played *biribisso* (much like modern roulette), *faro* (a kind of bacarrat) and *spigolo* (an earlier version of poker). Even outside the *Ridotto* gambling rooms existed everywhere around the city, in cafés, theatres and even barber shops. The entire city gambled, and many Venetians participated in the civic lottery in the eighteenth century, purchasing tickets at booths all over town. The government eventually closed the *Ridotto* in 1774 by order of the Council of Ten who saw it as a den of vice where impoverished nobles dug themselves deeper into debt, gambling away whatever crumbs of their patrimony or plots of land in the countryside they may have had left. Nevertheless, private casinos still numbered nearly 150 at the fall of the republic, and the remnants of their existence can still be found around town where the word *ridotto* appears in the names of various streets and palaces.

This was also the great age of the café. Perhaps the first documentary evidence we have of coffee in the West came to Venice in a letter from the *bailo*, or ambassador, resident in Constantinople in 1585: a discovery tied to Venice's long-standing relationship to and fascination with the East. Giovanni Francesco Morosini reported that 'The Turks, and among them both humble and important men, are in the almost continuous habit of sitting and drinking publicly, in shops and on the street, a black liquid, boiling as hot as you can take it, that is extracted from a seed called *cavée*, which they say has the virtue of keeping you awake.' Hot chocolate had been very popular in the seventeenth century – indeed the pope claimed to prefer it after he tasted coffee – but coffee soon became a craze. At the beginning of the seventeenth century Venetians began importing beans from Egypt for medicinal purposes and, in 1683, the first coffee house opened under the arcades of the *Procuratie Nuove* on the south side of the *Piazza San Marco*. Archival documents show that eventually there were over 30 cafés around the *piazza* alone, and over 206 in the city when the government decided that no more could be opened in an attempt to reign in the frenzy that had swept the city. Both Gozzi and Goldoni often mentioned the coffee craze in their plays, and one of Goldoni's most popular plays was called *La Bottega del Caffé*, or 'The Coffee House'.

The most famous café was, and still is, Caffé Florian, opened by Florian Francesconi on 29 December 1720. It was first called *Venezia Trionfante*, or 'Venice Triumphant', a somewhat ironic and unlikely name since at the time Venetians had little to feel triumphant about, having just lost their Greek empire with the Treaty of Passarowitz. Perhaps for this reason it was soon re-named after its beloved owner and quickly became the social centre of the city. Venetians and foreigners flocked to Florian, especially after the closing of the *Ridotto* in 1774, to drink their coffee from fine porcelain cups, show themselves off, gossip, discuss literature and hear the latest news. From the beginning Florian had an illustrious clientele of nobles, foreigners, merchants and artists. Frequented by the likes of Rousseau, Casanova, and the sculptor Canova in the eighteenth century, in the nineteenth century it attracted the most important European writers and artists of the day as well as nationalist revolutionaries and Austrian resistors. Indeed, Florian had played such a central role in the life of the city and so many events have unfolded both inside in its rooms and right in front of its windows that if its walls could speak, they could easily recount the history of the city.

In the eighteenth century, Venetians paid more attention to fashion, especially foreign fashion, than perhaps ever before, abandoning any former pretence of restraint in favour of the sensuous and playful designs from the North. Noblemen traditionally wore black in public as a sign of their modesty and submission to the Venetian state but, under their plain togas, they often wore the elaborate styles that hailed from France and which are now displayed in the museum at the *Palazzo Mocenigo* near *San Stae*. Men wore knee breaches, tight-fitting silk stockings, coats with tails, shoes with buckles, tunics with lace wrists and tricorn hats in black felt. Their finery came to rival that of women whose lavish fashions included bodices supporting, and revealing, ample *décolletés*, sleeves that finished in a cascade of lace, elaborate coiffures, gloves and fans. Wigs for men were also a must, so much so that when the nobleman Lorenzo Corner died in 1757, newspapers pointed out that he had been the last patrician to wear his own hair. The irony cannot be lost on us that while the Venetians followed and consumed French fashion with enthusiasm and rapt attention, the same cannot be said of their attentions to French ideas about political life. While their servants ironed their breeches and fluffed their lace, Venetian nobles disdainfully brushed off ideas about equality and liberty, even though forces motivated by these ideas were soon to sweep the entire continent of Europe and alter life in Venice forever.

Fashionable life at this time also included two new jobs or social positions, the *còdega* and the *cicisbeo*. Despite the fact that Venetians did their best to prevent night-time violence – in 1732 Venice became the first European city to provide street lighting – both Venetians and especially the numerous visitors to the city regularly hired a *còdega*. This was a lantern-bearing guide, a bit like a bodyguard, hired to take people safely from one destination to another through the dark labyrinth of the dangerous city at night. A *cicisbeo* was very different, being a gentleman (though not a lady's husband) who accompanied a noblewoman and was quite often her lover as well. He gave her his hand in public at balls and receptions, and attended her from when she awoke until when she retired. He ordered her meals, sat constantly by her side and even fed her if she so desired, making the *cicisbeo* the ultimate accessory in eighteenth-century fashion.

The most famous figure from the world of fashion and entertainment in eighteenth-century Venice is Giacomo Casanova (1725–98). Famous for his life of intrigue, gambling and seduction, he was the son of actors and an accomplished musician who became popular in the elite circles and high society of the city. He was suddenly imprisoned at the age of 30 for no clear reasons: the accusation was simply 'public outrages against religion'. Some suspect he possessed prohibited books but perhaps the authorities simply wanted him off the streets. He was taken to the prison called the *piombi*, or the 'leads' (so called because its roof was made of lead plates), above the Ducal Palace. Fifteen months later he made a daring escape through a hole in his cell and out on to the roof, eventually descending down though the building. He was mistaken for a civil servant and left the city by gondola, making his way to Paris, and eventually became the director of a library in Bohemia. He began writing his memoirs in the last decade of his life, producing 12 lengthy volumes that are among the best accounts of European life in the eighteenth century. His *Story of my Life* offers an endless stream of wild tales about courtesans, adultery, Carnival, gambling, balls, complicated plots involving gallant heroes and despicable villains, and life on the run from the police. While many European cities at the time maintained a decadent culture of excess and vice, Casanova's life and memoirs significantly helped fuel an image of Venice as the most decadent and lascivious city in Europe in the eighteenth century.

Festival and Ritual

Like most other medieval cities, Venice had a colourful array of civic rituals and celebrations. In addition to regular Christian holidays and saints' days, Venetians also had their own festive calendar rooted in the history of the city. Historians have long been fascinated by the cultural and political significance of Venetian festivals, such as the *Sensa*, the coronation of the doge and the various rituals surrounding the cult of St Mark. Venetian rituals served a wide variety of cultural and political purposes: they celebrated the powers of the doge and the noble class, reaffirmed the legendary free and independent nature of Venice and tied the history of Venice to the Christian calendar. They also made the lower classes feel as if they were politically important. The arsenal workers, for instance, had significant roles in both the coronation and funeral of the doge. By including a wide array of people and encouraging the lower classes to feel politically significant, Venetian rituals may have reinforced state stability and discouraged popular revolts. Of the many civic rituals on the Venetian calendar, two in particular stand out in the seventeenth and eighteenth centuries as being especially colourful and popular: the War of the Fists and the Carnival.

Venetians have long had deep feelings of attachment to their neighbourhoods. Especially in centuries past when only one bridge, the Rialto, spanned the Grand Canal, it was harder to move around town and the residents of one neighbourhood did not often visit other areas of the city. Even today it is common to hear older Venetians comment that they rarely leave their *sestiere* or local neighbourhood. Such feelings of local identity and pride manifested themselves in the *Guerre dei Pugni*, or 'War of the Fists': mock battles staged on various bridges without parapets throughout the city. These battles took place between the factions of the *Castellani* or *Arsenalotti* – mainly arsenal workers from Castello, San Marco and Dorsoduro – and the *Nicolotti* or fishermen who lived on the opposite side of the city in San Polo, Canareggio and Santa Croce. The goal was for a fighter, or group of fighters, from one faction to throw their opponents off the bridge, thereby earning honour, glory and fame. The battles were so popular that at times more than 30,000 people observed them, including patricians waving their handkerchiefs in the air in support of their chosen contender. We can still see remnants of this ritual around the city. The *Ponte Guerra* near *San Marco* and the *Ponte dei Pugni* just south of *Campo Santa Margherita* were some of the bridges on which these battles took place, bridges on the boundaries between the two factions. The bridges are marked with decorative 'footsteps' in memory of their significance. In addition, the church of *San Trovaso* in Dorsoduro is said to have several sets of doors and two façades because it stood in territory between the two rival factions of the *Nicolotti* and *Castellani* and needed to accommodate both of them, especially since their rivalry persisted through the nineteenth century. When there was a *Nicolotti-Castellani* marriage, the *Castellani* family members could enter through the south door and the *Nicolotti* by the side door. The War of the Fists was officially put to an end in 1705 as the state attempted to replace this violent ritual with more decorous ones such as a series of *regatte* or boat races, or the *Forze d'Ercole*, which means 'The Strength of Hercules': a competition to build human walls and pyramids with teams of people showing off their martial and acrobatic prowess.

The Venetian Carnival barely needs an introduction. Famous around the world for its masked balls, costume parades, concerts, public performances and night-time festivities, Carnival has long attracted foreigners to Venice. Records of Carnival exist as far back as 1094 when medieval chroniclers began to take note of public celebrations that took place in the days just before Lent. In 1296 the Senate made Carnival official by decreeing that the last day before Lent would be a public holiday. While today Carnival lasts for about ten days – a period notable not only for people wearing masks and costumes in the streets but for the fact that every Venetian *pasticceria* sells delicious Carnival pastries called *fritelle* – in the eighteenth century it lasted over six months. The festivities began on the first Sunday in October, became increasingly intense after the Epiphany in early January and culminated with the most brilliant festivities just before Lent. In the main *campi* of the city, along the *Riva degli Schiavoni*, the main quay facing the water by *San Marco* and in the *piazza* performers erected stages and people crowded around to watch jugglers, acrobats, actors and actresses, dancing animals and a great variety of other street artists play to the crowds. Venetians even chased pigs around the *Piazza San Marco*, captured and decapitated them, and then threw their ears to the crowd. Bull chases were also set up around the city. The main courtyard of the German Warehouse was open for public balls for three days and nights towards the end of the season. The final week was marked by the 'flight of the dove' when a courageous acrobat slid across a wire from the top of the bell tower of *San Marco* to the Ducal Palace, throwing flowers to the crowd, a ritual reenacted today with a wooden or plastic bird.

In the eighteenth century as many as 30,000 people came to Venice every year during the six-month Carnival season. The holiday was celebrated with particular verve and enthusiasm, and has prompted historians and anthropologists to question why this holiday was so popular, and what social and political purposes the ritual may have served. Carnival had no single meaning, but it was clearly a time when the world turned upside down: people dressed up in disguise and could ritually reverse the roles they played in day-to-day life. The rulers became the ruled, men dressed as women, and participants could express their social creativity and political critiques with no fear of repercussion, especially since people wore masks in public. Students could mock a rebellion when their professors lectured and fishermen could parody their patrician overlords by dressing in disguise like their noble rulers. Many nobles in the eighteenth century were particularly relieved when carnival season arrived since masks could disguise their poverty. It is said that such festivities promoted social harmony since they were a kind of social safety valve, a type of ritual inversion of the normal social hierarchy that allowed people to let off steam. The enormous number of gaudy mask shops that line the city's streets today trivialize and commercialize what was once a living and vibrant social ritual. Carnival offered a type of annual, cyclical commentary on the established social order and perhaps briefly allowed people to address their social grievances.

Carnival ended in 1797 with the arrival of Napoleon. French and later Austrian occupiers viewed its festivities with suspicion: a hunch that was perhaps correct if the safety valve theory is correct. It was only at the end of the 1970s that some people and civic associations in the city began to revive Carnival. Many Venetians say that it experienced a brief period of local splendour in the early 1980s before it was hijacked by international tourism once more, and by major international corporations who subsidized festivities and the concerts of famous performers in exchange for advertising sites in the city. (Volkswagon, for instance, had often placed large advertising posters and cars in various public squares around the city.) Carnival today remains a mixed bag; the city becomes extremely crowded, especially during its final days, and is often filled with drunken partiers and tremendous amounts of litter but, if you are lucky, you can still find local performers – palm readers, puppeteers, magicians and aspiring actors – performing on small, home-made sets in the quieter corners of town, offering a small reminder of what Carnival once was.

The Challenges of Change

Eighteenth-century Venice was an age of extreme wealth and extreme poverty. When King Gustav III of Sweden visited the city, the Pisani family put on such a great celebration for him at their villa on the mainland at Stra that they ruined themselves forever financially. The Labia family, Spanish aristocrats who bought themselves into the Venetian nobility in 1646, compensated for their status as new arrivals with elaborate displays of wealth. According to lore, during a dinner party held in their *palazzo* in the eighteenth century, they amused their guests by casually tossing every one of their heavy gold plates out the window and into the canal below (though some sources maintain they had cast nets to catch them). They cried out to their guests and to those who could hear them on the streets, '*L'abia o non l'abia, saro sempre Labia*', making a play on words to mean 'whether I have [money] or not, I will always be a Labia'.

While some were able to behave with such reckless abandon, the eighteenth century saw the formation of a new, impoverished social group in the city called the *barnabotti*. These nobles had become so destitute that they lived on small allowances from the Senate and often in decrepit housing maintained by the state. Nobles were increasingly impoverished since commerce had dried up. Even though some local industries still survived, nobles were forbidden to learn a craft or practice a trade. Many *barnabotti* lived in the neighbourhood of *San Barnaba*, from where they got their name and where there existed a well-known local casino where they played, still denoted in the passageway (the *Casìn dei Nobili*) through to the *campo*. There may have still been patrician families with ten gondolas tied up at their gate and more than 50 servants in their household, but there were also throngs of nobles with vastly diminished family fortunes, a whole class so financially ruined that they could no longer even afford the expenses of seeking or holding office. *Barnabotti* would rub shoulders with other nobles in the halls of the Great Council and then return to the shabby rooms of their tiny apartments. When Casanova went to visit the senator Zaccari Vallaresso in 1743, instead of finding an apartment suffused in patrician luxury, he found a room containing four worm-eaten chairs and a battered table. We can imagine scores of noblewomen in this period draped in jewels who passed endless, silent hours doing embroidery in the dingy corners of what had once been majestic palaces.

During this time radical and revolutionary ideas about politics and power began to filter down from the salons of the North. The Enlightenment was a political and philosophical movement born in Paris that encouraged Europeans to challenge traditional ideas about power and authority. The ideas that thinkers like Voltaire, Rousseau and Kant developed were diverse and complex, but these philosophers shared one common theme: they were revolted by the seemingly limitless political abuses practiced by the European governing class. Tyrannical kings, who were often also fanatical Catholics, regularly imprisoned and tortured their subjects for no clear reason and with no evidence of wrongdoing. English philosophers, such as like Thomas Hobbes and John Locke, argued that rulers could not be allowed to do as they pleased because the governed masses had inalienable rights – to life, liberty and property – that needed to be protected by contracts and constitutions. If governments or rulers attempted to rule absolutely or arbitrarily, they violated the natural rights of the individual and thereby forfeited the loyalty of their subjects. The language of documents like the American Declaration of Independence and the French Declaration of the Rights of Man and Citizen reflect these ideas. Such theories of natural law were used to justify liberal revolutions in France and America at the end of the eighteenth century. The Enlightenment encouraged Europeans to use reason to question traditional forms of authority – the clergy, nobility and royalty – and not to believe what they were told or to accept history at face value. These liberal ideas continued to inspire revolutions across Europe through the nineteenth century.

This vanguard intellectual and political movement in Paris, that encouraged the protection of the rights of man and the questioning of those in authority, might have rapidly spread to the rest of Europe and the Americas, but many Venetians either were not that interested or were hostile to such ideas. This radical new way of thinking and viewing the world directly challenged how Venetians had historically structured their state and their culture. In Venice every man owed his position to what his father had been before him, and the right to govern was given by God to nobles and remained theirs because of their patrician bloodlines. When confronted with revolutionary ideologies from the North, Venetians of all classes almost categorically rejected any ideas that challenged their medieval political system. In the eighteenth century most Venetians appeared to ignore the clashes, quarrels and debates raging among their European neighbours concerning political rights and representation. Only a small number of Venetians were interested in the ideas of the Enlightenment. Freemasons, for instance, were tolerated in the city in the second half of the eighteenth century. Masonic lodges were male organizations or clubs that often served as networks for political discussion and change. They became popular in Enlightenment France, and two Masonic lodges were founded in Venice, the Union and the True Light. They welcomed those who wished to discuss ways of infusing the state with new political life and vigour, and these ideas in fact did become popular among poor nobles.

Prior to the arrival of Enlightenment ideas, in 1627–28, the reform-minded patrician Ranieri Zeno had proposed that the government of Venice be opened to a broader base of people and that the dictatorial powers of the Council of Ten be curtailed, but the wealthy and conservative patricians around him were never open to such ideas. Similarly, in 1780, the senators Giorgio Pisani and Carlo Contarini, both impoverished nobles, made bold proposals before the Great Council to reform the government, restore the ancient power of the senate and curb what had become the inflated powers of several noble families and the Council of Ten. However, they received no real support and were thrown into prison. There was one final attempt in 1779–80 on the part of several patricians to shift the base of state power out of the hands of a few small, rich families to the advantage of the larger number of poor nobles, but many opposed ideas about the redistribution of power. Doge Paolo Renier (r. 1779–89), the second to last doge, called such proposals a form of agitation for conspiracy. Enlightenment ideas gained some ground in the lagoon as a fashion, much like the wigs and corsets that also came from France, but such ideas never took root with any seriousness and remained more of a curiosity than a real point of agitation from which to reform

Venetian culture and society. No real steps were taken to change way the state distributed power or the way the government functioned. Although the doge and the Venetian government were never as despotic as other eighteenth-century powers, such as Frederick the Great of Prussia or Catherine the Great in Russia, some resentment began to fester in the city among poor nobles and commoners who saw that there was no movement towards a broader political base. By the mid-eighteenth century especially, it became harder and harder to ignore ideas about liberalism and democracy, and what Venetians had once referred to as the great stability of their government appeared more like political rigidity and inflexibility.

In some ways, the Venetian political system was already dying. While in the fifteenth and sixteenth centuries there were at times around 2500 men in the Venetian Great Council, by 1797 it had fallen to around 1000. Disease and declining numbers of the patrician class because of the continued practice of just one marriage per family meant that, by the mid-eighteenth century, there were seldom more than 600 present to vote in the Great Council at any one time, and sometimes only half that number. Among these remaining patrician families, only a handful of the most powerful and wealthy actually ran the government at this time. The most prestigious government posts in Venice had become the most expensive so that, by the eighteenth century, only the wealthiest patricians could afford to hold high office. According to another count, there were about 450 patrician families in the eighteenth century, half of which were rich or very rich while the other half were often quite poor or just getting by. To make matters worse, the nobles were increasingly uninterested in fulfilling their civic duties. Many preferred to pay a fine for non-participation rather than undertake their governing responsibilities. In fact many nobles preferred to wear fashionable Parisian clothing and not their patrician floor-length robes to better blend in with the crowd. As Jan Morris has pointed out, the population of the city declined from 170,000 in the sixteenth century to 96,000 in 1797 (although others say the decline was less dramatic, dropping only to 138,000 or so), though the Hairdressers' Guild still had 852 members, an indication of where civic interest really lay.

Historians have long described Venice in this period as a frivolous city clearly in a period of decline, decay and decadence. It suffered, they say, from 'a great and incurable disease'. They cite Francesco Guardi's eighteenth-century paintings that show what it was like to see and be seen as a public partygoer rather than a senator or commander or the eighteenth-century Venetian painter Pietro Longhi who depicted Venetians placidly passing their empty days in luxurious patrician palaces instead of attending to business. The clouds gathering in the paintings of Giambattista Tiepolo, forecast the city's doom and announced the melancholy autumn that lay ahead.

While such claims are a bit melodramatic and clearly benefit from hindsight, many who lived in Venice at that time also saw the writing on the wall. Andrea Tron, for instance, a prominent and powerful politician in the second half of the eighteenth century, noted that trade had collapsed. Venetians, he claimed, had been,

> supplanted by foreigners who penetrate right into the bowels of our city. We are despoiled of our substance, and not a shadow of our ancient merchants is to be found among our citizens or our subjects. Capital is lacking, not in the nation, but in commerce. It is used to support effeminacy, excessive extravagance, idle spectacles, pretentious amusements and vice, instead of supporting and increasing industry, which is the mother of good morals, virtue, and of essential national trade.

In addition, many who visited Venice in the eighteenth century saw the city as decaying and doomed. Amelot de la Houssaie, the secretary to the French ambassador, noted the futility of Venetian neutrality and the way in which its cumbersome government took so long to make decisions. Other Enlightenment figures, including Voltaire and Cesare Beccaria, had similar observations.

The French philosopher Montesquieu lamented that Venice had 'no more strength, commerce, riches or law; only debauchery there has … liberty.' In 1794 Giambattista Susan, a priest from Chioggia, prophetically declared himself hopeful for the future when men 'would be liberated from the repression of sovereigns and would enjoy liberty and equality' as in France, where land and riches were shared, unlike Venice, 'where our lords have in income of fifty thousand ducats and many others have not even a piece of change.' A sonnet about Venice written in the eighteenth century by Angelo Maria Labia aptly proclaims:

> What luxury in people of all classes
> What cradle-like theatres
> What symmetry in the Piazza
> What regattas …
> What a Canal, what ferries
> Oh, God, what women!
> And yet, I don't know why, I could cry.

By 1700 Venetians had survived largely by doing the same things they had always done and by following age-old patterns that had always served the state well. In terms of changing political ideas and ideologies, Venetians seemed to encounter nothing outside their city that seemed worth emulating. They continued to support the rule of a closed caste of patricians. In addition, much like the Venetian reluctance to get involved in disputes between the pope and the emperor or to get involved in the crusading movement in the Middle Ages, Venetian international policy continued to attempt neutrality. Venice was a small state, and war was always bad for trade. The republic remained neutral during the Thirty Years War (1618–48) and managed to avoid the disputes of even close neighbours in these battles. Similarly, during the War of Spanish Succession (1701–14), when both the Bourbon and Hapsburg powers vied for the Spanish throne as the French aimed to unite the kingdoms of France and Spain under one monarch, war spread around Europe and involved almost every other European power, extending even into North America. The Venetians, however, managed to remain neutral once again, sparing themselves the ravages of war. But while Venice survived it was not building new ideas or a new political or economic infrastructure to move the city into the future. Venetians simply continued to do what they had always done. Such a view of the world was becoming outdated in the face of the sweeping changes unfolding in the rest of Europe, and this refusal to engage with the outside world and change would facilitate the republic's downfall. In an age of dramatic change – of democratic and industrial revolutions – Venice could no longer survive on the principles of neutrality and patrician control. All this, however, is not to say that a traditional political mentality *directly* caused the collapse of the Venetian republic. The cause of this can only be attributed to one thing: the relentless march of the charismatic and ruthless general who came from the North and swept across Europe, altering the fate of Venice forever.

Various monuments and shards of history around the city indicate the events and trends of the seventeenth and eighteenth centuries: a plaque outside the church of *San Stae* decrees the innocence of Antonio Foscarini; the wedding-cake façade of the seventeenth-century church of *San Moisè* exemplifies the dramatic grandeur of the baroque age in architecture, while the church of the *Maddalena* just off the *Strada Nuova* displays strange Masonic symbols on its eighteenth-century façade. The grandiose church of the *Salute* on the spit of Dorsoduro proclaims Venetians' gratitude for surviving the plague in 1630–31, just as the 'Bridge of Sighs', designed by Antonio Contino at the beginning of the seventeenth century and perhaps the most visited sight in all of Venice, supposedly allows you to hear the final gasps of prisoners as they were either thrown into their dungeons or taken to their deaths.

The monument that best captures the culture of Venice at this time, however, is the *Ca' Rezzonico* on the Grand Canal. This museum offers a reconstruction of life in a noble *palazzo* in eighteenth-century Venice. While the furnishings and decorations were brought here from many homes around the city, after conservationists gathered what was left after the destruction wrought by the French and Austrians, the composite effect offers a clear window on to the glittering world of Europe before the French Revolution. Its ballroom has two elaborate chandeliers, a *trompe-l'oeil* ceiling and porphyry statues of Ethiopian warriors with vitreous eyes. Wandering into the rooms beyond, we see Flemish tapestries, porcelain tea sets, carved and gilded furniture, wooden desks inlaid with ivory designs and marble tables. Tiepolo ceilings depict winged *putti* ascending into a seemingly infinite blue sky. A yellow lacquered door, original to the palace, shows a man with an umbrella riding a camel and a Chinese man sitting cross-legged, smoking an opium pipe, under palm and bamboo trees, a final testament to Venice's long-standing fascination with the East. Room after room contains images of the empty and superficial practices of the elite: pastel portraits of noblewomen with their bouquets, pale faces, and vague smiles besides men with powdered wigs; women preparing in their dressing rooms, or being served hot chocolate in their beds, curled up with their dogs as their correspondence is read to them. Here are laid bare the airy fantasies and delicate refinement of the leisured classes, living out what were to be their last days in their world behind the walls that shielded them from the increasing desperation of the common people and the forces of revolution outside. We can almost smell a whiff of tobacco coming from the study [or that of the unemptied chamber pot in the bedroom]. Though the house is now silent, we can practically hear the rustle of damask, the ping of the harpsichord, the clink of glasses as a servant clears a tray and the lessons of the French teacher. The palace offers an almost eerie snapshot of a fragile world in the moments before its collapse, just before its treasures were torn from their owners' hands and carted off by the forces of war, revolution and occupation that had at last arrived in the lagoon.

7

THE LAGOON IN THE MODERN AGE:
1797–1900

For better and for worse, Venetians had managed to keep their city, its economy and government much the same for a remarkable thousand years. In the nineteenth century, however, the city was forced through a series of wrenching changes when it had to confront modernity in all its forms. In 1797, seemingly overnight, the age-old republic collapsed with the arrival of Napoleon and the city quickly became a mere cipher of what it had been before. Venetians first fell under French and then Austrian rule, suffered a degree of poverty and economic desolation like never before, attempted a revolution to throw off their Austrian overlords and eventually joined the Kingdom of Italy in 1866 all while the Industrial Revolution was unfolding in the city. How can we – and how did Venetians – make sense of this dizzying sequence of changes that happened, especially by Venetian standards, in such a short period of time?

The French Occupations

Approximately one month before the start of the French Revolution in Paris, Venetians elected what turned out to be their last doge, Lodovico Manin (r. 1789–97). A native of Friuli, Manin was the first non-Venetian to hold this office in over 1,100 years. In fact Manin had never held any state office before but this gave him the advantage of having no real enemies in government and, in addition, he was spectacularly wealthy, which greatly appealed to Venetians during this period of economic difficulties at the end of the eighteenth century. At his coronation ceremony he threw more than 450,000 worth of lira in coins to the crowd, most of it from his own personal wealth.

Soon after, Venetians wilfully ignored the warnings of political change and military aggression that arrived from beyond the Alps, even as Napoleon and his troops arrived on the Italian peninsula in 1796. The regions of Piedmont and Lombardy almost immediately surrendered. Following tradition, Venetians claimed neutrality but several events soon made Venetian isolation impossible and gave Napoleon an excuse to move towards the city. On 9 April 1797 French soldiers were killed in an uprising in the city of Verona on the Venetian mainland, and then on 20 April Captain Laugier of the French ship ironically named the *Libérateur d'Italie* was killed when it attempted to enter the lagoon. Napoleon immediately exploited these events and supposedly exclaimed in his ancestral Italian that he would become 'an Attila to the Venetian state'. By 1797 Venetians were not capable of raising or leading an army to stop Napoleon, and he could no longer be appeased by negotiation. By 29 April French troops landed on the shores of the lagoon and, by 9 May, Napoleon issued an ultimatum: the republic must surrender to his forces completely, let his troops occupy the city and dissolve their government to form a provisional democratic council. On 12 May 1797, to the sound of French guns on the mainland, Venetian patricians cast balls into voting urns for the last time and voted to dissolve their age-old government. Once their votes were cast and the outcome decided, nobles threw off their traditional robes and fled the halls of state as quickly as possible, anxious to protect their families, property and especially their mainland estates. Legend claims that Manin walked calmly to his private wing of the Ducal Palace, removed his robes and *corno*, or ducal hat, with dignity and resolution, and gave them to his valet saying, 'take this, for I shall not be needing it again'.

Venice had only been seriously threatened with collapse twice before in its entire history: in 1310 with the Querini-Tiepolo consipiracy and in 1355 by the ambitions of Doge Marin Falier. In both instances, threats to the Venetian state were quashed in a matter of hours. The events of 1797, however, proved very different. Though boatmen and porters issued cries of protest calling out '*Viva San Marco*' in the streets, on 15 May 1797, for the first time in the history of the city, foreign troops led by the French general Louis Baraguey d'Hilliers entered the lagoon. While the figures cited vary, from 3,000 to 5,000 French soldiers boarded 40 longboats supplied by the Venetians and arrived in the city to parade victoriously in the *Piazza San Marco*.

French forces soon occupied the lagoon's islands, forts, arsenal and halls of government, abolishing the hereditary aristocracy of the Venetians in favour of a new governing municipality composed of 60 members. Though Venetians were appointed to this new government, none were consulted during its formation and no elections were held. The new government applied Napoleon's penal and civil code to the city, the French army garrisoned troops around the lagoon and the city of Venice was required to pay an indemnity to the French. At this point, however, Napoleon viewed Venice largely as a bargaining chip for other European territories that he wanted to get his hands on and, on 17 October 1797, he signed the Treaty of Campoformido giving Venice to the Austrian Hapsburgs in exchange for the Austrian Netherlands, freeing him for war against England. (The Museum of Naval History in Venice holds the silver inkstand that Napoleon used to sign this document.) The French left Venice in January 1898 and, for eight years, Venice was relegated to being a relatively inconsequential province of the Hapsburg Empire until the French later defeated the Austrians at the Battle of Austerlitz in 1805. On 26 December 1805, the Treaty of Pressburg once again placed all Venetian territories under Napoleon; the French returned to the city on 19 January 1806 and Venice became part of Napoleon's Kingdom of Italy. On 3 February Napoleon's 25-year-old stepson Eugène de Beauharnais entered the city where he was to become viceroy and make his home.

After the arrival of the French, Lodovico Manin supposedly never went near the *Piazza San Marco* or the Ducal Palace again by day and lived out the rest of his life shuttered in his palace, the *Palazzo Pesaro*, on the Grand Canal, going out only rarely for walks, accompanied only by a servant, to the more remote parts of the city. According to one story, during one of these walks on the *Fondamente Nuova* on the northern edge of town, an impoverished young patrician girl and her mother confronted him, protesting about their loss and hitting him with their hats and coats, shouting every curse known to man as he slowly trailed away. He died on 24 October 1802 – after leaving a generous 100,000 ducats to the state to be used for the care of orphans – and is buried in the church of the *Scalzi* next to the train station.

Whatever remorse Venetians felt about these dramatic changes in their city, Napoleon held some appeal and fascination since the French potentially brought with them the chance to experiment for the first time with democracy and democratic institutions. Many appeared excited about the arrival of the revolutionary ideas proclaiming political liberty and equality. Even before the French had arrived in the Veneto, mainland aristocrats – long excluded from Venetian political life – had echoed the slogans of the French Revolution and hung up liberty banners in their town squares. According to some stories, in the last days of Carnival in 1797, some *barnabotti* or impoverished nobles in their masks and costumes had approached French officials and revealed their hatred of the republic. They described their political oppression, inability to maintain their families and longing for the French to come and liberate them from the tyranny of the Venetian regime. On 4 June 1797 the first large-scale, public French celebration occurred a few weeks after the occupation of the city. Many Venetians sang and danced in the *Piazza San Marco*, including a number of prominent patrician women supposedly in scant clothing, where they erected a 'liberty tree' to embrace the French ideals of liberty and equality. They solemnly burned a printed copy of the *Libro d'Oro*, the book that historically recorded the names of patrician families (someone had thought to hide the original codices), and scribbled graffiti in praise of Napoleon on the columns in the *Piazzetta*. Crowds gathered in the church of *San Cipriano* on Murano to dig up the ashes of Doge Pietro Gradenigo, the mind behind the famous closing of the Great Council in 1297, and dispersed them into the wind. There were six months between April and October 1797 when some Venetians, committed to the idea of a new democracy, waited with baited breath and excitement to see how the ideals of the French Revolution would play out in the lagoon.

As in France, many changes took place in Venice to generate the new political order. Nobles gave up their titles and were instead called citizens. Many buildings and monuments in the city were renamed with more appropriate revolutionary titles. For instance, *Campo San Polo* became *Piazza della Rivoluzione* and the *procuratie* or archways around the *Piazza San Marco*, became the *Gallerie Nazionali,* or the *Galleria dell'Uguaglianza* ('Galleries of Equality') on the north side and the *Galleria della Libertà* ('Galleries of Liberty') on the south side. Caffè Florian was renamed *Caffè della Fratellanza Patriottica* or 'Caffe of the Patriotic Brotherhood', and the Fenice Teatro was modestly renamed the *Teatro Civico*. While the emblem of St Mark's lion continued to appear on civic communications, the traditional text in the book – *'Pax tibi Marce evangelista meus'* – held by the lion's paw, was replaced with the slogan 'Rights and duties of man and citizen', to which a cheeky gondolier supposedly exclaimed 'At last he's turned the page!'

The Emperor Napoleon eventually came to the city himself on an official visit in November 1807. He was greeted by a spectacular series of ceremonies, including the construction of a triumphal arch built across the mouth of the Grand Canal near the church of *Santa Lucia* where he arrived, the illumination of the *Rialto* and the *Piazza San Marco* with thousands of torches, and a lavish series of concerts, balls, banquets and boat races. For nine days he oversaw various inspections and held meetings aimed at creating order and efficiency in the city. Napoleon's favourite local architect, Giannantonio Selva (the designer of the Fenice), was commissioned to various modernizing projects, some of which were sorely needed. For example he designed a new civic cemetery on the island of San Michele so that the dead did not have to be buried in the city any longer. Napoleon also visited the workers in the arsenal, emphasizing how important their work was in preparing to give the English 'the lesson they deserved'. Always sensitive about his humble Corsican background, he was shown papers in the Marciana library that suggested his family actually descended from the ancient Roman family of the Bona Pars, with its long and notable history in Italy before settling on Corsica. Napoleon was clearly pleased.

However, the negative aspects of the French occupation clearly outweighed any benefits. Try as Venetians might to accommodate and impress the emperor, Napoleon was no fan of Venice since he thought the city embodied the evils of the aristocratic Old Regime. He punished Venice by making Milan the capital of the Kingdom of Italy, relegating Venice, once the 'capital' of the Mediterranean, to a regional port. Venetians were mortified at being subordinate to Milan, a city that for almost three centuries was only a provincial capital. French conscription was also devastating and virtually crippled the people of Venice and the Veneto when many of the region's young men were sent on disastrous campaigns in Spain and Russia. Furthermore, Napoleon's continental blockade, intended to isolate and punish England by depriving it of trade with Europea, devastated the Venetian economy as it deprived the city of commerce. In addition, in a city where so many had earned their livelihoods by working for the state government, the dramatic reduction in public offices under the Napoleonic regime left many Venetians without a state income, increasing poverty in the middle and upper classes. The lagoon essentially became the military zone of an occupying power. Napoleon and his troops demonstrated great contempt for Venice and sought to point out its failings at every turn, though this was not always effective. For instance, when the French arrived and flung open the cells of the state prison – much like with the opening of the *Bastille* in Paris – they could merely proclaim that they had found only four people to liberate from Venetian tyranny, and then they were just petty criminals and not political prisoners. One of them, in any case, was apparently so happy to be released from prison after 22 years that he gorged himself on wine and sweets and died four days later!

Most dreadful, however, was the degree to which the French vandalized and pillaged the city. Napoleon ordered all the public statues and sculptures depicting the Lion of St Mark, both in the city and on the mainland, to be removed since they were symbols of a despotic regime. They were added to his imperial wealth. He also shipped the four bronze horses above the doorway of the basilica of *San Marco* to Paris on 7 December 1797, placing them first before the Palace of the Tuileries and then on the *Arc de Triomphe*. He put the lion on top of the column in the *piazzetta* on the *Place des Invalides*. Newspaper cartoons around Europe depicted the lion of St Mark caught in a net or crushed beneath the feet of a crowing Gallic cock as Napoleon's troops systematically pillaged every corner of the city, including the mint, fleet and archives. They hired women to pick precious stones out of their ancient settings that they melted down. They took the diamonds from the Treasury of *San Marco* to be set in the Empress Josephine's crown. In particular, in the weeks just before handing Venice over to the Austrians in January 1798, the French desperately tried to remove anything and everything from the city that might benefit their Austrian enemies. Before departing the city, they destroyed the arsenal, bashing to the ground its plaster walls and marble staircases and, on 9 January 1798, they demolished the *Bucintoro* – the doge's ceremonial barge used in his marriage to the sea – smashing it to smithereens with axes on the island of San Giorgio Maggiore and setting what was left on fire. In early 1798 the French left Venice in a state of virtual anarchy and in great economic distress, consigning the city to the Austrians like a carcass.

They continued their pillage when they returned to the city from 1806–10. In a perhaps ironic reversal of much of Venetian history, the French methodically removed every last item of beauty or value from the city, literally down to the nails on which the city's paintings hung. They ordered the closure of scores of churches, monasteries, convents and all the Venetian *scuole* or confraternities, which Napoleon feared as sites of political insurrection. He converted these buildings into prisons, hostels and barracks or demolished them entirely. While figures vary dramatically, approximately 80–90 churches and around 100 palaces were razed during the French occupation. They carted off the valuable furnishings and artworks from both private homes and religious and charitable institutions to enrich French coffers and museums. Gold, silver, crosses, candlesticks, goblets and crowns were melted down and disappeared forever. Marbles, altars, paintings, relics, parquet floors, mosaics, frescoed ceilings, stuccoed walls, antique reliefs and inscriptions, furniture, porcelains, textiles, carpets glass, and entire libraries were dismantled, destroyed or sequestered by the crown. Through later auctions and resales these objects were eventually dispersed around the world. For example, some of the doors and ceilings in the *Villa Vizcaya* in Miami originally came from various Venetian villas and palaces.

Paintings probably represented perhaps the greatest of the city's treasures lost to French greed. Napoleon's agents, especially Peter Edwards – a scholar, painter, art critic and ex-inspector of public painting under the old Venetian republic – oversaw the collection and packaging of works of art to be sold off at auction or transported to Paris or Milan. Edwards compiled extensive inventories of the works collected. In the first month he and his assistants catalogued over 12,000 paintings, and eventually carted off over 25,000. The paintings of Titian, Bellini, Veronese and Tintoretto among others were systematically removed from the city. A sizable chunk of these treasures were sent to enrich Milan, the new capital of the Kingdom of Italy, which needed a gallery – the Brera – to match its new position. While the French left some artworks in place and eventually returned some to the lagoon after Napoleon's demise, the Louvre still proudly displays Paolo Veronese's *Marriage at Cana*, stolen from the refectory of *San Giorgio Maggiore*. According to one estimate, perhaps extreme but nevertheless indicative, only four per cent of the artworks that existed in the city before 1797 are still in the city today. When Venetians were asked if the French had stolen from Venice, the prompt response was '*bona-parte*' or 'a good amount'.

The only physical damage inflicted on the city before the arrival of Napoleon had been caused by fires. From 1797–1815, however, the city was virtually destroyed. By 1815, the city was devastated: impoverished, desolate and empty with blank walls, holes gouged into the sides and façades of palaces, and vacant rooms throughout the city's buildings that echoed with the cold emptiness of bare shelves, walls and floors. Within a generation after the arrival of the French, one-third of Venetian noble families were extinct and, according to one legend, the remaining families drew up a pact agreeing that none of their offspring would marry so that their pedigree would die out and prevent further humiliation. In all these ways, the city was altered more rapidly and dramatically during the French domination than at any other point in its history.

The Austrian Occupations

Venice was handed back and forth several times between the French and the Austrians from 1797–1814. The first Austrian occupation occurred after the signing of the Treaty of Campoformido in 1797 when Napoleon gave the city to the Hapsburgs. The Austrians arrived in the city on 18 January 1798 under the leadership of the Austrian general Olviero von Wallis. Everyone gathered in the *piazza* or along the Grand Canal, as they had for Napoleon, to witness the arrival of the Austrians, who were similarly greeted with fireworks, dancing and an array of civic celebrations. The city's walls were papered with announcements headed with the symbol of the Hapsburg double-headed eagle. Some Venetians hoped for better treatment. In particular, nobles who had fled in fear at the arrival of the 'democratic' French now returned to their palaces in the city. The head of every family was required to swear an oath of allegiance to the Austrian emperor before an official notary, and 907 patricians did so in the Hall of the Great Council on 23 January 1798, putting to rest any ideas about a democratic or popular government. The Hapsburgs were in the city for eight years before the French retook it in January 1806. It was not until Napoleon's defeat in Russia and his exile on the island of Elba that the Austrians occupied the city again when they really made their mark, fully developing Austrian institutions and policies here. They arrived in the lagoon for the second time on 19 April 1814 after a winter siege that lasted almost five months, when many Venetians died of starvation.

In the wake of the French Revolution and the Napoleonic Empire, The Congress of Vienna in 1815 and its conservative leadership attempted to set back the clock and erase European memories of democracy, equality and revolution. The Congress of Vienna gave Venice and most of Northern Italy to the

Austrian Hapsburgs. In yet another turn of history, public images of Napoleon were taken down around the city and Venetians once again swore allegiance to the Austrian Emperor, Francis II. In yet another dizzying change, Prince Reuss-Plaun, the Austrian governor of the Venetian territory, entered the city accompanied by celebrations, on 15 May 1814.

When the Austrians returned to Venice after over a decade of French rule, they found the city a shadow of its former self. Austrian authorities counted one-third of the city's inhabitants as impoverished and one-quarter as making their living from begging. Many were starving and in rags after the blockade, and many Venetian industries, such as the glass and textile industries, had virtually ceased to function. According to the historian Margaret Plant, the period from 1814–18 represented the nadir of the history of the city. Its population was reduced to around 100,000 as a result of malnutrition, migration to the mainland and a variety of epidemics including pellagra, a disease caused by vitamin deficiency, from which many went insane and had to be placed in an asylum on the island of San Servolo in the lagoon. When the Archduke Ranieri of Austria was nominated viceroy of the Lombardo-Veneto region in 1818, he sent a report to the Austrian emperor describing Venice as a city in ruins, with crumbling palaces and crowds of unemployed workers and beggars. Grass had invaded the streets and public squares of the city, and commercial life and civic services had become virtually non-existent.

The Austrians took several steps to try and alleviate matters. The Austrian navy revived the devastated Venetian arsenal, and Venice regained some dignity as both Milan and Venice became seats of the Hapsburg Viceroy. As the city once again became a regional capital, it regained its position as a centre of administrative offices, courts and the military. The Austrians built numerous roads to facilitate trade and connect rural and especially alpine populations to larger cities, and they made all of Venice, beyond just the island of San Giorgio, a free port in February 1830. This meant that ships could come and go free of taxes in an attempt to revive the port of Venice and re-integrate the city into the European economy.

Nobles permanently lost any vestiges of their antique privileges and were forced to work like everyone else. While some visitors dramatically claimed that they had seen ex-nobles working as porters or garbage men, in reality the vast majority developed professional practices and became doctors or lawyers. Nuns and monks were allowed to return to their cloisters, and monasteries and confraternities were allowed to re-open, all of which naturally generated some sympathy for the Austrians. As a significant symbolic gesture, in May 1815, as soon as the Austrians returned to the city, the four bronze horses were returned to sit above the central doorway of the basilica of *San Marco*. In 1816 they also brought back the winged lion to sit once again on top of the column that faces the bay in the *piazzetta*. It had been smashed into 84 pieces during its removal to Paris but was repaired and restored under imperial patronage. The Austrians experimented with gas lighting around the *Piazza San Marco* in 1843 and in the city at large in 1863, and built the railway bridge from 1841–46 connecting Venice to the mainland. It was also at the beginning of the second Austrian occupation that the convent of *San Nicolò delle Lattuga* and the *Scuola* of *Sant'Antonio* (both adjacent to the church of the *Frari*) were established as the site of the State Archives to contain all the documents of the fallen republic. With its 280 rooms, 50 miles (80 km) of shelves and, by some estimates, 700 million documents, the Venetian archive is the third largest in Europe, after the Vatican and Vienna.

Many aspects of Austrian rule however remained punishing for the Venetians. Even though the Austrians promoted Venice as a tax-free port, any positive effects were cancelled out by the fact that the Austrians continued to favour Trieste in the northern Adriatic as the main port of the Austro-Hungarian Empire. In addition, the Austrian penal code was harsh and did not allow public debate or criticism of the regime or the right of defense to those accused of crimes. Furthermore, though

Italian troops were not regularly made to fight for the Austrians they were subject to routine conscription – the most hated legacy of French rule that persisted under the Austrians – and often eight years of gruelling military service, frequently in the far away lands of the sprawling Hapsburg monarchy. Austrian military service involved such savage discipline, low pay and harsh and unpleasant conditions that many tried to avoid it by self-mutilation (forced hernias), smashing out their teeth and chopping off a finger. (The central command of the Austrian military was the *Palazzo Loredan* in *Campo Santo Stefano*. Looking closely at the main doorway to this palace, you can still see faded German over the entrance of what is now the *Istituto Veneto*.) The Austrians also brutally taxed the Venetians who had no political authority or voice to protest about the way they were being governed. All orders and decisions came directly from Vienna; Venice was completely subject to a distant imperial administration.

The Austrians enforced the support and subordination of the Venetians in large part through extremely harsh censorship laws. Venetian printers were ordered to submit all printed material, even single-page advertisements, to be vetted by the authorities. The Austrian police were in charge of the newspapers, the possession of foreign papers was prohibited and incoming vessels were searched for foreign literature as the Austrians maintained a constant vigilance for anything that might question their sovereignty. Since travel abroad was also carefully regulated and discouraged, Venetians had very little contact with liberal ideas from abroad. Austrian control of religion and public education also made sure that no one challenged their authority. For all these reasons, it remains harder to characterize the Austrian than the French occupation of the city. The Austrians were not not quite as ruthlessly exploitative as the French, and they tried in some ways to revive the Venetian economy. Although their rule was marked by relative peace with little political unrest and even some prosperity, this was still a repressive regime of policing, censorship and social immobility, as the Austrians treated the Italians like a subject population. Historians no longer tend to vilify the Austrians as great oppressors of the Venetians or the Italians, but they nevertheless recognize the great limitations the Austrians placed on Venetian growth and national self-realization.

The most lasting legacy of the Austrians, however, might be found in the city's official cocktail, the spritz or, in Venetian, the *spriss*. The spritz, made of white wine, soda water and the likes of Aperol or Campari is the drink of the city, consumed by Venetians every day. It is said to have many origins but most stories tie it in one way or another to the Austrian presence in the city. According to some, the drink originated in Austria with the Austrian Spritzer, since the Austrians liked to mix white wine and soda water, which they brought to Venice. Others claim that the drink originated when the Venetians began to water down the Austrians' wine, or that the drink was officially created in Padua in the early twentieth century with the addition of alcohol to this water-and-wine combination. Though its origins are unclear, it is highly likely that the Austrian presence in the city played some role in its creation and popularity, which is no small contribution in the city that consumes thousands, if not more, a day.

The Revolution of 1848

The most important and influential ideologies of nineteenth-century Europe were nationalism and liberalism, proclaiming that people with a shared history, language, religion and culture should have the power of political self-determination, and that suffrage should be expanded and constitutional checks erected to prevent monarchs from abusing their powers. These ideas motivated political organizations, protests and revolutions around Europe throughout the first half of the nineteenth century, primarily in the growing ranks of the middle classes. Such ideas were first expressed in Italy under Austrian and French rule (while the Austrians ruled North Italy, the Bourbon family ruled the Kingdom of the Two Sicilies in the south), and in Venice through Attilio and Emilio Bandiera. These brothers worked for the Imperial Hapsburg Navy but were interested in the ideas of the Italian nationalist Giuseppe Mazzini. They founded a secret society called *Esperia* in 1841 to support an uprising against the Austrians and form an Italian state. *Esperia*, however, found no real support in the city so the brothers decided to try to launch an insurrection in the south, in Calabria, instead. They were captured near Cosenza and shot on 25 July 1844 having failed to launch their revolution.

The example of the Bandiera brothers illustrates that, as in the Venetian republic before the arrival of Napoleon, there was no real tradition of opposition and insurrection in the city, unlike other parts of Italy. With the Venetians' unique history as an island community, nationalism initially seems to have had less resonance than for other Italians. The revolutionary ideas of Italian unity and Italian self-governance were slower to take root here, and Venetians may have associated the idea of an Italian state with a domineering government in Milan that would offer them no real advantages or benefits. Since the Austrians had been relatively reasonable overlords, the idea of exchanging the rule of Vienna for that of an Italian dynasty had only limited appeal. Ideas about nationalism, however, began to change towards the middle of the nineteenth century. Disastrous harvests occurred in 1845–46, resulting in high prices, poverty and the increased suffering of the poor, especially in the countryside. The Austrians did not appear to care and did nothing to ease unemployment or the tax burden. The middle classes in particular felt abandoned by the Austrians and started to show signs of hostility. By 1848 national and liberal revolutions swept through almost every country in Europe, and in Italy revolts broke out around the peninsula and constitutions were drawn up in Naples, Piedmont, Tuscany and the Papal States to protect the rights of the local citizens against the abuses of their foreign overlords.

Venice and Milan initially remained cautious because of the near presence of the Austrian army but, pulled along by the currents of revolution, Venetian feelings of nationalism grew

though they were still constrained by the censorship laws and
by the ban on reading nationalist poems, the singing or
whistling of patriotic songs and public gatherings. Nonetheless
Venetians began to articulate more fully their intolerance of
Austrian rule through various acts of resistance. They wore
patriotic ribbons, feathers and sashes, and carried patriotic
handkerchiefs in the *tricolour* of Italy: red, green and white.
They turned their hats around as a symbol of protest. They
refused cigars made by the Austrians and protested against the
Austrian tax on tobacco by smoking plaster pipes. They
avoided the *Piazza San Marco* altogether, a centre of Austrian
social life and military showmanship, and refused to frequent
cafés or celebrate Carnival in the spring of 1848. Some of the
most pointed moments of patriotism and protest occurred in
the Fenice Opera House during the winter of 1847–48. During
the fourth act of Verdi's *Macbeth* one evening, the words of the
chorus at the beginning of Act IV, 'Oppressed land of ours!
You cannot have the sweet name of mother now that you have
become a tomb for your sons ... My homeland, oh my
homeland!' produced an outburst of enthusiasm as spectators
threw flowers on stage. After a particularly noisy patriotic
demonstration on 6 February 1848 in celebration of the constitution being granted in Naples, crowds threw red, white and
green handkerchiefs on the stage, yelling wildly when the
Neapolitan dancer Cerrito appeared in a red, white and green
dress. Austrian troops ordered the evacuation and closure of
the theatre that night, after which Venetians refused to attend
at all in protest of foreign domination.

The city finally rose up against their Austrian overlords
under the leadership of Daniele Manin in the spring of 1848.
Manin was the son of a converted Jew. His original family
name, Medina, was changed to Manin when the brother of
Lodovico Manin, the last doge of the republic, sponsored his
family's conversion. Manin was a lawyer and liberal political
activist who argued that the Venetians had a legal right to self-
governance. He was also outspoken about the need to revitalize

the Venetian economy in the decade before 1848. For instance, he had petitioned the Austrian government to ask for trade from India to benefit the port of Venice rather than Trieste. He did not call for full political independence but he did support 'home rule' under the Austrian Empire that would give Venetians more political autonomy.

On 30 December 1847 the Dalmatian poet and nationalist Niccolò Tommaseo gave a lecture at the *Istituto Veneto* – a forum for intellectual discussions – denouncing Austrian censorship. A week later Daniele Manin issued a list of 16 demands for greater rights for all Italians under Austrian rule. On 18 January 1848 both Tommaseo and Manin were arrested and imprisoned indefinitely but, on 17 March, word arrived in Venice that a revolt against the Austrian government had broken out in Vienna. Venetians demanded the prisoners' release and the Austrian governor Aloys Palffy acquiesced as crowds carried Manin out on their shoulders and down the *Merceria* to his house in *San Paternian*. Manin then set up a civic guard of Venetian forces and demanded the complete expulsion of the Austrians from the territories of the Veneto. On 22 March the deputy commander of the arsenal, Malinovich – unpopular among Venetians for denying promotions and raises – was murdered by an angry mob. Manin rushed to the arsenal through the back streets of the city and while the civic guard held back the Austrians, he managed to distribute the contents of the city's armories to revolutionary forces. Manin and the civic guard converged on the *Riva* – the main quay on the south of the city – and marched to the *Piazza San Marco* shouting *'Viva la Repubblica! Viva San Marco! Viva la Libertà!'* They pulled down Austrian flags and raised the red flags of the former republic. Manin stood on a table in front of Caffè Florian and dramatically proclaimed a new provisional government.

The Austrians capitulated and their troops left the lagoon as Austrian governments in other cities on the mainland, including Milan, also fell to revolutionary forces. The provisional government immediately began to reverse the most hated aspects of Austrian rule. They abolished high taxes, including those on newspapers and the right to fish, they lowered and fixed the price of bread, established the right to a defense for all accused of crimes and, as their first important symbolic gesture, demolished the imperial box at the Fenice. Manin and his supporters hoped to pick up history where it had left off: where it had been interrupted 50 years ago by foreign domination.

The Austrians, however, were quick to retaliate. By the middle of June they had retaken the Venetian mainland. The provisional government under Manin sent requests for support to Paris. Manin hoped the French would help, both because of their own revolutionary experiences and history as a republic, but also because many Venetians felt the French owed them an immense debt for the shocking damage they had caused in Venice. In the end only Piedmont, Switzerland and the United States recognized the existence of the new republican government, but no aid or assistance arrived from any of them. Manin and his colleagues went so far as to draw up a list of 58 paintings, including some by Titian and Veronese, that could be sacrificed and sold to finance and preserve Venetian liberty, though they never went through with it. Rich and poor alike tried to support the revolutionary government but the Venetians were no match for the Hapsburg army.

The Austrians blockaded and besieged the city, bombarding it with canons for weeks on end. With revolutions all over Europe petering out, by the spring of 1849 Venice found itself alone against the Austrian Empire. Lombardy, Tuscany and Palermo had all been retaken by Austrian and French forces. Although the Austrian canons pointing at Venice were not that effective since they were firing from the mainland, and although the Austrians made a failed attempt at dropping bombs from air balloons (that often fell on their own forces), the Venetians quickly began to suffer from food shortages and famine. A chicken cost a worker's weekly salary and butter was inaccessible even to the rich. The little remaining flour, beer and wine slowly disappeared, wood for cooking was nowhere to be found and all the city's *osterie* and food markets closed by July. As the bombing continued, blasting holes in the roofs around the city, gondoliers courageously ferried the wounded to get medical assistance and to safety around the lagoon.

By mid-summer cholera raged through the city: the factor that decisively defeated the Venetians. As people fled the quarters of the city where bombs were landing, overcrowding in Castello and the safer parts of the city helped spread the disease. By the end of July, nearly 3,000 had died of cholera, their bodies being piled up in the square in front of the church of *San Pietro* in Castello when it was no longer possible to bury them all. In the Hotel Daniele on the *Riva* where the richest families took refuge during the siege, a group of Venetians finally formed a petition on 3 August 1849 asking Manin to surrender the city. Manin must have known long before that there was no way he could withstand the Hapsburg Empire, but he fought tooth and nail until the bitter end until the spread of cholera finally made Venetian resistance futile. In the depths of their misery in the first weeks of August, Venetians accidentally discovered a cache of fine wines and spirits that had been hidden in the palace of the Austrian governor Palffy – 1,471 bottles of Bordeaux, champagne, Marsala and more – but this certainly was not enough to save them. Unable to hold out any longer, on 19 August two gondolas approached the mainland with white flags and, three days later, the Venetians surrendered. On 24 August 1849 the Austrian marshal Radetsky solemnly re-entered the conquered city as Venetians watched sadly and silently, their thin faces displaying just how much they had suffered from the long siege. The Austrians expelled all the leading revolutionaries from the city, including Manin and Tommaseo, but otherwise demanded no harsh reprisals as Venice fell back under Austrian rule for the third time. In *Campo Mario Marinoni* next to the Fenice theatre, there stands a little-noticed site as a unique memorial to these dramatic years: a building designed by the engineer Carlo Ruffini in 1869 whose façade is decorated with the cannon balls, shells and guns used by the Austrians in the siege of 1849.

Daniele Manin's wife died of cholera the day after the city's surrender. He went to Paris and supported himself by giving Italian lessons. His son Giorgio went on to fight in Garibaldi's army, seeing his father's hopes for national revolution come to life, and living to see Venice join the Kingdom of Italy in 1866. Lodovico Manin died in Paris in 1857, but Giorgio returned to live out the rest of his life in his native city. Daniele Manin is forever honoured by the Venetians, and his tomb is among the lions on the north side of the basilica of *San Marco*. His remains were transported from Paris to Venice by rail, followed by a night-time procession that conveyed his body through the city along the Grand Canal in a gondola decorated with bronze statues depicting the state of Italy consoling a grieving Venice.

Venice becomes Italian

When the Austrians returned to Venice under the command of Radetsky, it was no surprise that they carried on as before except they now maintained a much greater military presence after the events of 1848–9. Their troops appeared everywhere, especially in endless military exercises held in the *Piazza San Marco*. They even built the Accademia Bridge across the Grand Canal in 1854 so that their troops could quickly rush from one side of the city to the other in an emergency. This was only the second bridge to be built across the Grand Canal. Their main artillery garrison was on the island of San Giorgio, where they fired a canon every day at noon to symbolize the defeat and oppression of the city. Annulling all the laws of Manin's provisional government, the Austrians tried to eliminate any remaining signs of resistance and opposition. They removed all the anti-Austrian graffiti on the walls around the city, prohibited Venetians from carrying weapons or holding any type of political meetings and reimposed harsh censorship laws. The Austrians even confined the privilege of free trade to just one island, San Giorgio. Over 4,000 Venetians went into exile to resist and avoid Austrian rule.

Among the first foreigners to come to the city from the outside world and witness its impoverishment and desolation first-hand were the Ruskins. John Ruskin was an art historian who drew and catalogued much of the art and architecture of the city, famously championing the Venetian gothic style above what he considered to be the barbaric forms of the Renaissance. He despised, for instance, the work of Palladio and preferred the buildings on Torcello and other Byzantine architecture around the city, and published his drawing, findings and opinions in his famous *The Stones of Venice* (1851–3). Ruskin is a central figure in the history and historiography of Venetian art, but it was interestingly his wife, Effie, who first noticed and depicted in detail the plight of the Venetians during the third Austrian occupation. While her husband was off sketching, she described urban life to her friends and relatives back in England. She described how she regularly saw impoverished women, whose sons had been conscripted into the Austrian army, selling lace to try and earn an income. In November 1849 she noted that,

> many of the Italians here appear to have no homes at all and to be perfectly happy. At eight o'clock in the evening when we return from hearing the band we see them all lying packed together at the edge of the bridges, wrapped in their immense brown cloaks and large hoods as warm as fires. Then in the morning there are little stands on all parts of the quay where they can get hot fish, rice soup, hot elder wine, all kinds of fruit, cigars, and this eating al fresco goes on the whole day … The other day an immense fire and a large cauldron was put in the square where they burned all the paper money issued by the Provisional Government here while it lasted. I saw the ashes of above 2,000,000 notes.

Despite the fact that she witnessed such painful events as Venetians warming themselves by the fire that burned the money from their failed revolutionary government, both Effie and John Ruskin had mainly positive things to say about the

Austrians, especially since Effie was excited to be admitted into Austrian social circles in Venice. Other visitors to the city, however, were more critical of the Austrian mistreatment of the Venetians. The writer George Sand, for instance, regularly reported the many things that the Austrians did to make themselves hated, including urinating on her gondola.

Continued unemployment and the misery of foreign occupation served to build feelings of nationalism more than ever. While Caffè Florian had long been and continued to be a nationalist bastion, the Austrians frequented Caffè Quadri across the *piazza*, smoking and watching their military drills. No Venetian ever applauded when the Austrian band played in the centre of the *piazza*. The Fenice once again became a rallying point for nationalists during the occupation, as audiences threw symbolic red, white and green bouquets on stage. *Viva Verdi* – standing for Vittorio Emanuele Re D'Italia – became the code for defiance against the occupation and in support of Italian unification. On 22 March 1858 – the tenth anniversary of Manin's revolution – Venetians acknowledged the date by dressing in red, white and green, but the Archduke Maximilian of Austria and his wife had planned a visit on exactly that day and as they promenaded in the *piazza* with the Austrian military band, every Venetian left, and once again the Fenice closed in protest against Austrian rule.

However, the drive for Italian national unification – the *Risorgimento* – was gaining momentum up and down the peninsula. In 1859 the territory of Piedmont in north-western Italy gained the support of the French and they went to war with the Austrians. Other news helped maintain morale in Venice: reports of *La spedizione dei mille* (Garibaldi's conquest of the Kingdom of Two Sicilies), the inauguration in Turin on 18 February 1861 of the first national Italian parliament and the proclamation on 17 March 1861 of the Kingdom of Italy. As they saw what was happening, the Austrians prepared for their departure, once again removing everything they could possibly take from Venice, just as Napoleon had done many decades before. On 19 October 1866 Italian troops entered Venice and shortly after a plebiscite based on universal male suffrage made Venice part of the Kingdom of Italy. On 7 November 1866 the Italian King Vittorio Emanuele II entered the city amidst frenzied celebration, and the Fenice opened once again for a gala evening dedicated to the new sovereign. By December the Veneto had communal and provincial elections so that, by January 1867, Venetians could finally begin to work out among themselves how to fix all the things in their city that had been neglected and broken by almost 70 years of foreign occupation.

The Modern Economy

Though Venice's economic development was clearly hampered by the prolonged Austrian presence in the city, industrialization had nevertheless been developing in the city through the nineteenth century. Factories had been opening and industries growing, reflecting the new industrial age that began to extend right across Europe at this time. To give just a few examples, in 1848 a tobacco-processing factory opened in the neighbourhood of Santa Croce that eventually employed thousands, most of whom were women. A cotton and textile factory opened in the neighbourhood of Santa Marta in 1882, and a flourmill, the Mulino Stucky, opened in 1884 and still today offers the best example of industrial architecture in the lagoon. It sits monumentally on the western end of the Giudeccca, and though flour production ended in 1954 it has recently reopened, not surprisingly, as a luxury hotel. The Giudecca became somewhat like a little Manchester in Venice as this island on the southern edge of the city became the site of many factories, including a watch factory, brewery, ice factory and textile factory (belonging to Mariano Fortuny). By 1850 the city had approximately 50 factories that employed thousands of Venetians, and by the beginning of the twentieth century Venice was thoroughly industrialized. In panoramic photographs of Venice from this time, smokestacks shot up around the city.

Growing public services also fed the Venetian economy, including the introduction of a gas network for public lighting, an aqueduct for drinking water and the inauguration of the first *vaporetto* line in 1881. A French company won the first concession to build motorized boats to transport passengers around the lagoon, and the first eight of them came down the Seine and around the toe of Italy to start the first mechanical transport service in the city. Before the arrival of *vaporetti*, large boats would row passengers from the train station to *San Marco*, so not surprisingly the introduction of *vaporetto* services provoked a wave of protest among boatmen and gondoliers, especially around the time of the trial run of the first *vaporetto*, the *Regina Margherita*, along the Grand Canal. Motorized boats had connected the city with Chioggia, Fusina, San Giuliano and Jesolo since 1872, but they functioned outside the city and were not seen as a threat. When the regular service began on 15 September 1881 tension in the city grew and, on 31 October, the city's boatmen began to strike and argue with the police. Resigned to the *vaporetti*, however, the gondoliers went back to work within a few days and the *vaporetto* found its place in the modern city. In the 1890s there was further discussion about building a subway – an underground railway – to connect the centre of the city with the islands of the Giudecca and the Lido, a discussion that has resurfaced in the twenty-first century as Venetians have grappled with the best way of moving tourists between the city and the airport. No serious steps have ever been taken to realize such a project.

The industry that would transfix and transform Venice forever, however, was tourism. Tourism had played a role in the local economy for centuries, with visitors travelling to this mythic city to see its relics and shrines, to use its port when going on crusade, to revel in the delights of courtesans, opera, gambling and the Carnival, and to get an education when taking the Grand Tour. But tourism in the city took two decidedly different turns in the nineteenth century. First, after the fall of the republic and the waves of foreign occupation that virtually destroyed the city and its inhabitants, Venice became the quintessential 'romantic' city. After nationalism and liberalism, romanticism – the artistic and literary movement that focused on the sublimity of the emotions as they extended far beyond the rational mind – was the third main ideology of the nineteenth century. Rejecting the intellectual focus of the age of Enlightenment, romantic writers, composers and artists sought out and embraced the full range of human feelings, especially those of pain and longing. Romantics were also attracted to the foreign and the unfamiliar, the macabre and the misunderstood. Venice by the nineteenth century was all this and more. During the Napoleonic occupation, Venice became a dead city and a city in ruins. Indeed, the idea that Venice was disappearing encouraged many visitors to come and see it before it disappeared (just like today). It was also, of course, an Eastern city, and a once great place that had fallen into a state of desperation and at times, despair, a place that encouraged intellectuals to think about the function of memory. I embodied exoticism, sadness, melancholy, nostalgia, loss, longing, decay and death. No wonder, then, that Venice became *the* centre of artistic pilgrimage in the nineteenth century and a virtual magnet for European artists and intellectuals who wanted to embrace it body and soul.

It is impossible to list them all, but Venice attracted the likes of the poets Lord Byron (who stayed from 1816–19) and Shelley (1818), and the painter Turner (1818–19, 1829 and 1840). Byron was among the first to see the city after the departure of the French, and he described meeting the proud survivors from the Venetian republic. According to Jan Morris, Byron swam home along the Grand Canal after a long night of revelry while his servant carried his clothes in a gondola behind him. Other famous visitors included Corot, Mendelssohn, Liszt, Browning, Dickens, Henry James, Manet, Whistler, Sargent, Nietzche, Renoir, George Sand, Walter Sickert and Wagner. The growing numbers of visitors meant that old patrician palaces were either converted into grand hotels or rented out. In 1822, for instance, the *Palazzo Dandolo* on the *Riva degli Schiavoni* was refurbished to become what is still today one of the city's most elegant and luxurious hotels, the Hotel Daniele, where both Sand and Dickens lodged. Venice was copiously studied, painted and written about in depth in the nineteenth century, though by this point (apart from a handful of artists, such as the painters Giuseppe Bernardino Bisson and Ippolito Caffi) rarely by Italians or Venetians.

The masses followed the artists and intellectuals in the second great wave of tourism that hit Venice in the second half of the century. After Italian Unification, almost overnight, mass travel to the city grew exponentially. While rich tourists had begun to come to Venice in larger numbers in the 1830s – their gaiety and wealth at odds with the misery of the Venetians – after 1866 Venice began to attract everyone. In 1867 the tour agency Thomas Cook began operating its first tours to Venice, Baedeker's guidebooks helped more people navigate the city and, by 1880, the Lido – previously nothing more than a grassy sandbar with a Jewish cemetery and a series of deserted fortresses – became a fashionable European beach. Salt water bathing had become such a craze in Europe that entrepreneurs established enormous bathing platforms – huge floating docks where tourists could sun themselves and swim – around the lagoon, one in particular moored just off the *dogana* in front of San Marco. By 1845, in a city with little more than 120,000 residents, around 110,000 tourists were already visiting per year, helping Venetians begin to find a way out of their economic plight.

Anxious to claim the admiration and fame associated with the different types of great exhibitions that other cities had begun to enjoy (the Great Exhibition in London being the best example), Venetians also began to promote their city as a centre of contemporary art and culture by opening the Venice Biennale in 1895, an avant-garde contemporary art festival that is still one of the most prestigious venues for contemporary artists. The city continued to express its cultural influence at an international level later in the twentieth century by opening the Venice Film Festival in 1932 and the Theatre Festival in 1934.

Venetians also revived some of their traditional arts and crafts, largely to profit from the growing number of visitors who wanted a local souvenir. The city revived its reputation as a centre for glass making and, in 1859, the Austrian entrepreneur Antonio Salviati established a productive new glass factory on Murano. In 1871 the countess Andriana Marcello opened a lace school under the patronage of Queen Margherita of Italy, reviving this centuries-old tradition on the island of Burano. By 1882 it had over 300 students who were paid to attend and develop this craft. Though it closed at the end of the 1960s, you can still visit the school's museum and watch the lacemakers at work. Furthermore, some of the earliest photographs of life in the lagoon depict women with trays of glass beads in their laps, stringing them on to threads with long needles. These bead-stringers (called *impiraresse*) and lace-makers were able to supplement their household incomes without straying far from home or toiling in a factory. Their products were exported around the globe, and became a curious component of European colonialism as Venetian beads became a currency in colonial Africa, used for exchange by the French in their colonial territories in Senegal. These women, sitting in the courtyards with their beads and lace soon became another tourist attraction themselves, as foreigners flocked to see what Venetians did and how they lived.

The Nineteenth Century Made Visible

The nineteenth century marks a great turning point in Venetian history. Whereas the city had long maintained its separation from the rest of Europe, both in its island location and its traditional form of government, it had now been wrenched into the modern world and made to function much like other European cities, sometimes willingly and sometimes against its will. We can see how and where this happened all over the city.

French rule dramatically changed the appearance of the *Piazza San Marco*. When Napoleon's stepson arrived in the city, he immediately decided that there was no space near the *Piazza* grandiose enough to house him and his retinue. The *procuratie* – the buildings that lined the north and south of the *piazza* – were too humble for a French viceroy since a royal palace needed the likes of a grand staircase and a ballroom that these existing buildings did not provide. French planners therefore knocked down the church of *San Geminiano* on the western side of the *piazza* on 19 May 1807, though patriotic painters such as Canaletto, Guardi and others often continued to depict the *piazza* as if the church was still present to protest against Napoleonic destruction. French builders knocked it down to make room for the *Ala Napoleonica*, or Napoleonic wing, of the *piazza*, which now stands opposite the basilica on the far western side of the square. Look up at the upper frieze of this building and you will see 14 statues of Roman emperors along the attic storey. A statue of Napoleon was intended to grace the central position but it was never mounted, so the gap in the centre symbolically marks the ultimate emptiness and failure of Napoleonic schemes.

In addition, beyond the *Piazza San Marco*, whenever you find yourself in a broad street or a wide-open space that is not a *campo*, or public square, note that such a space was most likely carved out in the nineteenth century. Nineteenth-century kings and leaders all over Europe were concerned, if not obsessed, with making new, open public spaces out of the dark, irregular and labyrinthine streets left from the Middle Ages. These open spaces served many functions: they allowed light and air into cities to improve public health, they offered spaces in which rulers could show off themselves and their entourages, they permitted new forms of public transport and they facilitated easier and quicker movement of troops in urban centres when the use of force was necessary. The most famous example of such urban renewal happened in Paris under Baron von Haussmann who opened up wide avenues all over the city in the second half of the nineteenth century. In Italy new ideas about urban planning resulted in the *Piazza del Duomo* in Milan, and the *Corso Vittorio* and *Corso del Rinascimento* in Rome. As Venice underwent similar changes in urban planning, it became like other nineteenth-century cities.

At the start of the century, Napoleon's main architect and civic planner, Giannantonio Selva, organized the clearing of many spaces in the eastern part of the city, namely the *Via Eugenia* (now the *Via Garibaldi*) and the city's first public park adjacent to it, to the east. Like other city planners, Selva's intention was to open up a dark, cramped, medieval section of the city to let in more light, air and traffic. The creation of this wide, new avenue demanded the demolition of several large churches and religious complexes and the filling in of canals to make a wide street, a process that similarly continued around the city into the twentieth century. One of the churches demolished was *San Antonio Abate*, the church that held the tomb of Vettor Pisani, the great hero of the War of Chioggia in 1380. The monumental arch from the Lando Chapel was saved and is the only remains of this church. It sits quietly back in the shade of the gardens, a strange and displaced shard of history. Despite what were perhaps the good intentions of Napoleonic planners, Venetians' reactions to these changes were largely negative since, as Franz Liszt put it when he visited the city, 'to be a Venetian is to prefer marble to foliage, a palace to a garden'. Later, in 1867, Venetians voted to open a wide, new artery between the churches of *Santi Apostoli* and *Santa Fosca* – the *Strada Nuova* – to facilitate movement in the northern part of the city. They later cleared areas like the *Calle Larga XXII Marzo* (to the west of San Marco) and the *Merceria Due Aprile* (near the eastern base of the Rialto Bridge), naming these newly opened areas after important dates in Manin's revolution and again demolishing parts of the medieval city centre in the process. While many Venetians welcomed this increased pedestrianization (indeed, many of the modern *sottoporteghi* or underpasses around the city were first carved out in the nineteenth century to improve pedestrian routes), but restoration experts and urban planners today tend to condemn these avenues because they are out of scale with, and lacking in sympathy for, the historic nature of the city's urban layout.

It is important to note that nineteenth-century urban planners constructed or 'invented' buildings as much as they demolished them. Invasive and destructive restoration projects were one of the hallmarks of the nineteenth century. To cite just a few examples, the old Turkish warehouse – the *Fondaco dei Turchi* – on the Grand Canal was badly restored from 1858–69 by planners who hoped to make it look antique or Turkish while largely ignoring the building's original construction, façade and appearance (the building was originally a patrician palace and not a Turkish warehouse). The head of this restoration, Federico Berchet, placed triangular crenellations inspired by the mosque of Ahmad ibn Tulun in Cairo on the façade of the restored *fondaco*, even though such forms were most likely never on the original building. Similarly, in 1884, the remains of the *Palazzo Querini* (where the rebels collected their weapons before the Querini-Tiepolo conspiracy of 1310) were removed to create a new *pescheria* or fish market: a long, metal-roofed, tent-like structure that was so unpopular that it was soon destroyed to rebuild a *pescheria* or fish market in a gothic style that still exists today.

Nineteenth-century architects and urban planners were famous for attempting to construct buildings in traditional Venetian styles that appeared authentic or traditional, but as imitations and reconstructions they were not always entirely successful. Modern experts of restoration and conservation have long criticized the nineteenth-century penchant for willfully failing to preserve original structures and appearances. Throughout the city we can find buildings that were recreated rather than preserved in the nineteenth century. They are easy to spot (the *Palazzo Franchetti*, just to the east of the Accademia Bridge, is a perfect example) by the way in which their façades handle gothic elements in ways that appear almost too confident, harmonious, tidy and pristine, just as overdone plastic surgery produces a face that is wrinkle-free but pulled too tight. In fact there is something very appealing about the faded and dilapidated states of many of the city's venerable buildings. When over-restored they are deprived of their history, as the restorer Gianfranco Pertot put it, end up looking like a corpse rendered clean and decent in a funeral parlour.

The nineteenth century was also the great epoch of memorializing the events of the age in bronze. All around the city bronze plaques and statues point out the tumultuous events and charismatic leaders of the nineteenth century. For instance, *Campo San Paternian* was renamed *Campo Manin*, and a bronze statue of Manin made by Luigi Borro in 1875 now stands in the centre of this square, not far from the doorway to his family home. Just a short walk towards the Accademia Bridge in *Campo Santo Stefano* there is the 1882 sculpture of Niccolò Tommaseo by Francesco Barzaghi. Locals have another name for this statue that cannot be repeated here, so the curious reader will have to ask a waiter at one of the several surrounding cafés what it is really called. At the entrance to the Napoleonic Gardens you will see an 1885 statue of Garibaldi by Augusto Benevenuto, and another of Vittorio Emanuele II, the first king of a united Italy, on the *Riva degli Schiavoni* by Ettore Ferrari (1887). In a little noticed but fascinating corner of the city behind the *Piazza San Marco* and the *Ala Napoleonica*, an array of bronze plaques that plaster the walls, side to side, commemorates the great Venetian heroes of the nineteenth century, those who contributed to civic self-realization, the building of national identity and the *Risorgimento* or forging of the Italian state.

Indeed, when you note the presence of these statues and plaques in bronze around the city (sites to which we might normally not pay much attention or even see in a city so rich in medieval and Renaissance art and architecture), you get the sense that it was only towards the end of the nineteenth century that Venetians could finally stop and take a breath and remember, after all those extraordinary changes that affected the city. These monuments clearly express the sense of public pride and patriotism that emerged at this time. Venetians were certainly left battered by the events of the nineteenth century, but their struggles to become independent also left them with much to be proud of and hopeful for, as these bronze memorials communicate.

Though not particularly visually inspiring, of all the monuments and remains from the nineteenth century around Venice the most important emblem of this age (and the greatest footprint of the Austrians in the city) is undoubtedly the railway bridge built to connect the city to the mainland. The Austrians wanted the bridge to better connect Venice to the rest of the Hapsburg Empire. As ever, several palaces and churches had to be destroyed to make space for the new railway station, namely the church of *Santa Lucia*, which gave its name to the station. After five years and the work of a thousand labourers, Venetians and Austrians completed the bridge that is just over 2 miles (3.2 km) long, cheering the first trains into the city in January 1846. (The adjacent *Ponte della Libertà* for cars and pedestrians was built in 1932.)

As we can imagine, reactions to the bridge both at its opening and over time were mixed. On the one hand the bridge increased Austrian control over the city, and it also immediately ruined an entire class of boatmen who had long earned their living transporting people and goods to and from the mainland. The decline of the historic role of gondoliers and ferrymen began with this bridge. There was, on the other hand, much to be said in its favour. After the revolution of 1848, for instance, when supplies had run out and Venetian trade in the Adriatic had been completely stifled, the bridge undoubtedly facilitated the recovery of the city by enabling food to be brought in quickly, as well as the new tourists who helped revive and restore the Venetian economy. Ruskin protested against the bridge by continuing to take a gondola every time he came to the city, but Wagner was so ecstatic to see Venice for the first time from the window of a moving train in 1852 that he threw his hat out the window and into the water in a fit of excitement.

Appreciated or hated, the bridge represents one of the most radical changes in the entire history of Venice. Though the city's traditional government had fallen and the city had experienced the brutal disregard of its own government, culture and economy as a result of foreign occupation, in some ways these events, though devastating, remain less significant in the overall history of the city than its permanent connection to the mainland. Almost overnight, considering the long history of the lagoon, Venice lost its most fundamental and defining quality as an island to become, somewhat mundanely and drably, an extension of the land. Of course Venetians fortunes were always tied to the land in one way or another: the city's initial rise came from trade up the rivers on the mainland, and its food and labour supply came in part from the nearby *terraferma*. The island and the land had always been economically and politically intertwined. Spatially and culturally, however, the island had always been far removed from the rest of the world, even the nearby mainland. Whereas it traditionally took over four hours to reach the city by gondola, after 1846 it took only minutes. As we take the train into the city today and stare out the window on to the vast expanse of the lagoon, we cannot fail to realize the monumentality of this change. A melding of brick, stone and mortar was erected across the waters to link the island to the land, as if attaching it to a leash that reined it in and tethered it to the rest of the world forever.

8

VENICE:
A BRIEF HISTORY OF LIFE ON WATER

At 9.53 am on 14 July 1902, the *Campanile* of *San Marco* collapsed in a heap after showing a large crack for several weeks on the north wall. Though debris came right up to the base of the columns of *San Marco*, no one was injured or killed (except for the caretaker's cat) and the church was spared. Sergei Diaghilev – the creator of the *Ballets Russes* and a frequent visitor to Venice – liked to tell of how a Venetian ship returned to the lagoon the day the bell tower collapsed and how, when its captain saw that it was no longer there, he went mad. This story is most likely apocryphal, but both the collapse of the bell tower and the shock it generated ushered in the twentieth century. The bell tower was rebuilt to look the same as before but, in retrospect, the collapse represented a sign of things to come. The twentieth century would present the inhabitants of the lagoon with a series of problems that were by no means new but gradually became much more grave: the challenge of managing an economy, an ecology and an existence in a lagoon where up to hundreds of thousands of people visit every day and, in addition, the water is rising.

After the unification of Italy, Venetian history largely came to echo the history of the rest of the Italian peninsula much more closely. As the city became woven into Italian politics more broadly, it tended to share more experiences with the rest of the mainland so that the story of the city to a large degree becomes less unique. Venetians like their Italian neighbours on the mainland also struggled through the wars of the twentieth century, the rise and fall of fascism, the construction of a demo- cratic regime and the challenges of rebuilding their economy in the wake of the Second World War. But Venice's history diverged sharply from the history of other Italian cities because it increasingly had to confront the health of the lagoon, its rising waters and mass tourism. And that raises the question, how and why have the waters of the lagoon risen, threatening life in the city? And what is being done to protect the way of life of the Venetians who live there today?

Venice and the Wars of the Twentieth Century

Before we turn to the lagoon and its ecological management, let us briefly look at the first half of the twentieth century. Much of the fighting in the First World War took place very close to the city, in the territories of the old republic on the mainland to the west and north of Venice, just a few miles away. Venetian casualties were large as the front between Austria-Hungary and Italy was for some time along the Piave River to the north of Venice. The Battle of the Piave in 1918 was the final, decisive battle on the Italian front. Italian forces were victorious and the Austro-Hungarian forces had to retreat but only after, as Italians still remark today, the River Piave ran red with the blood of hundreds of thousands of the dead and wounded.

In the city itself, after war was declared, the Venetians removed the four horses of *San Marco* to an undisclosed location, churches and galleries were emptied and their paintings taken to the mainland, and scaffolding and sandbags encased the walls and windows of the Ducal Palace and *San Marco*. Statues around the city were also encased in padding, and Venetians used seaweed from the lagoon to wrap up smaller statues and to stuff mattresses to protect valuable, fragile objects. All the canals that led to waters outside the lagoon were blocked, and lights had to be switched off at night causing many to fall into the canals in the dark. Shells fell on several churches, most seriously on the church of the *Scalzi* near the train station, though bombs launched on *San Marco* and the Ducal Palace miraculously did not explode. From 1915–18 the city suffered 42 air attacks and was hit by over 1,000 bombs while Venetian gunmen fired back at Austrians planes from the rooftops. The greatest damage during the First World War, however, occurred when tourism evaporated. Hotels and theatres closed and, in addition, commerce came to a halt since mines made it too dangerous to navigate the Adriatic. Two-thirds of the population left the city. In March 1919, after the defeat of the Central Powers, Venetians dragged prisoners of the Austrian fleet into the bay of San Marco to be publicly viewed and humiliated, an event that must have evoked powerful emotions for Venetians with the memory of 70 years of Austrian rule still in the minds of many.

In the 1920s and 1930s fascism took root in the city as it did elsewhere in Italy. Mussolini offered the hope of revitalization and renewal that attracted people in the wake of the First World War but, while anti-fascist groups consolidated in other cities, Venetians seemed much more compliant and showed less interest in resisting fascism than the residents of Naples and Florence, for example. Hitler and Mussolini staged their first historic meeting in Venice in June 1934, greeted and cheered on by thousands of fascist followers. As the story goes, Hitler was advised to travel in civilian clothing and he disembarked from his plane on the Lido in a crumpled suit to be humiliated when he found Mussolini in his full military regalia. After the *Manifesto della Razza* or 'Manifesto on Race', the first anti-Semitic legislation published on 4 July 1938, Italians and

Venetians began to limit Jewish participation in commercial and public life, and the deportation of Jews to concentration camps began in December 1943. Of the more than 2,000 Jews who lived in the city on the eve of the Second World War, 212 were deported and most of the rest managed to escape or find refuge in non-Jewish homes. Of these 212, only 15 eventually returned to Venice, and about 600 Jews live in the lagoon today.

Once again, after war was declared, *San Marco* was enclosed in a cage of wood and sand bags as Venetians transported their artistic treasures to the mainland while the contents of the state archives were taken to a castle near Padua. Armando Gavegnin, the most vocal partisan activist in the city, addressed Venetians from a table top in the Caffè Florian in the summer of 1943, but that did not stop the Germans who arrived on 8 September. They dealt harshly with any acts of resistance and the *Riva dei Sette Martiri*, or 'Quay of Seven Martyrs', the waterfront to the east of *San Marco*, is named after seven men who were shot by the Germans in 1944. While the city was not bombed in the Second World War, as both sides tried to protect the city's artistic treasures, the rest of the Veneto and the industrial zone of Marghera on the mainland was hit hard by bombs. Venice suffered dramatically from overcrowding since so many came to the lagoon for safety, in an almost eerie modern echo of the founding of the city when the original inhabitants fled here from the barbarians on the mainland. Food shortages and high prices plagued the city, and the winter of 1944–5 was one of the coldest in memory. The city was eventually liberated in 1945.

Sinking and Rising: Water, Ecology and the Fate of the City

As we have seen, Venice was dramatically and laboriously founded on water when the first Venetians decided to make their lives on the marshy mudflats of the lagoon. Venetians have a longstanding and particular relationship with water, with only about eight per cent of the lagoon's surface being land. However, the waters that once protected these refugees and later allowed medieval merchants to make the city among the richest in the world now threatens the city's wellbeing if not its existence. From the very beginning, Venetians faced unique challenges to their survival, and a brief review of how some of these challenges have been managed will help us understand how Venetians are now confronting the threats of rising water and possibly a sinking city.

From the start and throughout their history, Venetians found many ways to adapt to and manage their watery environment to keep it habitable, safe and profitable. Their existence, in many ways, was a give-and-take between the forces of water erosion and their ability to build up their shores.

The lagoon seems to have been formed by a series of rivers as they came down from the Alps and flowed into the Adriatic: the Adige, Bacchiglione, Brenta, Sile and Piave all once naturally flowed into the lagoon. However, over the course of the centuries, from the Middle Ages and right through the fourteenth and seventeenth centuries, Venetians diverted the course of these rivers by digging wide canals that forced them to enter the sea outside the lagoon. The city employed local workers on the mainland in winter, when tides were lower and labourers were not needed for farming, to undertake the backbreaking job of digging these canals. This prevented the lagoon from silting up and resulted in the creation of the lagoon as it is today: a kind of sea water lake that is regularly cleansed and kept in motion by rising and falling Adriatic tides.

These tides once entered the lagoon at nine points or inlets among the barrier islands between the lagoon and the Adriatic, but in another act of manipulation the Venetians reduced these inlets to three – the inlets that still exist today – to better control these currents. In addition, by 1700 Venetians had filled in several of the natural channels on the lagoon floor so that the tides, when forced through fewer channels, would flow more quickly and scour them out to keep them cleaner for regular use as shipping lanes. Later in the eighteenth century, from 1744–82, Venetians built up the *Murazzi*, the banks of the Lido, reinforcing the Adriatic side of the lagoon against storms and flooding by transporting massive Istrian stones from the opposite coast of the Adriatic and piling them up to build sea walls on the eastern side of the barrier islands of the lagoon. Such construction represented a monumental accomplishment when you consider that the Venetians had no access to cranes or heavy machinery for transport, and this was one of the last great efforts of the Venetian republic before it fell. But perhaps the most basic component of Venetian water management concerned draining the land and sinking supports into the mud so that inhabitants could build lasting structures on it (see Chapter 3), a procedure still practiced today almost exactly as it was in the early Middle Ages.

Venetians have always had to manipulate the balance of water and land through the use of canals, the Venetians' primary means of transport through the city. Before the construction of the *Ponte degli Scalzi* (the bridge in front of the train station) and Accademia Bridge in the nineteenth century, only one bridge, the Rialto, crossed the Grand Canal. So to get from one place to another, and especially between distant neighbourhoods, you had to travel by boat though a dense network of canals. City streets were entirely inferior to water travel and, if you need proof, just look at the main façades of Venetian palaces and their splendid entrances that face the water and not the street. Street access to buildings was just a secondary means of entry. In fact part of the reason why Venetian streets often seem so illogical, which is why so many tourists get so lost, is precisely because the city's original inhabitants and planners never meant people to get about much on foot. The city's canals are laid out in a much more logical fashion. Today the gondola and the canal-facing façades of Venetian *palazzi* are the main remaining evidence that water was originally the primary means of transport.

Gondolas are one of the most curious legacies of the Venetian republic, and their eerie black forms still make their way through the canals much as they did hundreds of years ago, though now they are exclusively for tourists. There are also far fewer today than there once were. According to the sixteenth-century Venetian historian Sansovino there were as many as 10,000 gondolas around 1500 compared with 500 today though its design has barely changed, if at all.

The Venetian Senate recognized early on that the physical survival of the city depended on the free movement of the tides through the canals, and for this reason Venetians created the *Magistrato alle Acque* in 1501 to oversee all hydraulic matters. The city regularly maintained its network of canals to meet both the transport and sanitary needs of the city. The city's' vast network of canals allowed the Adriatic's tides to flow into the city centre every day and flush out the sewage, and for this reason magistrates typically rejected most requests to fill in canals. The fall of the republic in 1797, however, Venetians increasingly began to fill in canals. The invading French and the Austrians were used to living on the mainland and wanted more pedestrian routes. Napoleon's architect Selva, for instance, had numerous canals filled in to create gardens and thoroughfares, namely the *Via Garibaldi* where a wide, paved area was substituted for a large canal.

Canal closures also often occurred because of individual whims and desires, as a result of landlords, for instance, no longer wanting to be taxed and pay for dredging the canals outside their houses or because they wanted them closed since silting made them smell. Under the period of Austrian rule in particular, so many canals were filled in that their combined length exceeded that of the Grand Canal; the authorities eventually decided that it was, in fact, cheaper to close a canal than maintain it.

From the time of the fall of the republic to the formation of the Italian government, the roles of land and water travel reversed with more canals being filled in and the fundamental principles underlying the construction of Venice being rejected in favour of modernization. Some estimates claim that close to 50 canals were closed in the nineteenth and twentieth centuries, a total of 4 miles (6 km). When foreign powers moved in after 1797, the greatest rupture in the history of Venice also meant that the Venetians' relationship to their watery environment changed. In the nineteenth century Venice became more like a pedestrian city in a manner that would have been once unimaginable.

You can see where these canals once existed where streets are now called *Rio Terà* meaning 'canal filled-in'. You can also sometimes spot the results of filled-in canals because the buildings will have tilted since the filled-in canals are not as firm as the land that had been laboriously built up and stabilized. Canal filling continued until the 1950s, but in the late twentieth century there has been a move to excavate and re-open some canals since many ecologists and conservationists recognize the crucial role they play in the functioning of the city and its ecology.

This brief overview illustrates how Venetians have manipulated (and usually protected) the lagoon to maximize their commercial capabilities, protect their way of life and benefit from the fact that they live on water. At times they found themselves in conflict with their watery environment as they struggled to control it, since land and sea are always in conflict in the unstable lagoon, though their lives have also been in harmony with their environment as they adjusted their habits, their ways of building and their way of doing business in order to survive here. They overcame the obstacles associated with living on water and turned them to their advantage.

In the twentieth century, however, dramatic changes began to take place that permanently altered the city's ecology. Industrialists thought that greater industrial expansion could take place on land reclaimed from the marshes around the perimeter of the lagoon which led to the industrial port and complex of refineries around Mestre and Marghera, on the mainland to the west of Venice. Much of this development was overseen and encouraged by one particular person, Count Giuseppe Volpi, a businessman and financier who wanted to make the Venetian mainland a massive industrial complex.

Volpi had a vision of a city where the old and the new, the historic and the modern, could come together. He wanted to pull Venice out of its economic torpor after the First World War. By 1939 Volpi had overseen 63 factories and plants on the mainland that employed more than 19,000 people in various chemical, naval, metal-refining and electrical plants. Marghera was based on the idea that removing heavy industry to the periphery of the lagoon would protect the historic centre of Venice from industrial development. Venetians also realized that they needed to support industries other than tourism, and thought that this new industrial port would serve this purpose without threatening either tourism or the city's cultural past, despite the fact that visually, as most readily admit, Marghera remains an extraordinary blight on the city and its skyline.

The *raison d'être* behind such a massive industrial port on the shores of the Venetian lagoon was questioned, however, after the dramatic flood of 1966 saw the tides rise in the lagoon in an unprecedented way. On 4 November 1966 the city awoke to find itself completely submerged. There had been a high tide the day before, but nothing unusual, when a powerful *scirocco*, a front of warm air coming up from North Africa, swept in to cause the disaster. At the time when the tide would normally recede, it continued rising to 6.3 ft (1.94 m) above the average sea level and stayed that high for 24 hours instead of the usual six hours of high tide. There was 3.9 ft (1.2 m) of water in the *Piazza San Marco* as the waves lapped high up against the sides of the buildings. Boats ripped away from their moorings and smashed through windows. Anything and everything turned up in the water, including fruit and vegetables, drowned dogs and cats, the contents of shops, documents from the archives and endless garbage. The island of St Erasmo, to the north-east of the city, disappeared entirely beneath the waves.

Finally, towards 9 pm, the wind died down and the water began to recede. Venetians came out of their houses with flash-lights and candles to peer and step tentatively back out on the streets. Many recall that it was a clear night with no moon and you could see all the stars. No one slept. By morning they saw the full extent of the damage. Debris was everywhere. Everywhere seawater had risen above the impervious Istrian marble bases of buildings and seeped into the more porous and fragile brickwork above it. A massive amount of water managed to climb up the walls of the city through capillary action, allowing salt to crystallize in the bricks and eventually make them disintegrate. Electricity and phone lines were interrupted for a week. Even more dramatically, heating tanks that had been overwhelmed by the high tide leaked their contents into the water. The floodwater had become covered with a stinking layer of surface oil and left a black streak over buildings and streets as it receded. The flood represented a dramatic turning point in the history of the city since it forced Venetians to confront the threats of a changing natural environment. That day, Venetians and the world started to wonder if life in the lagoon could continue in the long term.

There was no single cause behind the dramatic flood. There had been abundant rains combined with an atmospheric depression, strong winds and the normal tidal pull in the Adriatic. But many argued that the city had already been sinking as a result of industrial development. From about 1925, Volpi's industrial complex was permitted to pump ground-water for industrial use, deflating the water table under the lagoon and the city. This was finally halted in the 1970s, but the full effect remains unknown even today. Furthermore, the extra deep dredging of a shipping canal between Marghera on the mainland and Malamocco on the Lido – to support mainland industry – altered the city's water table. Different sources produce different statistics but many suggest that, on average, the city has sunk by 1.5 inches (4 cm) over the past century. According to another measurement, the city has sunk by 9 inches (23 cm) since 1897, when measuring devices were first placed near the church of the *Salute* at the end of the Grand Canal to keep track of the 'zero' mark or median sea level. Many of the city's public squares, including the *Piazza*

San Marco, have been raised and repaved numerous times in an attempt to fight this sinkage.

In addition, Venetians began to understand that the sulphur dioxide emitted by the smokestacks of Marghera corrodes the stonework of the city and also creates an umbrella layer of pollution that traps other pollutants (for example, from central heating) in the city. In 1969 a UNESCO report declared that environmental threats in Venice, including the changing water table, the danger of pollution and the corrosion of the lagoon environment, were 'much greater than the League of Cambrai' that had famously threatened the city's destruction at the start of the sixteenth century. Since the fall of the republic, Venetians had been attempting to make a city just like many others: a modern, commercial metropolis with an industrial future. The flood of 1966, however, made them see things afresh. Many began to realize that the city was special and different, and that it had to develop in different ways to mainland cities. It needed cultural (and not industrial) development based on tourism, concentrating on the city's archives, libraries, university, Biennale, museums, theatres and civic foundations. The city's relationship with tourism was, and is, by no means unproblematic, but if the gravity of this flood was in any way linked to industrial development, Venetians needed to think hard about how economic and industrial growth threatened the city.

In addition to the danger of sinking, scientists have been keeping track of the rising sea level. You can see in museums around the city the occasional, fascinating paintings and photographs of the lagoon when it was frozen over. In the rare moments over the centuries when it was so cold that the canals and lagoon became ice, these images show Venetians skating, playing winter games and even walking out to Murano with the peaks of the snowy Alps in the background. According to legend, Venetians built fires on the ice and roasted oxen in the middle of the Grand Canal. Of course, the lagoon could easily freeze over again but, as we are painfully aware, global temperatures are rising. The effects of global warming mean that surface temperatures around the world are increasing, melting the world's ice caps and glaciers, simultaneously affecting sea levels and threatening coastal communities. Venice is most certainly at risk. When the city was founded, the sea level was 16 ft (4.8 m) below what it is today. When John and Effie Ruskin visited the city around 1850, the *Piazza San Marco* only flooded around six or seven times a year; towards the end of the twentieth century water has risen to be knee deep often 100 times a year. At the current rate that the water is rising, some predict that in 2055 many of the streets and ground floors in Venetian buildings could be under water on a daily basis if new measures are not taken to protect the city.

By the 1980s engineers had come up with a possible solution, the MOSE project (standing for *Modulo Sperimentale Elettro Meccanico*), whose name directly recalls Moses, the parter of seas. MOSE is a series of gates pin-jointed together at their base on the seabed in the inlets between the lagoon and the Adriatic near Chioggia (18 gates), Malamocco (19 gates) and the Lido (41 gates). The gates are like giant teeth that lie flat on the lagoon floor when not in use. When extremely high tides are predicted, they are inflated with air to rise up and rotate on their hinges to an angle of forty-five degrees, and emerge out of the water to create a physical barrier between the lagoon and the sea. The gates are designed to go up when a tide rises above 3.6 ft (1.1 m) and protect the lagoon against a tide of up to 6.5 ft (2 m). They will never protrude more than a few feet above the water, and most of the time are entirely invisible beneath the surface. The gates also have locks on their sides to allow boats and fishermen to pass, if necessary, when the gates are up. The cost? From three to five billion Euros.

From early in its planning phases, from when the prototype for the gates was launched in 1988 and exhibits were placed in public squares around the city describing the proposed gates and their function, Venetians and the world at large have protested angrily and vociferously, arguing that the gates represent a huge threat to the lagoon. MOSE's critics argued first and foremost that the gates would present an enormous threat to the lagoon's ecosystem since when raised they would stop the natural tidal flux between the lagoon and the sea on which the lagoon's wildlife depends for its survival. They also say that, based on current and projected measurements of tides and sea levels, the gates would have to be raised possibly over 150 times a year, maybe even day after day, dramatically upsetting the lagoon's equilibrium since pollutants will not be flushed out and marine life will not receive enough fresh seawater. The continuous cleansing of the lagoon is crucial since the city, regularly infused with enormous numbers of tourists, has no system for sewage collection and treatment. Sewage and contaminants (unbelievably) are regularly discharged directly into the canals of the city and into the lagoon, and the curious visitor can witness with this by patiently observing the pipes near the surface of the canals. If sewage is not flushed out by the usual tidal flow, the results could be disastrous.

The opponents of MOSE argue that we need to maintain rather than block the tidal flow, and that Venetians should build up the ground level of the city instead of blocking the tides. In addition, many argue it simply will not work. Tides could easily be higher than the gates, which even their designers admit will function for only a century or so until a better, more long-term solution is found. And if the rate of the rising sea level is higher than predicted, the gates could quickly become obsolete. All of which means that MOSE just buys time, and very expensive time, while people look for a better, long-term solution. What we should be doing, the critics argue, is look for that solution *now*. Many Venetians are also angry about the vast sum allocated to MOSE when so much is needed for social services – for day care, parks and schools, restoration and conservation, and transport and sewage management – to support the everyday lives of Venetians. Extremists also worry that collapsing gates could generate a kind of tidal wave if they are let down too quickly, and that they are therefore at risk from a terrorist plot. Massimo Cacciari, the philosophy professor turned mayor of the city of Venice from 1993–2000 and in 2005 once proclaimed '*Veneziani, compratevi gli stivaloni*', or 'Venetians, buy your tall boots', meaning that he had little faith in the success of the project.

Those who support MOSE, by contrast argue that Venetians have manipulated their watery environment from the very beginning by diverting rivers, digging fishing valleys and shoring up the banks of their islands to survive in the lagoon, and that there is little that's 'natural' about the lagoon and its environment. The lagoon is an almost entirely artificial creation. For decades Venetians have reconstructed salt marshes around the lagoon and protected them from wave action by shoring them up with wooden piles or stones, have built breakwaters around the edge of islands to prevent wave erosion, and have brought sand to the lagoon's barrier islands to lessen wave damage. Had the lagoon not been regularly managed by humans, it would have filled in by now and become dry land, a process that could have happened 500 years ago. MOSE is simply the natural and necessary continuation of such protective action. The gates, they say, would only need to be raised about nine or ten times a year for three to five hours a time, and would not do any permanent damage to the ecology of the lagoon. In addition, MOSE's supporters point out that it will employ 1,500 people a day. Like it or not, in any case, work on the gates continues and, given the right funding, could be operational in 2012.

In addition to the sinking city and rising waters, mass tourism also threatens the delicate and watery environment of the lagoon. Ever since the time of the crusades, the city has attracted artists, intellectuals and tourists, but the degree to which tourism has exploded in the city in the past several decades is shocking. The statistics speak for themselves. On 1 February 2009 the BBC estimated that 15 million people visit the city every year (80 per cent of whom come only for a day trip). Clearly, tourism is by now the city's main industry, if not its lifeblood, since it accounts for 70 per cent of the city's economy. So many people arriving in the fragile city, however, also threatens its survival. On an average summer day tourists tend to number around 30,000–40,000 and, on special holidays, there are closer to 50,000–80,000. An influx of more than 100,000 visitors a day brings the city to a standstill and that easily happens, for instance, during the last days of Carnival. (An infamous Pink Floyd concert in July 1989 saw over 200,000 visitors in one day, and in bars around the city you can occasionally see photographs of the piles of rubbish that they left behind.) The more people that come, the more Venice's infrastructure and services are overwhelmed, including rubbish collection, public transport and toilets. The dramatically increased levels of human waste and sewage produced by such large numbers puts incredible pressure on the lagoon, and this will only worsen if the city does not manage to introduce a more sustainable sewage system.

The rising tide of tourists is in stark comparison to the declining number of native Venetians in the city. The population of Venice declined from around 150,000 (and over 180,000 according to some accounts) in 1950 to near 60,000 today largely because Venetians moved to the mainland in search of work and more affordable living conditions, and this needs to be set against the daily arrival of up to 100,000 tourists. Many businesses and offices in the city closed in the 1990s, including *Alitalia* and *Assicurazione Generale*, a large Italian insurance firm, bringing Venice to the lowest per capita income in the Veneto. The flight of younger people from the lagoon has also had the collateral effect of producing a dramatically aging population in the city with a significant proportion of the city's inhabitants now being over 65.

As Venetians continue to grapple with their age-old questions of identity – trying to balance modernization and the drive for economic vitality with preserving their unique past – the city's future remains uncertain. Meanwhile, the engineers on the MOSE project continue slowly laying the doors to the great gates on the floor beneath the lagoon's surface and

Venetians carry on, pushing their way through tour groups to shop at the Rialto or take their children to school. They run into one another on the street and stop to drink a spritz and chat, an increasingly rare breed among the tourists shopping for masks. But if history is any guide, they do have reason to be hopeful. If their ancestors were able to beat back the Franks and the Genoese in their own lagoon, to rule the entire northeastern Mediterranean from Pavia to Constantinople, to survive the Portuguese discovery of the spice route around Africa, the pillaging of the French and the assaults and sieges of the Austrians, then surely there is hope. As the waters rise, and in the face of confident predictions of the city's certain demise, the world watches with baited breath in the hope that Venetian's will save the city once again.

BIBLIOGRAPHY

Brown, Patricia Fortini. *Art and Life in Renaissance Venice*. New York, Abrams, 1997.

Davis, Robert C. and Marvin Garry R.. *Venice, The Tourist Maze: A Cultural Critique of the World's Most Touristed City*. Berkeley, Los Angeles, and London: University of California Press, 2004.

Howard, Deborah. *Venice and the East: The Impact of the Islamic World on Venetian Architecture, 1100–1500*. New Haven and London: Yale University Press, 2002.

Keahey, John. *Venice Against the Sea: A City Besieged*. New York: St Martin's Press, 2002.

Lane, Frederic C.. *Venice: A Maritime Republic*. Baltimore and London: The Johns Hopkins University Press, 1973.

Lorenzetti, Giulio. *Venice and Its Lagoon*. Padua: Edizioni Erredici, 2002.

Mentzel, Peter. *A Traveller's History of Venice*. Gloucestershire: Arris Publishing, 2006.

Morris, Jan. *Venice*. London: Faber and Faber, 1960.

Norwich, John Julius. *Paradise of Cities: Venice in the 19th Century*. New York: Doubleday, 2003.

Pertot, Gianfranco. *Venice, Extraordinary Maintenance*. London: Paul Holberton, 2004.

Plant, Margaret. *Venice Fragile City*. 1797–1997. New Haven and London: Yale University Press, 2002.
Zorzi, Alvise. *Venice, 697–1797: A City, A Republic, An Empire*. Woodstock, NY: The Overlook Press, 2001.

INDEX